Also by the author

Motorcycle Journeys Through Baja

Motorcycle Journeys Through California

Motorcycle Journeys Through California & Baja

Honda VF and VFR Interceptor

101 Road Tales

All photos taken by, or for, the author unless so noted. Book design and main illustrations by Sue Salvadori. Additional illustrations by Gary M. Brown as noted.

Cover: Designed by Liselotte Posson of Posson Art. Photo depicts the author dealing with an often encountered dilemma — a no-thru-road situation. See *Guatemala 1975* chapter.

This first edition published by:
Trovatello Press
8240 Toloso Road
Atascadero, CA 93422
U.S.A

ISBN: 978-0-9906459-0-0

Printed by CreateSpace, an Amazon.com Company
Available from Amazon.com and other bookstores.

Leonard—
My wife is from Minnesota—
she likes California!

NO THRU ROAD

Confessions of a Traveling Man

Original Sahara photo by Arnie Friedman

CLEMENT SALVADORI

[signature]

A Trovatello Book
Trovatello Press
Atascadero, California

Dedication

I have great love and appreciation for my wife, without whose hard work this book would never exist. I commend her highly for her computer skills — which I lack — and her ability to stay cheerful in the presence of an often grouchy husband. The photo I have chosen was taken on our wedding day.
— Clement Salvadori

Table of Contents

Foreword

No Thru Road is a book about travels. The author, my husband, is considered by some to be an expert on that subject. Though I've done a share of traveling, I'm no expert. Also, though I've spent the majority of my working life in the motorcycle industry — publishing and motorcycle safety aspects — no expert there either. But, after 25 years with Salvadori as a last name and having worked with Clem in the industry since 1980, I come as close to 'expert' on Clement Salvadori as you are likely to get.

The Salvadori household has a tradition, well-known locally: Thursday Night Pasta Night. Guests are invited to share a simple Italian dinner. True, everyone likes a good meal but the real draw is good conversation. Clement would rate a successful evening as one where conversation is amusing and informative, and flows effortlessly. With his former State Department training and knack for diplomacy, he can make this happen. We've never adhered to the edicts of 'political correctness' so at our table good conversation is not the same as polite conversation. Politics and religion are not off-limits, much like an old-fashioned salon, but most often the subject turns to travel and travel is all-encompassing, rife with politics and religion, rich with interesting people, places, and intimate experiences — hence the story-swapping begins. Clem, having circled the globe and having a penchant for finding out-of-the-way places, easily holds his own when telling a good traveling story, so we let him hold court — for a time. Even after all these years I still hear tales I've never heard before and am fascinated.

Many people are avid readers of Clement's touring magazine articles. This means that they are familiar with some of his travels, however, these excursions necessarily conform to pre-determined agendas set forth by the publishers and editors — based on specific motorcycles and destinations. Many colorful side trips, personal opinions, or backroad experiences simply don't fit the formula, weren't necessarily on a motorcycle, and therefore never see the light of day. Also, Clement has been searching out the no-thru roads on this planet most of his life, thus the stories go well beyond his days as a moto-journalist. Before that time, he had already gone 'round the world, traversed the so-called Hippie Highway from Istanbul to Kathmandu, played chess in Afghanistan, found a girl finding God in Kashmir, adventured deep into old Africa, been rescued in the Sahara by the French Foreign Legion, been offered a slave-girl bride in Tanzania, freightered himself and bike to Australia, and had seen Vietnam several times, to name a few.

Having said this, I invite you to a Pasta Night here in the pages of this book to listen to stories from Clement – unedited. Pull up a chair. Grab a glass of wine. Let the stories begin.

— *Sue Salvadori*

Introduction
Confessions of a Traveling Man

Travel is what interests me, seeing places I haven't seen before. It can be as simple as a stretch of tree-lined road in Maine or a small town in Nebraska, as dramatic as a crusader fortress abandoned on a Turkish hill or a sweep of snow-capped Himalayan mountains running jaggedly from horizon to horizon. It could be looking at the sign in Zagora, southern Morocco, which points the way to Timbukto, noting that it is 52 days by foot, three days by motorized transport — with no gas stations in between. My five-gallon tank won't make it.

There is no real profit in this passion, other than personal pleasure, no real purpose, other than seeing some place new. But it's what I like to do. Bowlers bowl, hunters hunt, football fans watch football, philanderers philander; I travel. Also, I am a great believer in the fact that the more one travels, the more tolerant of others one becomes.

This book is a collection of stories about some of my travels since I first went off on my own at age 17, about the places I've been, the things I've seen, the people I've met. Perhaps the *No Thru Road* title is not entirely accurate, as most times I did get through, but often I have been told, "You can't get there from here." Perhaps. Perhaps not.

Travel is the unifying theme of this book, and as is true of most travel writing, this is as much about me and my personal perceptions as it is about the places I went to. I mix in a bit of history, a bit of culture, some politics, even economics and sex.

Of secondary importance is the idea that somewhere in all these chapters a motorcycle is mentioned. A motorcycle is merely my preferred instrument of travel, a way to move about. Some travelers have walked to wherever it is they want to go, others taken a horse or a camel or a mule. Some travel by jeep or truck, others go by train. Some go by boat, some by plane. Some by bicycle. I go by motorcycle . . . crossing the Sahara being the one exception.

Any form of travel has its own restrictions. Boats need water, trains need tracks, planes need landing fields, legs get tired. I have been limited by the need to follow some sort of road, but with an estimated 30 million miles of highways, byways and dirt tracks criss-crossing the six continents, I have had a good deal of scope. I will leave the seventh continent, Antarctica, to the truly adventurous. On the map a road may be denoted by a fat red line, a middling blue line, a thin black line, or even, best of all, a dotted line. And I have been on some roads which I never saw on any map.

I find a motorcycle a convenient tool for following these lines. It can carry me hundreds, thousands of miles, distances that would defeat my legs. When I turn off the key I don't have to give it water or hay. It consumes relatively little gas, and as it takes up little space when necessary can be squeezed onto any ferry. It can go down narrow trails, be carried across unbridged gaps, hoisted over a fallen tree. If it gets properly stuck I don't need a wrecker to get it unstuck, just a couple of brawny locals.

And when I come to the edge of a continent and face the Big Water, I can usually convince some passing ship to winch it aboard. Or load it into the belly of some cargo plane. It is my own mechanical Passpartout.

How did I become interested in motorcycling in the first place? Perhaps the devil made me do it. Or perhaps it was my Uncle Erminio, who gave me my first ride on a motorcycle at eight impressionable years. He was an Italian country doctor who, on a warm summer's evening thought it preferable to do his rounds on an aged 250 Sertum, rather than be cooped up in a car.

One afternoon he asked a very bored visiting nephew, American to the core, if he would like to come along. Having nothing better to do with my time, I said yes. And off we went through the Italian hills, going down dusty white roads with me bouncing along on the pillion seat.

The memory is hazy, but as a child who had usually traveled within the confines of a sedan this was a very new experience. I could see all around, see overhead, see cobblestones passing beneath the wheels, see the respectful looks of pedestrians. This was certainly a good way to see the world.

Stopping at a lonely farmhouse, the good doctor would park, retrieve his black bag from the saddlebag, and tell me to stay close to the motorcycle. I always heeded such advice, as a farm dog or two would be barking ferociously, chain taut and seemingly ready to snap.

I would seat myself on the front saddle, to give the aura of ownership, the motorcycle secure on the centerstand, and look at what was around me. White oxen would be working the fields, women doing washing in an outdoor trough, local children peeking out at me from behind walls. They were obviously envious.

Eventually my uncle would reappear, stash his bag, start the engine, and off we would go. Il Dottore (R.I.P.) can take the rap for my motorcycling passion.

For better or for worse, and I always presume the worst, which negative focus has often saved me from disaster, I have been riding motorcycles steadily since the age of 16. I reduced my mother to tears on occasion. Myself, too.

I once sat beside a little-used two-rut dirt road in the hinterlands of Zambia, some miles southeast of Tunduma, on the back road to Lake Malawi, contemplating my bruised body and broken motorcycle. Miles from anywhere, I was feeling suitably miserable at the immediate hopelessness of everything. Speaking to the gods, the African savannah, and to whatever wildlife was around in the tall grass, I screamed, "Damn it! I don't have to be here!" A few tears probably dripped down my dusty cheeks; I must have been a pathetic sight. Fortunately there was nobody to see me.

If I could have abandoned bike and baggage and magically transported myself back home, I would have.

But it was merely a passing aberration. I overcame the problems and continued on my way.

While a motorcycle is a very practical conveyance, it does require more attention than a Jeep or Land Cruiser. Gas supply is limited, and a length of clear plastic hose becomes an essential accompaniment; any passing non-diesel vehicle can provide aid and succor. No spare tire and wheel is carried, so a repair kit and the ability to use it make common sense. The weather can be contentious, with unexpected snow and ice or a 100-degree dust-storm.

Not least of concerns is the inherent danger of riding a motorcycle, where a minor distraction might cause a spill and a broken leg. Normal traffic in places like Mexico City and Tehran can be, in a word, intimidating, and a foreigner had best learn to join in the fray. There are no Marquess of Queensberry-type rules in most of the driving world.

In what is loosely referred to as the developed world motorcyclists are a definite minority, and often discriminated against. Policemen have harassed me, commanding officers threatened me, doctors damned me, hotel keepers denied me a room, ambassadors harangued me, psychiatrists questioned my sanity, children laughed at me, mechanics robbed me, priests prayed for me, women scorned me, all because I rode a motorcycle. Instead of driving a Ford or a Mercedes.

In the less affluent countries, where much of my traveling has taken place, 90-plus percent of the populace aspires to owning a motorized two-wheeler, like a Honda 90 or a simple scooter. Possession means not only status, but liberation ... the freedom to travel, if only a few miles to grandmother's house to celebrate her birthday. And when they see me they understand that I am indeed a traveling man, and maybe have tales to entertain them about strange and exotic places they have never imagined.

— *Clement Salvadori*

Afghanistan 1973

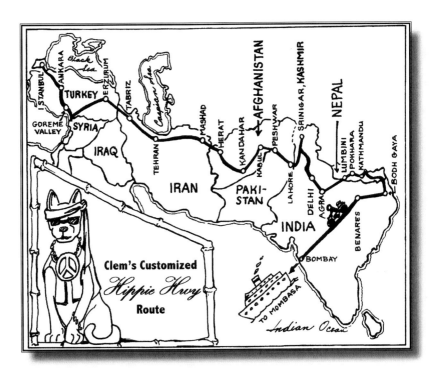

    "Why do you come to Afghanistan?" the sweaty-faced, middle-aged immigration official asked. He stared at me over the top of his glasses, sucking at a cigarette.

    Why does one come to Afghanistan? In this case it was that I was on my way to somewhere else. This was 1973 and I was riding my motorcycle along the Great Hippie Highway, stretching for some 4,000 narrow miles between the affluent West and impoverished East, between Istanbul and Kathmandu. The late Sixties and early Seventies were the heyday of this thin ribbon of reasonably good asphalt, the Asian Route 66, with the long-haired youth of Europe and North America going to the East to find — whatever. It could be spiritual salvation, or drugs, or profit, or wanderlust, or all four.

For me it was wanderlust. While working at the American embassy in Rome I decided that after five years I did not want to continue my career as a diplomat. After tendering my letter of resignation I sent my personal belongings to my parents in Massachusetts, got on my BMW R75/5 and headed east. A ferry took me and the bike across the Adriatic Sea to Greece, and then a road led over the top of the Aegean Sea to Istanbul, where Europe meets the East.

This was September of 1973 and the first bridge to be built across the Bosphorus was almost complete, but would not be open for another six weeks, so to get from Istanbul to Asia Minor involved a short ferry ride. Not a problem, as dozens of boats were vying for customers. Once on the Asian continent I headed east along the Hippie Highway, through the Turkish cities of Ankara, Erzurum and Dogubayazit, entering the royal domain of Iran (the Shah still ran the place) at Bazagan. Then it was on to Tabriz, where I acquired an unexpected passenger, an American woman hitch-hiking her way to India, and we motored together to Tehran and along to Meshed, in the northeast corner of the country.

We left Meshed one sunny morning, crossing the high, dry desert to the Afghan frontier, then spending the requisite several hours at the border. An artificial line of nationalist demarcation had been arbitrarily drawn in the sand several hundred years before, and gradually a sentry box had grown into a town. This border community was not a town that any sensible person would want to live in, but nevertheless a town. Bureaucrats and police and soldiers provided a semi-transient, financially stabilizing population, but the bedrock was the merchants who sold food and clothing, and the smugglers who existed along any international frontier. The prices of camels, oranges, auto parts and a thousand other items varied from one side of the border to the other, and good businessmen were quick to take advantage of these economic vagaries. As were officials who were willing to turn their heads ... in order to count their money.

There were also the shysters who preyed on the unwary. At one time the country bumpkins had been ignorant Iranians and Afghanis, but of late the Western innocents had provided extraordinarily good pickings. Many excuses could be found to delay the traveler a few days, even weeks, and all this meant profits for the hoteliers, the restauranteurs, the money changers.

The key to minimizing unpleasantness at a border crossing was to know what is expected from the bureaucrats. I had my paper ducks all in a row: passport, visa, vaccination certificate, proof of ownership of my BMW R75/5, international driver's license, and a wad of travelers' checks. The only thing I lacked was Afghani insurance, and for $10 the office next to immigration sold me a two-week policy, a very minor shakedown in the larger scheme of things.

"I am on my way to Pakistan," I said to the official, "merely passing through."

"Good! Enjoy your visit." He slammed a rubber stamp down on my passport.

He turned to look at my traveling companion, a six-foot specimen of womanhood discreetly covered in motorcycling gear. "You travel with him?" he asked.

"Yes," she said.

"Good. Enjoy your visit." Slam! Had Cass been alone, obviously the process would have been far more complicated. Women traveling by themselves were a mystery to Afghanis, and they were generally presumed to be of ill-repute. But a woman with a man ... that was understandable, especially as these Westerners had rather immoral standards.

Border towns often have their own particular fascination, and deserve a day's visit, but not this one, which was hot and bleak and not a tree to be seen. We left in the mid-afternoon and crossed the hundred sun-blasted miles to the oasis city of Herat.

As an historical note, I was at the border a few months after the king of Afghanistan had been deposed by an army-backed cousin who proclaimed a republic. In truth the country was run by a collection of warlords, each one protecting his own financial turf, but promising not to war on his neighbors. Then the Russians invaded in 1979 and screwed everything up, and the place remains screwed up to this day.

Herat was full of ruins of reasonably great antiquity, dating back to the time of Alexander the Great, which could be seen as we entered. The city had blossomed in the 15th century, decayed in the 17th. Still to be seen were the remnants of old walls that Alexander had built, crumbling, but considering that they were some 250 feet in width at the base, it would take a long, long time to obliterate them.

The citadel in Herat was built a thousand years ago, and though the city was occasionally ravaged by the likes of Tamerlane and Genghis Khan, the place remained a pivot point for the meeting of Central Asian cultures.

To one side was the Old Town, where things had not much changed in 15 or 20 generations. Narrow alleys led into the warren, each occupation an open door: cobblers, butchers, gunsmiths, doctors, greengrocers, cloth merchants, tobacconists, saddle-makers, letter-writers. Every one was lord of his little domain, with a retinue of small boys to do his bidding, to sweep the shop, carry messages, fetch tea. The only real indication of the 20th century were the electric light bulbs and the lengths of wire running overhead.

But city planners had been at work a century ago, and I was headed into New Town along a broad, tree-lined avenue, backed by a number of buildings which served as the local hotels. The two-storied versions were considered high-rises, exceeded in height only by a dozen minarets scattered around the metropolis.

The long-haired, low-budget tourists had created a considerable economic stir in the place. Herat was the first town along the Hippie Highway in which one could buy and ingest all the hashish and marijuana one wished without much fear of government (in the form of police) reprisals. A lot of stoned freaks got this far, and no further. Anyone who had $400 could stay happily zonked for a year, room and board included.

The New Super Behzar Garden Hotel had been highly recommended to me, with an enclosed courtyard where the motorcycle could sit unmolested. The youthful concierge cheerfully indicated that I should ride across the shiny tiles of the lobby. It was one of the higher-priced hostelries in town, at $1 a night for a room. That meant it had more of a transient crowd, as the low-bucks rip-heads were mostly at the $3 a week dives. The place was clean, always a consideration in this milieu, with the floor swept and the sheets reasonably white, if a little ragged. A pond was shaded by a large tree, and several European travelers were sitting in chairs industriously writing in their journals. A journal was as essential as a passport on this route, although I must admit I failed miserably in my effort to keep one.

Journal writing is a discipline which does not seem to lend itself to my traveling. I've met camel-riders on safari, trekkers in the Andes, libertines in Thailand, all with a carefully kept journal in the bag. Myself, I end up with a thick notebook with a long entry at the start, a short one or two afterwards, and then page after page of brief notes, names and addresses of fellow travelers and locals, recommendations of places to stay and to see, phrases heard or read, the little bits and pieces which serve to open the correct filing drawers of the mind's memory.

However, this shorthand works for me, which is why I can recall the name of the hotel.

The main street was partially paved, and the local transport

11

of choice were pony-powered carts and a few bicycles. On the nearest corner was a curio shop, obviously established to cater to the Euro-trade. In the window were displayed hand-wrought saddles, marvelously ornamented bits of harness, knives of all length and curvature, swords, muzzle-loaders, hammered tin lanterns, ceramic dishes, artifacts of a different era. The gentleman behind the counter, a suitably hook-nosed, rascally looking devil, was acquiring the abandoned pieces of common culture as his countrymen moved into the age of internal-combustion engines, automatic rifles, and plastic utensils.

I poked about, and the proprietor leaned on a glass case, smoking Marlboros, sizing up his customer. As I moved closer, admiring the aged prayer rugs hanging from the wall, he reached down and brought forth a crunched up piece of newspaper, spread it out, and showed me a large chunk of hashish. No thanks, I said. He scrunched the paper back up and stuffed it under the counter, then beckoned me to come into the back room.

A small armory was hanging from the walls, leaning in the corners, lying on boxes. British Enfield 303s, American Garands, Belgian FNs, shotguns, and the ubiquitous Soviet-design AK-47 assault rifle. Webley revolvers, US Army issue .45 caliber automatics, and pistols I had never seen before. "You want?" he asked. No, I said, picking up a Sten submachine-gun, compliments of some British arsenal. "Cheap," he said, noting what I had in my hand; true, I thought, wondering who would want a weapon whose accuracy was limited to some 12 feet. It probably did get a good deal of use in later years, when Afghanistan became a nation at war.

My Swiss Army knife would have to do if ever I needed to defend myself or my possessions.

Another motorcyclist was at the hotel, Kenny from Detroit. He had fled his hometown two steps ahead of some irate business competitors, gotten on a flight to Germany, and bought himself a BMW. His vague appreciation of geography, remembering the two-dimensional maps in his textbook, was that if he headed east, eventually he would get home.

For a while we would ride together. We were both going

in the same direction, after all. He was a marvelous traveling companion, never harried, always patient, willing to overcome any problem. He never despaired, never lost his temper. In many respects he was an innocent abroad, but as an innocent who had been raised in Murder City, USA, nobody ever put anything over on him.

We went to Pardees Restaurant for dinner, not quite what one would expect to find recommended in a Michelin guide, but the local hot spot. The dining room was thickly carpeted, the tables arranged around the edge, everybody sitting with their backs against the wall. Mutton stew poured over rice was the popular dish, but a variety of vaguely Western dishes were also available. The distaff side of a French couple was earning room and board by working the kitchen, turning out omelettes and steaks and anything else the local market could provide the makings for. Her boyfriend sat whacked in the corner by the tape recorder, alternating The Grateful Dead with Edith Piaf.

Kenny and I plotted our next move. Cass, my passenger, was a temporary traveling partner. The agreement was that any time she did not like where I was headed, she could find another ride.

She was heaven-bent for India and spiritual salvation, while I was more leisurely in my aims.

Three roads fanned out from Herat, one graded dirt stretch went 400 miles northeast to Balkh and Mazar-i-Sharif; it was considered to be of strategic importance and permission to travel it had to be granted by the authorities. A second, very rough road went due east to the lakes of Band-i-Amir and the Buddhist temples at Bamian; a Land Rover couple staying at the hotel said we would have to carry enough gas to cover at least 250 miles. The minimal traffic they had seen on the road was all diesel-powered, which would not suit our engines. Plus the road was a real sump-buster, with broken, rocky sections where lots of ground clearance, more than we had, was highly advisable. Scratch that one; neither of us were interested in roughing it. The third route went along good concrete highway southeast across the charmingly named Desert of Death to Kandahar, then up to Kabul.

13

We decided we would try for the northeast road; I wanted to go to Balkh and Kenny had no preference. In the morning we presented our reasonably well-groomed selves at the police station, where the chap in charge was quite cheerful and talkative. Of course he dreamed of owning a motorcycle like ours, and sadly showed us the decrepit Russian two-stroke he had to put up with. He would like very much to give us permission to travel this road, but first he would have to ask Kabul, and that might take a week. Or possibly two. And there was no guarantee that the permission would be granted. Perhaps it would be better to go ourselves to Kabul to seek the permission, and then come back.

The Kandahar option looked like it. But first we wanted to go and have a look-see at this forbidden road. We rode out of town to the roadblock, where the soldier in charge was happy to let us through if we left our passports with him. There were four of us on this afternoon spin. Cass and myself, and Kenny had a hitch-hiking Australian who was also staying at the Super Bezhar.

Afghani landscape tends to the austere. The road, well-graded, traveled along a broad alluvial stretch, then began to climb into

Off-roading had its hazardous aspects, and here friend Kenny congratulates himself on getting my BMW unstuck.

the mountains. After we motored along for a while, my passenger pointed off to the east. Look, a village! A half-mile or so from the road was a collection of roofs, practically invisible against the hilly backdrop except for the unnatural right angles of the buildings. We had no destination other than to see something slightly different, and this perhaps was the goal. No road led that direction, but with the motorcycles we felt we could find a way.

It wasn't easy, but in half an hour we had arrived close to these brown mud walls. No broad avenue, no street, not even a lane led into the village, just a bumpy goat-path sliding narrowly in between the houses. Kenny and I were intent on keeping the bikes upright; our passengers could afford to look around. Up was the only way. Shy heads were poking over the rooftops, catching quick glances of us, then retreating. A faint cry could be heard, obviously alerting people further along. There was nobody on our little alleyway, only brown walls and small closed doors.

Push on. We arrived in what amounted to the village common, a small dirt square with one small leafy tree. No store, no cafe, no movie theater. We stopped, parked the bikes, got off. It was hot; we doffed our helmets and jackets. We were a colorful foursome; I had a beard, Kenny a long blonde ponytail, the Aussie a bright red Fu Manchu mustache, and Cass an obvious bosom.

Within minutes the little square was filled with people, others looking down from the rooftops. Old people and young children were on the ground; women of a sexual age wore burkhas, enclosed as tightly as in a bank vault, peered through veils from above. The working men were obviously off somewhere, working.

Nobody spoke any language any of us could communicate in. A white-haired man took over the task of moderating this meeting.

We indicated thirst. Orders were given. Four bottles of warm, orange-colored pop appeared on a tray, a young boy presenting them to us. We drank, they stared.

It was an interesting stand-off. I was accustomed to urban children fingering the motorcycle, but here they were far more interested in us than with the machines. The lines were clearly drawn, with four of us and two motorcycles on one side, several hundred villagers on the three other sides as well as looking down on us.

We tried to come to some sort of understanding. The map meant nothing to them. After several tries at different pronunciations, the white-haired man understood Herat, and proceeded to inform the crowd that that was where we were from. A congenial sigh of recognition came from the audience. But no open arms, no sign of fraternity, no welcoming us into the life of the village. I felt the opposite was true.

Nobody wanted us around; obviously the idea was to get us out of there before the men-folk came home from the fields and the herds. Here were not only four strangers, but one was a woman who wore tight jeans and was probably not familiar with the Koran. Our presence was more than a tad disturbing to the local elders, and life proceeded better without such interruptions. We took the hint. There was no souvenir shop to buy a postcard defining our arrival, no quaint antiquary where we might purchase a momento. With empty soda bottle in hand I approached the boy with the tray, and proffered what I thought (by Herat standards) to be a suitable amount for the four sodas. He looked at the old white-beard beside him, who nodded, and he took the money. Obviously such flatlanders as ourselves were not to be privy to the fabled Muslim hospitality. And I was just as glad. This was not a remote town, we were not in need, and we were leaving. Pay up and get out.

Afghanis lead a rough life. If you were strong, you were okay; if you were weak, somebody smacked you and took what you had. When in doubt, throw him out. No possible good could come of these strangers being in town.

We shook hands quite formally with the patriarch and loaded up. The white-beard directed us, not down the alley we had come, but one at right angles to it. It was slightly wider, but we still poked along in first gear. The rooftops as we left were lined with people, god knows how many. And behind us the narrow lane had absolutely filled with children, trotting along behind, having as much excitement as they had probably had in six months or more. The children were yelling, the roof-toppers were crying out. I felt rather like the British expeditionary force that was massacred while attempting to flee Afghanistan in 1842.

We made it back to the road, back to Herat, picked up our passports, and celebrated our adventure with beers at the hotel. Two days later Kenny and Cass and I left for Kabul, via the Desert of Death, though no longer very death-like as a new concrete road covered the 300 miles to Kandahar.

Much of Afghanistan is desert, with long, long stretches between gas stations and the local versions of Denny's restaurants. Roads in the Seventies tended to be good, being built mostly by the U.S. and Russia.

At Kabul we checked into the Friends' Hotel, well known among the traveling set. It was a converted mansion surrounded by ill-kept gardens, where rooms went for a dollar a night. Its greatest attraction was the shower room with a wood-fired water heater, so the place was toasty warm and had as much hot water as one cared to heat. The restaurant served hamburgers and apple pie, and though the cooks went off at nine o'clock, there was always somebody who, for a small extra charge, would fix anything you wanted at any hour.

Kenny disappeared into the kitchen one day. He liked the local hashish, but found that smoking it in the short, fat pipes called

Afghanistan 1973

Going north from the 11,000-foot Salang Tunnel the road descended from one narrow canyon to an ever narrower one — but there is a gap in that wall, and beyond that the opening of the Asian steppe.

Camel caravans were still in use crossing the Turkestan plains of northern Afghanistan, which stretch north to the Oxus River and beyond to the Arctic Circle — 2500 miles away.

chillums, as was the local habit, was tearing his throat up. The way around that was to ingest it in food, and what could be better than a chocolate cake. The two large lady cooks were absolutely entranced at watching this pony-tailed foreigner whipping together his ingredients, pouring it into a pan and popping it in the oven. I came by to see how he was doing and licked the mixing bowl. Which seemed to be a good idea at the time. So good that I followed it up with a large slice of cake after it was baked. The rest of the evening passed unremembered.

In the morning Ken and I left some gear, and Cass, behind and headed north to visit the ancient city of Balkh, reputed to have been Alexander's temporary headquarters around 2300 years ago. Ken had never heard of the place, but was happy for any excuse for a ride, while I still had the visions my history teacher had instilled of this political and commercial center.

Leaving Kabul and rolling northwards we went through some of the more fertile land in the country, with apricot orchards and vineyards and fields of millet. A few trucks were on the highway, many horses and camels off on either side. We went higher and higher, heading up for the Salang Tunnel, at 11,500- feet, a mile and a half-long unlit hole through the Hindu Kush. At the north end it opens onto the great Asian steppes that stretched all the way to the Arctic Circle ... though it was a good ways off, some 2,500 miles.

The long ride down the northern slopes was stupendous beyond belief. I try to use these exaggerations advisedly. After switch-backing down the mountain, the road entered a broad valley and continued dead straight north. The valley narrowed, a gap appeared, the road went over a little hump, and down into a slightly smaller valley. And on and on and on, each valley decreasing in size. No towns, no villages, no habitations, an occasional herdsman with a flock of sheep, only sparse grass, rocky walls, and glimpses of a small river to our right. Finally we came into a valley which was no more than a hundred yards wide, steep cliffs going high on either side. No traffic, straight road, we were running about 50 mph side by side, and the highway was headed right into a solid wall.

Over 2300 years ago
Alexander the Great, a Greek,
temporarily subjugated the
tribes of Afganistan, and made
his capital in the northern
city of Balkh; these walls are
what remain of a much later
fortification.

I had visions of being an outlaw trying to escape a posse and running into a box canyon. We weren't going to get out of there. We must have taken a wrong turn and were headed for a dead end. Looking at the sheer walls closing in on us, I figured that somewhere I had screwed up.

Slowly the road merged with the riverbank, both heading for the blank spot ahead. The grey-black rocks were now looming above us, and I was reaching for the brakes. Then the narrowest of cuts appeared, no more than 15 feet wide, and a low overhang to our right. We went through the cut, the river ran under the overhang. — And then we were out, onto the steppes. Two thousand miles of golden grassy plain was before us. The road veered west, and a brilliant red autumn sun sat low on the horizon; if we could crank up to 1,000 mph, we could keep up with it. We couldn't, and we didn't.

Balkh was a city once on a par with ancient Babylon, a Zoroastrian and Buddhist center, but on the decline since being sacked by Genghis Khan in the 13th and Tamerlane in the 14th century. A dusty brown landscape stretched to either side, very flat. Trees appeared, and I realized that the brown in front was not just horizon, but melting mud walls, the crests worn smooth by wind and rain. On the north side an abandoned caravanserai was slowly rejoining the earth from whence its mud bricks came.

As we stopped for a closer look at the wall, an elderly man with a cane came forward, speaking a rather old-fashioned English. Would we like a guide? No, we would not, but we got one anyway. He was full of wonderful misinformation, mostly concerning Alexander, whom our instructor emphatically believed that on his way to India in 329 B.C. had indeed wintered here. But I should not be critical; history books can be wrong.

To prove his point, our guide reached into a baggy pocket and took out a small coin. He stated convincingly that this he had found as a young man while tilling the fields, and if we wished it would be ours. It was a Bactrian Greek coin, or more probably a reasonable facsimile thereof, and since the price we negotiated was about 25 cents, I felt that I, too, would believe that this had fallen out of Great Alex's pocket lo these many years.

But for all the romance that my high school teacher had given the place, all second-hand, I might add, from books he had read, I found Balkh rather dull. The dirty 20th century streets had no charm, nor did the inhabitants. I preferred to leave the images from Robert Byron's "Road to Oxiana" undisturbed. We got on our motorcycles and headed back.

We slept in Mazar-i-Sharif, a commercial center a few miles east of Balkh, whose only real reason for existence was its proximity to the USSR. Anything that was made across the Oxus River was superior to goods made in Afghanistan for the simple reason that nothing was manufactured in Afghanistan; it was a prime market for Soviet exports. And Soviet seconds; leaky inner tubes and trousers with legs of different lengths were major items on the local market. Next day we returned to Kabul.

On our last night Kenny and Cass and I went down to Chicken Road (where a poultry market had once existed), and settled into the cushions at Siggi's, a tea shop full of hip travelers, progressive

21

Along all the trade routes in Afghanistan the local chieftains would build imposing fortresses and collect taxes from the merchants — this one is between Kabul and Jalalabad. The third bike belonged to a New Zealander who joined us.

That is the Khyber Pass, connecting Afghanistan with Pakistan, the sign directing vehicles to the left, camels to the right; we stayed on the pavement.

jazz, and occasionally even members of the Afghani elite. Out in the garden was a giant chessboard, with wooden chessmen five feet high, which I went to look at.

An English-speaking Kabuli asked me if I played. I did, albeit at a rather rudimentary level. Plus I was used to plotting my strategy on a conventional board, where all pieces were in easy sight.

My opponent was a doctor, worked with the Afghani Olympic team, and had studied in England. He asked me what my profession was; I told him I was traveling. I called him Doctor, he addressed me as Traveler. It was easier to talk knowing we were merely strangers on a chessboard, that we would never meet again.

As we roamed around the board (knight to rook three) we discussed the state of the world (pawn to bishop four), the future of Afghanistan (queen to knight three), the problems of a Westernism versus Muslimism, (bishop to king four) and the politics of maintaining neutrality while living next to the Russian bear (rook to knight four).

"Russia would never want Afghanistan," said the doctor, "because there is nothing here for them. And because they would have to kill every single Afghani." He was wrong, but he was right.

Perhaps as a portent of the future, I avoided a total loss by provoking a stalemate.

Two days later we were riding over the Khyber Pass into Pakistan.

Back in 1973 the Khyber Pass was a beautifully desolate cut through the Hindu Kush, reaching a modest 3500 feet; today it is rife with gunfire and landmines.

NO THRU ROAD

CLEMENT SALVADORI
confessions of a traveling man

Trovatello Press
8240 Toloso Road
Atascadero CA 93422 USA

805-462-0833
salvadori@charter.net

Here is my latest effort at becoming rich and famous: NO THRU ROAD. The book describes 29 motorcycle trips, and one in a VW van, that I have taken over the last 50 years on six continents, in places like Afghanistan and Zimbabwe, Peru and Texas. Now available from Amazon, Whitehorse Gear, and many booksellers.

Alaska 1976

The last frontier was my destination! "Last frontier" is a trifle exaggerative, although that is Alaska's unofficial state motto. Following World War II the light plane, a lot of roads, and the discovery of large amounts of oil had rather put paid to the frontier aspect, but the appellation would have to do. Also, Alaska was the only U.S. state I had not been to. Seward's Folly it was called back in the 1860's when U.S. Secretary of State Seward paid a whopping great 7.2 million dollars to the Russians for this unprime piece of real estate   that was about $12 a square mile, a deal even in post-Civil War dollars. The bargain price was due to Russia worrying that the Brits would merely march in from Canada and take over the place without so much as a by your leave; $7.2 mil looked better than nothing.

My departure for this frontier was in the aftermath of the nation's Bi-Centennial celebration. I — and some 50 others — had gathered for a week-long extravaganza at a ranch in western Oregon to hail the 200th 4th with American beer and native-born steaks. The company of celebrants was slowly dispersing, all heading their own ways. My eventual way was to Massachusetts, but a detour via Alaska promised to make the trip more interesting. My transportation to the 49th state was to be on a high-mile BMW R60/5, which deserved a check-over. I laid out my little toolkit on the saddle. The party's host was John Muir, an engineer who bought the ranch after making an immodest profit on a how-to book on keeping Volkswagens running. Being interested in all things technical, he pulled up a milk-crate to sit on and proffered sage advice, mostly concerning the vulnerability of motorcyclists when traveling in areas inhabited by bears. Be foolish to camp out in such a place, he noted, when a bear will smell your food and come to visit. "You'll wish you had a nice VW to crawl into and shut the door"

Change the oil. Clean the air-cleaner. Check the oil in the driveshaft. Check the differential by moving the rear wheel back and forth. Felt like too much play. The wheel came off to reveal some very worn teeth on the essential gear. Calls to several BMW shops revealed they didn't have the necessary item in stock, and a call to Butler & Smith, the semi-competent U.S distributor, had the clerk saying that they didn't have that part, but were expecting some from Germany in three or four weeks.

Somebody recommended a shop in Seattle. Over the phone the owner listened to my description of the problem, said he can fix it, bring it in tomorrow. A quick pack, a round of goodbyes, and I was off — with John's final recommendation that I get rid of the bike and buy a Volkswagon. At the shop the next morning the owner wheeled the bike away, telling me to come back in two days. "Don't bother calling; it's just a waste of my time."

True to his word, the bike was ready to roll through the wilderness. And I needed to get to Vancouver to meet a friend at the airport. No point to have one person enjoying a foray to the last frontier when two could enjoy it just as much. Getting from Vancouver to Alaska with a motorcycle could be done via either the Marine Highway (ship) or the Alaska Highway (road). Since my passenger was not very familiar with passengering on a motorcycle, I thought the more leisurely seaborne marine way would be best.

Meeting at the airport, we ferried over to Vancouver Island and made a leisurely run up to Port Hardy at the northern tip. Big ships cruised up the Marine Highway, filled with cars, trucks, and motorhomes that all required reservations. Motorcycles were small, and could show up at any time and be welcomed aboard. Apparently that is no longer true in the 21st century.

The ships avoided the open ocean and went up narrow waterways, very close to the forested mainland and many islands, with moose and bear and eagles on the shores. For the first day passengers were constantly oohing and aahing, but by the third, they were almost bored.

It was very early on the third morning when the ship sailed up the Chilkoot Inlet and docked at our destination, Haines. This small port town of a thousand or so year-round residents, sat at the northern tip of Alaska's panhandle with a road connection through Canada to the much larger pan part of our 49th state. The road had to go through Canada as the skinny piece of American land between the pan and the handle involved two large glaciers, which do not make for a reliable road surface.

The ship's ramp went down and the cargo-master waved my motorcycle as the first off. On the town's main street the few shop- and cafe-owners had opened early to greet the tourists; better to miss a little sleep than to miss a sale. A plaque informed interested visitors that Haines had been named after a New Jersey woman who had raised money to build a school for the local Indian children. Mrs. Haines never set foot in Alaska, but was more famous here than she ever was in New Jersey.

Not wanting to swallow the dust and diesel fumes of the motorhomes that were disembarking, we had a short look-around then headed up the Haines Highway. This good graveled road would pass quickly out of Alaska, go into Canada, and connect with the Alaska Highway after 150 miles.

Initially the road ran alongside a narrow finger of Chilkoot Inlet, crossed over a bridge, and approached a low range of mountains. A wide spot in the road, with a couple of dozen houses, was once the boisterous gold-mining town of Porcupine. The gold had mostly played out by the time World War I started and the town dwindled, but a cafe offered hot, strong coffee.

"I see the ferry came in," said the broad-shouldered woman flipping pancakes on the griddle. Not for us, but for a pair of husky men sitting at a table. "Ferry traffic always means a little extra action here, which I can always use." The road into the mountains was dry and in good condition, we were told, "but do pull over to the side when you see a truck coming. Some of them don't brake too good."

The Boundary Range of mountains were bleak and treeless, with snow on distant summits. Some 65 miles from Haines the road crossed Chilkat Pass, having gone from sea level to 3500

Alaskan photos courtesy of Road Rider magazine, 1976

An unpaved stretch of the Alaska Highway near Destruction Bay in Canada's Yukon Territory shows that the big trucks can throw up a heap of dust; it is all paved now, but under constant repair.

A hundred years ago a miner or two or three would have been living in this cabin, snowed in for four months out of the year, hoping to strike it rich when the weather cleared.

28

feet, and we entered Yukon Territory. After the pass the road dropped into the flat, lake-dotted land to the north. No towns out here, as there was no way to earn a living, no lumbering, no mining, nothing much but road maintenance.

On-coming traffic was minimal, perhaps a vehicle every 20 minutes. A car came around a curve in front of us and flashed its lights. In the Lower 48 I might have thought that he was warning me of a police presence, but here? It was obviously just a hello. I flashed back, continued around the curve and met a bear. A big grizzly, standing tall in the middle of what was essentially a wide one-lane gravel road. Braking was not a good solution, what with the loose surface, so I chose to shoot on past Mr. Bear, and then applied the brakes.

"Why are you stopping?" queried my passenger.

"To get a photo of the bear," said I, fumbling in the tankbag for my little Rollei camera. Travelers' tales on life in this northern frontier often wrote of beggar bears who had learned that they might get a cheese sandwich if they flagged down passing motorists, and this bear was obviously in on the game.

"Get going! He's coming this way!!"

Turning to look, sure enough Mr. Bear was galumphing towards us. John's words about having a nice VW to retreat into came to mind. Our crash helmets might not prove to be very digestible, but perhaps Mr. Bear would merely scoop the innards out. We sped off in a shower of gravel. Never did get a bear picture.

At the aptly named Haines Junction the road hooked into the graveled Alaska Highway. Passing Kluane Lake we saw a sign for Destruction Bay, so named, we found out, for a great storm which had swept through in 1942, destroying housing and equipment used for the workers building the highway. Back then this was a real frontier.

At the Alaska border the Canadian fellow merely waved us through. The American, more than a bit bored and obviously a mild motorhead, stopped us to have a chat. And to admire the well- loaded BMW. He had seen two Hondas come through two days before, but motorcycle traffic seemed low. He recommended

We were incredibly fortunate at McKinley/Denali National Park in both getting a campsite and in having clear weather; Denali can be seen in the middle of the picture.

This was Portage Glacier, 50 miles southeast of Anchorage, back in 1976; in 2010 most of the ice just beyond this parking area has become a lake.

a campground a short ways up the road.

The official "Highway Map of Alaska" showed that the state ran almost 200 campgrounds, many on the edge of picturesque lakes. We were the only campers at that first stop. The sites were spacious, firewood available for the taking, and no mosquitoes. An Alaska summer can be a mozzy misery, but that year the blood-suckers were hardly noticeable. Which meant that we could enjoy our meals outside, rather than hiding in the tent. As self-designated cook I opted for the simple fare, like a can of soup or stew. With a bottle of wine, though the wine choices in stores were quite basic: red, white, or pink. Night never really came, as even after the sun set, about 11 o'clock, there was still light enough to read by.

The next morning we arrived at Tok, where a left turn on Highway 1 went southwest to Anchorage, while Highway 2 went straight on to Fairbanks. We went straight, an easy 200-miler with not much of great note to see along that stretch. It offered lots of trees, small towns, the occasional little museum to attract the passing tourists, and a photo stop at the cutely named village of North Pole (zip code 99705) was mandatory.

Were one to imagine the last frontier, it probably would not have a gleaming strip of asphalt heading arrow-straight through the towering pine forest. Alaska might not be chock-a-block with people, but the transportation infrastructure was in excellent shape. Thanks to the taxes from the oil coming out of Prudhoe Bay; the state government had cash in bucketloads.

Every second or third night we found a hotel or motel; hot water was always appreciated. Costs for beds and food were a good deal higher than in the Lower 48, but only to be expected. A can of Dinty Moore stew had to come a long way to sit on a shelf in a store, as did the hamburger at a diner. Moose meat was cheaper than beef. With such a short growing season there was little in the way of fresh fruit or veggies especially as this was only July. I had no real thought of trying to get to Prudhoe Bay, up north of the Arctic Circle, which today is a destination for many travelers. Back then the haul road, being privately owned, was not open to public use. Permission could be requested, but

This is Palmer Creek Valley on the Kenai Peninsula, looking north towards the little town of Hope and the Turn Again Arm of the Cook Inlet.

I'm close to the border between Alaska and Canada, looking east towards Tombstone Mountain in the Yukon Territory; yes, the Top of the World Highway was not paved.

the oil company was decidedly not keen on having motorcycles interfere with the truck traffic. Motorcyclists could fall down, motorcycles could break down and truckers would waste precious time helping them.

The road south promised to be far more interesting, past Mt. McKinley National Park and on to the Kenai Peninsula. For me Mount McKinley was by far the biggest attraction, not to climb, just to see. For hundreds of years the local Indians called this great mountain Denali, meaning simply The High One — well deserved at 20,000 feet. Then in 1897 some feckless outsider fellow who obviously wanted to curry favor with his president decided the name should be McKinley. And so it was until the mountain officially reverted to being Denali in 1980.

A hundred miles south of Fairbanks we arrived at the park entrance — to find out that this was where all the tourists were. I had presumed we could ride into the park, camp, and hike around. Except a sign at the visitor center announced that all campsites were full; I had never thought of that being a problem. This was Alaska, the last frontier, with lots and lots of room — but a very limited number of campsites inside the park. A ranger explained that the only way into the park, unless one had a camping reservation, was to take a bus on a day-trip; camping might be available at some of the private campgrounds outside the park.

Miffed, I found my passenger talking to a back-packing couple who had just arrived by train from Anchorage, and they did indeed have a camping reservation. Good for four people. Would we care to join them? You betcha! I'll make dinner; a large store catering to the touring types sold steaks and red wine. These particular camping permits were exceptionally good, being at the furthest campground, some 70 miles inside the park, and the closest to Mt. McKinley/Denali. Clear skies provided a most dramatic view of the snow-covered High One, standing well above any other mountains in the Alaska Range.

Our back-packing hosts arrived by bus several hours after we did. Over dinner we exchanged traveling stories; they were school teachers in the Lower 48, spending the summer seeing the 49th

Above: Coming up the Taylor Highway from Tetlin Junction north towards Dawson City one sees this huge dredge; I could only presume the amount of gold found justified the expense of bringing the contraption here and then abandoning it.

That's the ferry which crosses the Yukon River, taking the traveler from Alaska to Canada's Dawson City; it's a free ride — or at least it was in 1976.

state — on the cheap. We hiked around the area for several days, and The High One remained highly visible. A ranger allowed as to how this clear weather was quite exceptional, as usually the peak was shrouded in clouds. The mountain was about 30 miles southwest of us, and since the broad McKinley River lay between us, we did not get much closer. Close enough for me.

On the third morning we packed up the motorcycle, bade our hosts a fond farewell, and rode south towards Anchorage. Passing by a little town called Wasilla, which would garner headlines 32 years later as the home of a vice-presidential candidate.

Time was a'wasting, as my companion had to catch a flight home in four days, and urban Anchorage held no appeal. Continuing south, Highway 1 looped around the east end of Turnagain Arm, the body of water which almost makes the Kenai an island rather than a peninsula. The town of Portage lies at the narrowest bit, and as the name implies, ships would dock here and the cargo portaged a few miles across this narrow neck of land to be reshipped on the east side. This strenuous effort avoided a long sail, or steam, around the entire peninsula. Highway 1 went on to Homer, the southernmost end of the road in Alaska's pan; definitely not a thru road. This was a pleasant seafront town where the inhabitants had figured out that more money could be pulled from the tourists than from the sea. We were looking for a place that would be somewhat more remote.

Our schoolteacher friends had told us they had camped in a little valley a few miles west of Portage, near the village of Hope, and recommended the place. A dirt road led to the village of Hope, right on Turnagain Arm, and then inland along Palmer Creek. This was the site of the first gold rush in Alaska, starting in 1889, although it lasted only about ten years. Much of the mining equipment was left here when operations were abandoned, gently rusting back into the earth, forming its own kind of beauty. Our rough camping was surrounded by purple lupine on the valley floor and the hillsides, so quiet that even a gentle zephyr was notable. The only real sounds were those of birds, large and small, winging their way through this small paradise. Perfect for our last two nights on the road. A single

I'm looking down from Canada's Top of the World Highway to the Yukon River and Dawson City, an old gold-mining center, now dedicated to mining tourists for a few months every year.

Some of the old log cabins in Dawson City have been salvaged, like this one where Jack London might well have spent a lonely winter and written some of his stories.

interruption was one car that drove to the end of the road, turned around, and left us in peace.

My passenger had to catch her plane. We returned to Anchorage and spent a night in a motel owned by a man who had made his money laboring on the oil pipeline. The motel had a bar, with a piano, and the owner regaled his guests with endless renditions of "To Dream the Impossible Dream." Fueled by endless glasses of cheap bourbon. Our room was far enough away so as not to be bothered.

Passenger gone, it was time to head back to Massachusetts, some 4500 miles east. In the motel parking lot I checked over the BMW. The differential was holding up great. The rear tire was worn, but should last until British Columbia, where the price would be a good deal cheaper. While I was loading the bike another motel guest came out to watch. He was Swiss, owned a BMW, had come to Alaska to catch salmon, and was flying back the next morning. He gave me a package with some freshly smoked fish, which I tucked in my tankbag and nibbled on for the next few days. That was the best food to be had in Alaska!

Highway 1 took me back to Tok, but while the smell of the barn was strong it did not stop me from doing a major deviation. Instead of heading down the Alaska Highway I turned north at Tetlin Junction onto the Taylor Highway. Alaskans like to use the term "highway", even if it is just a gravel road, which this was. The lure was that it led to the Top of the World Highway, a justifiably famous, or infamous, 80 mile stretch of gravel that crossed a low range of rounded mountains. Though the highest the road reached was 4100 feet, it did give the impression of being at the top of the world, the view over the thinly treed slopes creating a seemingly endless panorama.

At the east side the road dropped down to and stopped at the Yukon River, where the Canadian highway service ran a free ferry. On the far side was the town of Dawson, a boomtown in gold rush days, with a population estimated at 40,000 in 1900, now down to about a thousand. Although annually hordes of tourists made their way to this romantically dilapidated community in the summer months. The old buildings were being fixed up by

The Klondike Highway runs alongside the Yukon River almost to Carmacks, where I turned off to take the Robert Campbell Highway east to Watson Lake.

There was no Triple A up in Alaska in the 1930s, so if your truck broke down and you couldn't fix it, you left it.

the Yukon Territory's administration, as it understood the appeal of the history to those who journeyed north to find at least a little piece of that last frontier.

One of the cabins in town had reputedly been lived in by Robert Service, the Yukon's poet laureate. Outside a man with a good voice, hired by the tourist bureau, was reciting Service's poems:

"This is the law of the Yukon, that only the strong shall thrive;
That surely the weak will perish, and only the fit survive."

I was enjoying a nice 70-degree day in July; in six months it would probably be 80 or 90 degrees cooler; too cold for the likes of me.

That evening I pitched my tent at a campground called Flat Creek, near the Klondike River, and thought briefly about going north 450 miles along the Dempster Highway to the end of the road at Inuvik. Morning came, and I gave up that notion, but one more minor deviation was in order. Instead of going south to meet up with the Alaska Highway, which would be full of trucks and motorhomes and afflicted with miles of construction, I turned east at Carmacks.

That put me on the Robert Campbell Highway, 400 miles of good dirt more or less paralleling the Alaska Highway, ending at Watson Lake, on the Alaska Highway. Campbell was a fur trader, and apparently one tough hombre, who explored much of the Yukon Territory back in the 19th century. This last little indulgence world provide an adequate frontier experience, with the advantage of having very, very little traffic.

The village of Ross River, with a store and a few houses, was 170 miles along the Campbell Highway, and had the last gas before Watson Lake. Another 230 miles. I put the Beemer on its centerstand to make sure that I could fill the gas tank all the way, and bought a one-gallon container just in case. After filling the tank and the container, and lashing that to the passenger seat, I went in to pay.

"It's a good road," said the shop keeper, "you shouldn't have any problems."

Rolling the bike off the centerstand, there was a depressing

"Squish!" Flat rear tire. A close look at the tread showed some cord showing, but no nail was apparent. It must have been a sharp stone that did the damage. I had definitely made a false economy by not replacing the tire in Anchorage. Nothing to do but go forward.

The shop keeper, having seen all this, came out to offer commiseration, a complimentary soda, and a couple of rags. I took the wheel off, took the tire off, patched the tube, and then stuffed a folded t-shirt between the tube and the most worn part of the tire. "Good luck," said my host, and I believe he truly meant it. I rode the next 230 miles slowly, making the distance without need of the spare can of fuel. Proof that an easy hand on the throttle does extend mileage.

Watson Lake had a big campground, where I found two motorcyclists from New Jersey who were headed home. Dropping my gear with them, I went into town in search of a new, or even a used, tire. Nothing. A garage owner said he could order one up from Dawson Creek, the southern terminus of the Alaska Highway, pre-paid, and it might take two or three days to arrive.

I returned to the campground, bereft and depressed. John Muir was right; I'd get a flat tire somewhere in the wilderness, be unable to repair it, and end up eaten by a grizzly.

"Don't worry," said the Jersey guys, "we'll stick with your. You won't be alone. You get a flat, we'll all fix it. Worst comes to the worst, one of us will run ahead to Dawson Creek, get a tire, and come back. We won't abandon you."

Two slow days, one more flat, lots of newspaper stuck in the tire to protect the tube, and we got to Dawson Creek. Salvation came in the form of a motorcycle shop, and the tire was changed in front of the motel. I paid for a celebratory dinner to thank my companions. Next morning we went our separate ways. Wish I could find those Jersey guys again, and thank them again.

Baja California 1975 & 1980

Baja beaches are incredibly varied and can be found from the Playas de Tijuana in the north to Cabo San Lucas in the south, some more accessible and crowded than others like this secluded idyllic cove.

My first trip to Baja was entirely accidental. In 1975 a friend and I were riding up from Panama on a pair of BMW /5s and spent a night at a campground in Puerto Vallarta, on the Mexican mainland Pacific coast. This being late January, a number of American motorhomers were snow-birding at this pleasantly tropical latitude, and one fellow came over to chat with us. We said we were planning on continuing north to Arizona, and he asked if we knew about the new weekly ferry to Cabo San Lucas at the tip of Baja California. And the newly paved Baja highway. We did not. He had just driven down the length of Baja on the

41

Above:
In the northern third of Baja, the Sierra de Juarez and the Sierra San Pedro Martir are mountainous zones with heavy evergreen coverage; the Picacho del Diablo is over 10,000 feet.

Between the 29th and 30th parallels is the Parque Natural del Desierto Central di Baja California, about 15 miles wide and 100 miles long, home to the cirio cactus, often known as the boojum tree.

fresh asphalt and had found the trip quite exhilarating…and recommended it. And the ferry was due in tomorrow. Next evening Kenny and I loaded our bikes on the ship, spent a comfy night sleeping in lounge chairs, and rolled off the ramp into Cabo at dawn. We had both been on the road for two years, and the idea of getting back to the U S of A appealed to us. We boogied.

The thousand miles was a minor hindrance, and instead of exploring the delights of the peninsula we just cruised on through, covering the thousand miles in two days. It was rather eerie, following this pure black ribbon for hundreds of miles, passing tiny villages, the occasional town, and black cows sleeping on the warm black asphalt.

The first night we spend camped amongst the palm trees of San Ignacio, an oasis-like setting. It was a nice old town, with a mission church on the square, good food for very little money, and friendly locals. But truth be known, we were headed for the barn, as the horse folk say, and just gave the place a quick look, a snooze, and away in the morning.

Late that afternoon we got to the northern port of Ensenada; it was just before dusk and we decided to wait until the next day to do the last 70 miles up to US Customs in Tijuana. We looked for a place to pitch our tents.

On the north side of the harbor we found a faded, peeling sign which read ENSENADA CAMPING. The place was on its way out of business, a 1950s travel-trailer park with several dozen decrepit little plywood trailers warping on weed-surrounded concrete slabs, sitting on a cliff overlooking a beachless ocean. We were just in time for a nice sunset view, but not much else.

An elderly Mexican gent was honchoing the place. He appeared in serape and wide-brimmed hat, speaking a rather polished English. Of course there was room, and he showed us to a vacant concrete slab. Not quite the greensward that a tenter desires, but we both had free-standing tents. And air mattresses.

Unfortunately, said our host, there was only cold water in the bathhouse, as there was not much business, and nobody in residence, and the cost of heating water could not be justified. No problem.

He told us where to find a good, cheap restaurant in town. We went, ate to surfeit, and returned to the campsite with a bottle of Santo Tomas red, a local wine which might not be to the oenophile's taste, but suited us just fine.

Kenny and I were going to split up the next day, go our separate ways, so we appropriated a couple of elderly deck chairs and began to reminisce and make promises about the future, sipping the wine out of our tin camping cups, admiring the stars.

The host appeared, trusted that he was not intruding, hoped that everything was satisfactory, lack of hot water notwithstanding, and enquired as to our travels. We invited him to pull up a chair, and if he cared for some wine, he could swig from the bottle or find a glass.

Excusing himself, he went off into the dark, to reappear a few minutes later with a tray, a bottle of tequila, salt, lemons, and three glasses. We were well on our way to getting schnockered.

He had been a school teacher when Pearl Harbor happened, and then had served as an interpreter for the war-time American presence in this natural harbor. After the war he had married, seen the future, and bought this piece of land. But financial success had evaded him. Mexicans and Americans "with connections" were making great profit, but he had "missed the boat." His mastery of American colloquialisms was excellent.

He wasn't sorrowful, or self-pitying — he admitted he wasn't a good businessman. He would sell the land and go and live with a daughter in Tijuana. But, he ruminated, how different things would have been if the United States had acquired Baja California as well as Alta California in 1848.

Ensenada could have been another San Diego. I was just as glad it wasn't.

Baja California is an accident of just about everything — geography, geology, history, politics and economics. It is a bit of the third world belonging to the second world with a border on the first world.

The narrow peninsula is 1059 miles long, measured along Mexico Highway 1; it is a 100 miles wide in the northernmost section, while down by the Bay of La Paz it is less than 30 miles

thick. A spine of mountains runs down the length, from the Sierra de Juarez in the north to the Sierra de la Laguna in the south, the Pacific Ocean on the west, the Gulf of California (also known as the Sea of Cortez) to the east. It is predominantly a rocky, dry, inhospitable finger of land, with little green spots

This is a good part of the old Westside Highway — good except for the annoying corrugations that tend to rattle your teeth as one bounces along.

Though a map actually shows this as a road called La Cuesta de la Ley, or The Slope That Rules, I wouldn't try this on a rainy day. Street bikes with low clearance wouldn't fare too well on any given day of the year.

around water sources.

Until the early 1970s most of Baja was a rather wild place, generally ignored by the federal government in Mexico City. La Paz and a few tiny towns struggled along in the south, while up by the American border there was a little fishing, a little truck farming, and a little tourism. In the 1960s Americans began coming down and holding motorcycle and car endurance races that tore up the cactus and sand from one end of the peninsula to another.

If you weren't interested in racing, to travel from north to south was a reasonable facsimile of an adventure, with bad dirt roads, minimal services, and cold beers few and far between. That changed in 1974 when Route 1 was paved all the way from Tijuana to Cabo San Lucas — two narrow lanes of overly thin asphalt. Two trucks could barely pass each other, though they often tried this feat at speed, with both vehicles sometimes ending in the cacti.

The road was a political victory for Baja California Sur. The peninsula is divided between BCS and the northern state, called simply Baja California, two of the 31 United Mexican States. Little love was lost between La Paz, capital of BCS, and Tijuana and Mexicali in the north. The northern cities basically existed as economic colonies, poor relations of the United States of America, while La Paz was limited by its reliance on ferries to the Mexican mainland. Building the road meant that BCS could peddle fish and produce in the north, and attract motorized tourists to the south. You could get a better price for a head of lettuce in San Diego than in Mazatlan, a ferry-ride away from La Paz.

I've been back to Baja many times, and each trip shows me something new, whether it is prehistoric cave paintings, remnants of the Spanish mission era, or merely a road I had never been on. In 1980 I took the ferry from Topolobambo on the mainland over to La Paz, and thought I would ride up the old West Side Highway.

Before the paved road was done, connecting all the towns of note along both shores of the peninsula, the most popular route

Usually Baja is very dry, but after a stormy winter there will be some water crossings along in the back country; this is on the way to the beach portion of the old Westside Highway.

Locals often use dry river beds as roads, easy with a donkey, somewhat harder when getting a motorcycle through soft sand and around rocks.

for the long-distance truckers was to stick to the west coast, avoiding having to cross twice over the mountains that are the backbone of the peninsula. The West Side Highway was a pleasant euphemism for 150 miles of bad road and 50 miles of smooth beach. My motorcycle, a Suzuki GS850G, was intended for asphalted roads, but I thought it could handle the lack of pavement. And the gas tank was big enough.

At Insurgentes the paved road turned east, the dirt road, well-defined but washboard rough, went north along the west coast. I've been told any number of times what causes washboarding on a dirt surface, but I still don't understand the process. Baja has thousand of miles of such road, and the constant worry is that such shaking will loosen nuts and bolts and cause the untimely demise of the vehicle.

San Juanico, the last village before getting to the beach, sat on a bluff overlooking the ocean; I stopped to reassure myself of directions and get some food for supper. One store seemed to have the entire retail business for the community sewed up, selling tinned food, stale bread, and soda pop. I hoped that the bottle of wine I had in a saddlebag had survived the beating.

My map of Baja was put out by the American Automobile Association, which does do good cartography. Even little-used dirt roads were marked down to the tenths of a mile. However, for every line on the map there were two or three versions on the ground. I knew that I was going to have to go some miles beyond San Juanico to find the turn to the sea, and if I made a mistake I would end up in the mountains rather than on the beach. No road signs out this-away, and dozens of tracks that could lead nowhere.

"Senora," I asked the lady behind the counter, "can you tell me how to find the road to the beach?"

"No," she replied, "but he can," pointing over my shoulder. The caricature of a Mexican bandito was coming in the door, with cowboy boots, jeans, an old and torn denim shirt, and a large, black mustache. Here was I about to divulge my route and whereabouts so he could follow along and murder me and take the motorcycle. Ah, well.

We've just crossed the peninsula from Mulege on the Sea of Cortez on over to San Juanico, better known as Scorpion Bay, one of the prime surfing spots on the Baja Pacific side.

On the dirt road going south from San Felipe, near Gonzaga Bay, an enterprising fellow, Coco, (shirtless) who retired some time back, set up shop to cater to the travelers. Though out in the middle of nowhere — or often because of that — he gets a regular flow of customers stopping in for cool refreshments.

We went outside and leaned on the fender of his very beat-up Ford pick-up, which sported a worn decal announcing that the truck had once been part of the support team for the Baja 1000. His distances weren't too precise (undoubtedly his odometer didn't work), but he had all the topographical features that anyone would need. I would go more or less inland along the road for some miles, pass a very small cooperative farm, drop into a gully, climb out and drop into another gully, go by a rancho, and then I would climb out and onto the plateau. And after three, maybe four miles, there would be a turn to the left marked by a little pile of rocks. And a million broken beer bottles. The racers would come through there, using the place as a refueling stop, and along with filling gas tanks, everyone, especially the pit-crews, refreshed himself.

The directions were spot on. The rancho was typically Baja, with a small house, several scrawny cows, some prickly pears, and a barking dog. At the intersection there was enough broken glass to warrant setting up a recycling plant. When I got to the edge of the plateau I could see the dark ocean beyond reflecting the late-afternoon sun, and I began scrabbling steeply downhill.

At the bottom the track pitched and heaved, winding in and around a lunar landscape filled with large boulders. Finding a secluded campsite along a dried-up creek, I pitched my tent, prepared my lavish meal of sardines, stale rolls, and wine, and watched the stars come out on a moonless night. Somewhere, far off, I could hear the sounds of tinkly bells, the kind one associates with domestic animals. Though what animals would fatten in this waterless land I did not know.

In the morning I loaded up and after a mile I came upon a hut and two half-sized corrals, and two small boys herding quantities of goats around. Their little operation was somewhat beyond the back of beyond.

"Is this the road to the beach?" I asked.

"Yes, yes," they chorused, rushing close up.

A one-eyed man came out of the hut. He corroborated the information and asked, "Do you want coffee?"

"With great pleasure," I replied, and dismounted.

When a man's got to eat, a man's got to eat — and I usually choose open-air places where the locals go. That way I know the food is bound to be fresh and you can't get more authentic to the region.

Below:
Repairing a tire is a very necessary skill to have in Baja, as a puncture can happen anytime, anywhere.

The hut was too low and small for me to enter, but rustic seating accommodations were in front. The fellow brought two chipped enameled cups outside, a tin-can with boiled coffee, and some sweetened, condensed milk.

"There is a spring here," he said in reply to my question, "and in this season I bring my goats to feed, and my family. My cousin has a truck, and every week, two weeks, he brings supplies and takes some goats to market. Do you want food? My wife will fix you cabrito and frijoles."

"No thank you, the coffee is enough. How much do I owe you?" "Nothing. The coffee is free. If you had eaten my food, I would charge you, because it costs me to bring beans and flour here. But to share a cup of coffee is to show that we are all brothers, all friends."

I had not seen his wife, but the two boys were standing close by, eyes riveted to the stranger.

"Come here," I said, going back to the motorcycle. I would be home in 36 hours, and I was on my last clean clothes. But in the dirty laundry were several T-shirts, and I felt that the family would accept a gift in the spirit in which it was offered — rather than the soiled condition. The older boy received a stunning Harley-Davidson shirt, and the other a black and turquoise number extolling the wonders of a New Orleans jazz festival.

I left a small-time entrepreneur who could become the Colonel Saunders of the fast-food goat-meat world, and two kids who would never grow enough to fit the XL T-shirts.

And then the beach. It was half a mile or more wide and 50 miles long. No traffic lights, no turns, no directions, no nothing. Keep the ocean on your left. To find a stretch like this in the backyard of the United States is rather overwhelming. The sand was flat, hard-packed, the surf rolling gently in the distance, the beach backed by dunes and hills and mountains. Nothing out there, no park rangers, no concessions, no signs telling me not to litter. Just the motorcycle and the beach and a half-full tank of gas. Speed and solitude. Just don't crash.

The setting was not 20th century. It would be easier to imagine a horse and rider on this expanse, but a lone motorcycle was an

Up at the north end of the Gulf of California, a.k.a. Sea of Cortez, is the town of San Felipe, where many boats have spent their final days.

That is Land's End out there in the Pacific, the very tip of Cabo San Lucas at the southernmost bit of the Baja peninsula.

anomaly. When the Baja 1000 took this route, scores of vehicles would pass at full tilt. But wind and weather had wiped away all traces of that event, and now I was on pristine ground. It was a road unlike any road I have ever been on. Well defined by sea and dune, but wider than any highway known to motorized man, and completely free of traffic. Civilization could have disappeared, and but for my need for gasoline, I could have gone on forever. Or at least until the beach ended.

A mile on this beach, whether at 10 or 100 mph, was entirely different than a mile on any sort of paved surface. I could go straight, I could zig and zag between the surf and dunes, do U-turns without slowing down. I have ridden on many other beaches, but the great appeal of this one was that it was merely a long day's ride from San Diego. Though I appreciate the technical and scientific advances of the last hundred years, I like to know there are places where I can pretend that I'm a real traveler.

After 20 miles I passed by a temporary fishing camp, men and women cleaning the night's catch, a truck with ice containers waiting to take it to some distant town. Fifteen miles further along a small community of stilted houses stood a thousand yards off to my left. After 50 miles the beach ended at the Bay of the Whales, celebrated by a collection of fishermen's shanties. I had to leave the sand and wind bumpily along the rocky road through the hills to San Ignacio.

As on so many of my trips down to Baja, life doesn't get much better than starting the day with a fresh shrimp taco and all the trimmings, such as here at Rice & Beans, a family-run establishment in San Ignacio.

And then back to the pavement of National Route 1. Asphalt is useful when one is in a hurry, like truck drivers trying to earn a living, but it is not very romantic.

The central part, the best part, of Baja has not much changed over the past 40 years. Or 230 years; the mission at San Ignacio has been holding services since 1784. On the coast at San Jacinto a freighter was wrecked 30 years ago, and still slowly succumbs to time and rust. In the Mulege plaza the fisherman opens his taco booth at ten o'clock, the locals come for the fish tacos, and he closes at two to go home and be with his family, and sleep before getting up at 4 a.m. to go out to sea to catch the fish he puts in his tacos. In the mountains west of town are bad roads and rocky tracks which lead to little ranchos where the family might get to town once a year, and should a couple of motorcyclists show up, they might well be invited to share their meal.

Baja is friendly and hospitable — except for the tourist areas. Stay away from them is my advice.

∾∾∾∾

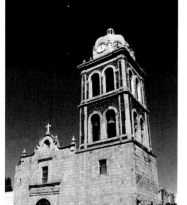

Throughout Baja one encounters venerable old missions: that on the left is the mission in Loreto, rebuilt after the devastating earthquake in 1877 that flattened the town. On the right is Santa Rosalia de Mulege, a more original structure. Most of the old missions still hold regular religious services.

Bavaria 1964

The Special Forces emblem, and Latin speakers know the words to say:
To Free the Oppressed.

Military service was what many young men did back in the
early sixties, in that draftable era, and while many suffered, in
truth I could not have asked for a nicer posting. Uncle Sam was
sending soldiers to thankless places like a freezing Korea or a fetid
Vietnam, and I got sent to the Bavarian Alps. And issued a pair
of antiquated cross-country skis, no less. I lived in a handsome
kaserne (barracks) that we had inherited from the German army,
which was a short half-mile walk to a gondola lift that went up
the mountain, the Brauneck, that loomed behind us.

The 10th Special Forces stationed the three "killer" companies — killer meaning operational as opposed to the administrative company that was up the road in Bad Tolz — in Lenggries, a German army post that had once housed ski troops. Old postcards (above) show barracks at Jaeger Kaserne, the name by which the earlier complex was known.

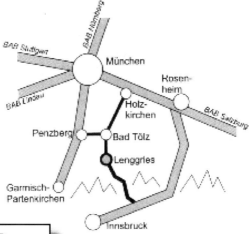

Clement in full Special Forces regalia, with Green Beret and paratrooper wings on his chest.

The little town of Lenggries was just across the Isar River, with a population of about 2000 and three small breweries — the way things should be. A train ran from there to the city of Munich four or five times a day. In May of 1964 the station-master called up to say that a crate had arrived from the Triumph motorcycle company in England. After opening the crate about the only thing I had to do was bolt on the handlebars and front wheel, and connect the battery. Plus put some gas in the tank. I was back on the road.

My assignment in Germany was with the US Army's 10th Special Forces Group (Airborne). When I joined the army I had thought I would be going to Officer Candidate School. At the end of basic and advanced-individual training several specialized schools gave presentations in an effort to lure in some recruits. OCS was done by a weedy second lieutenant wearing an unflattering garrison cap; he impressed me not a whit. Next on the program was a solidly built sergeant wearing a very handsome green beret. President Kennedy had recently authorized the wearing of the beret, and with this added interest from the government Special Forces was busy recruiting new members. The sergeant ended his talk by looking around the auditorium and saying, "I doubt if any of you can make it, but you're welcome to try." I volunteered.

In the 1950s you had to be pretty much a career soldier to get into Special Forces, but after Kennedy embraced them in 1961 they were taking volunteers from those of us who had been in the army for a mere four months. Vietnam was heating up and Green Berets were much in demand.

First I had to qualify for my airborne wings, which I got after a two-week jump school down in Fort Benning, Georgia; the nicest thing about being a paratrooper, other than the exhilaration of stepping out of a perfectly sound airplane while in flight, was that it paid an extra $55 a month, no mean sum back in those days. My base pay was $78 a month. Jump pay would go into the motorcycle fund. From jump school I went north to Fort Bragg, North Carolina, home of the Special Forces Training Group, where I became a demolitions expert. "Expert" was perhaps too

Even while training stateside for Special Forces the seemingly accident-prone Clement had had his trials, breaking his wrist, which did not keep him from riding. Shown here in 1963 on a very trusting friend's BSA.

To impress the local frauleins a GI was advised to dress well — and when at all possible, to act in gentlemanly fashion.

strong a word, but I did learn to blow things up without blowing myself up. After many months there was graduation, with the ritual burning of the fatigue caps and donning of the berets. Some of my classmates stayed stateside, others went to Vietnam, or Panama, while I lucked out with Germany.

Arriving in September of 1963, I was just in time for Bavaria's Octoberfest, which was merely an excuse to drink lots of well-brewed beer. So far I really had no complaints about the hardships involved in defending my country.

The autumn was good, and I was saving my bucks to buy a new Triumph Bonneville come spring. I did go down to the Fischer ski factory in Austria and bought a pair of down-hill skis, inexpensive as they were seconds, having a minor blemish. In my off-time I'd take the lift up the Brauneck and ski down. Beyond the upper gondola station and restaurant were two rope lifts which would take the dedicated even higher up the mountain. I was way up high one Saturday afternoon.

The Germans did not have the carefully groomed slopes that American lawyers demand, but let nature take her course. Sometimes there was fresh snow, sometimes the snow had been blown off, leaving a rather hard surface. As it was that Saturday. The upper slope was merely a swath cut through the pine trees, perhaps 70 or 80 yards wide, where the reckless could go schuss-booming straight down, confident of their ability to stop if necessary. The more cautious, like myself, could do a series of stem turns, providing a modicum of control by choosing the angle and speed. My risk-taking was more in tune with jumping out of an airplane at night, blasting caps secured in a breast pocket, than in zipping straight down a 30-degree slope on a pair of thin skis.

I hit an icy patch, skidded, attempted to regain control, but with my sliding about a binding let loose, putting me on my butt. I got back up, put the tethered ski back on, and, stupidly, tightened the binding, the classic mistake of a novice skier. I arrived at another icy patch, skidded, and again the binding let go…but this time a split second too late. Sitting on the snow I realized that my ankle hurt, and would probably hurt a lot more in a little while. Getting

Bavaria 1964

Clement had a 1964 Triumph
Bonneville shipped over to Bavaria
from England, and was happily
riding it around the Alps until the
day of his accident.

Back in the Sixties the C-rations that
troops ate in the field came with packs
of cigarettes — not so in the 21st century.

up I skied gently to the restaurant, gondola'd down the rest of
the mountain, and then limped gingerly back to the barracks. A
medic said I should go have an x-ray. An ambulance took me up
to Munich, where the army doc said I had indeed lopped off the
bottom of my left tibia, and that I would need a cast. I should not
have tightened that binding.

While lying in bed a German orthopedic doctor who worked
in the U.S. Army hospital came to see me, with my x-rays in hand.
"Mr. Salvadori, I am doing a book on broken bones, and you
have the classic ski fracture. Would you mind if I used this x-ray
in the book. Your name will not be mentioned, but I consider it
polite to ask permission."

All I could think of was the novel by Thomas Mann, *The Magic
Mountain*, in which a young man at a tuberculosis sanatorium in
the Swiss Alps falls in love with a fellow patient and carries an
x-ray of her around with him. The doc got my permission.

Winter passed and I ordered up the Bonneville. My unit had

a bad reputation for accidents, and some psychiatrist writer had done an article saying that Special Forces types had mind-sets similar to race-car drivers. Both professions appeal to risk-takers, those who like living a little closer to the edge than do most folk. And being trained to parachute behind enemy lines at night did involve some riskiness. We also had some fast cars on the post, including a Ferrari and an E-type Jag. And two guys had BMW motorcycles.

Crate arrived, bike assembled, I was on the road with my own transportation, tearing around the mountains, Garmisch, Berchtesgaden, day trips and weekenders. My only unfortunate incident was on a damp day on a small road near the town of Gmund that had a sharp S-curve combined with disused railroad tracks, where I low-sided. Nothing drastic, just a bent footpeg.

One June afternoon I was in Bad Wiessee, a little resort town on Tegernsee, a lake not far from Lenggries, and happened to meet Gretchen, a charming fraulein. Her English was excellent, as was our compatability. We talked, and she said she was dating a GI, but had no exclusivity. After a few questions I figured out that the GI was a boring "leg" (non-airborne soldier) who drove a boring car, and she liked the romance of the motorcycle and Special Forces. Several weeks went by, everything was going well, and we had a date on July 3rd.

I showed up in Bad Wiessee, and she looked subdued. She told me that her "leg" friend had proposed, and she has decided to accept. A proposal of marriage!? That was not fair, not fair at all. That was just not done! Not in the rules! Of course I said none of this, as I was not willing to propose. Gretchen was very gracious, and apologetic, and we did have a pleasant last supper. Late in the evening she kissed me goodbye, we wished each other well, and I headed back to post, via Gmund.

And there was that same S-curve I had crashed on once before. Wanting to see how fast I was going this time I looked down at the Smiths speedometer. But at night it took a bit longer than expected to read the figures, especially with six-volt lighting, and while I was looking down at the speedo I saw dirt coming up under my front wheel. I was headed for a ditch, and not

Clement on the Bonneville in Massachusetts in the spring of 1965, after both he and the motorcycle underwent extensive repairs.

Look closely at that lower right leg; this is what Clement's 1964 salad fracture looked like in 1972. Can't say it has changed much to-date either.

wanting to bend the bike I put it into a slide bringing the front end back around 90 degrees and heading towards the pavement. My sideways movement was faster than my forward motion, but I believe I would have made it safely if a Nazi tree had not intentionally jumped in my way. I hit the tree going sideways, with my right leg taking the blow right behind the knee.

I ended up sitting in the road, in shock, with my right foot strangely flopped over. That looked odd, so I reached down, picked it up, and it flopped the other way. Not good. My Bonneville was sitting upright in the ditch, the tranny having somehow gotten into neutral, ticking over at idle. Cars appeared and stopped, ambulance arrived, a hit of morphine and I was off to the hospital. X-rays showed that while the ankle and knee were in good shape, the femur was broken into two pieces, the tibia and fibula together were in 15 pieces. The army docs put a steel rod in the femur, said I would be in traction for six weeks, and probably in plaster for six months. After traction was over they would med-evac me to the US Navy hospital in Boston, the closest facility to my home town. Looked like my military career was ended.

Gretchen heard the news and came up to Munich to visit me in the hospital, a very nice gesture. I thanked her and told her not to bother wasting her precious days off by coming to see me; she had other things to do and I would soon be history. My buddies from the 10th came up and told me that they would take care of the Bonnie, make sure it got shipped back to Massachusetts.

And the German orthopedic doctor appeared again in my room. "Very interesting, Mr. Salvadori. In your lower leg you now have what we call a salad fracture, like a tossed salad, and I would like to include an x-ray of that in my book as well. With your permission." Permission granted.

Nine months later I was out of the hospital, out of the army, and back on the Bonneville. Only regret is that I never did see the book.

Big Sur, California 2012

The road passes Hearst Castle, the ornate construction sitting high on a hill a mile off to the east, glittering in the early morning sun. It's certainly not a real castle, built for defensive purposes as they did in Europe hundreds of years ago, but a vanity built by a very rich man to entertain his mistress and his friends. It is now a state park, and definitely worth a visit, if only to see how huge piles of money do not necessarily translate into good taste. Cattle and zebra graze in the fields; Mr. Hearst liked having his foreign animals to impress his guests.

Yes, that sign indicates 74 miles of twisty road ahead — best taken early on a spring morning, but good all year round.

I'm headed north on California Route 1, a seaside road running most of the length of the state of California. The 100-mile stretch I am on, between the towns of Cambria and Carmel, is popularly known as the Big Sur Highway. Though its official name is the Cabrillo Highway, honoring the Portuguese explorer Juan Rodriguez Cabrillo who sailed up the coast in 1542. This is one of the most entrancing roads in North America, and it is part of my extended back yard.

I have written about many far-off places that I've been to on a motorcycle, but I can get the same pleasure close to home. It's not that I have to see some place new, like Rajasthan or Australia's

Cape Desolation, merely a road that changes each time I ride it. I've ridden the Big Sur Highway well over a hundred times, and never tire of it. Although sometimes, after a big rain or an earthquake, a landslide will block the road and it does not go through for many days, even weeks..

Hearst Castle, a few miles beyond Cambria, is an hour's ride from my house, and then the good times begin. The road curves gently along the coastal plain swooping by the old Piedras Blancas lighthouse, which used to warn ships to stay away from the rocky coast. Nowadays the idea of a rotating light has become a bit old-fashioned, with radar and GPS taking over the task — which are, admittedly, far more useful in a heavy fog. This is early on a winter's morning, and the day is as clear as the tone of a well-cast bell, the sun just climbing over the coastal range of low mountains, the Santa Lucia, where the highest peaks are a little over 5000 feet.

A long straightaway is ahead and the speedometer runs into triple digits, until I back off on the throttle as the road bends and gently climbs, then makes a devious right-hand downhill turn into the little valley of San Carpoforo — for the next 70 miles the Santa Lucia mountains come right down to the ocean's edge.

To the Spanish this mountainous area was merely referred to as the Grande Sur, or Big South, now a combination of the two languages. In the 18th century their regional headquarters for Alta California was in Carmel on the Monterey Peninsula; they never bothered to explore this rough and tumble section as there was not so much as a horse trail; only the native Chumash Indians knew the way on their footpaths. Spaniards chose to either sail along the coast, or take the easy walk along the Salinas River valley to the east.

All that changed in 1937 when a road was finally finished, connecting Carmel with Cambria. We could thank the Great Depression for that, as the government funded much of the construction in order to keep a lot of men busy; a silver lining to the Depression's black cloud.

Going north the road curves around and goes over the bridge crossing San Carpoforo Creek, then climbs recklessly up the face

The construction of Bixby Bridge in 1932, using the newly designed reinforced-concrete open-spandrel arch, was the key to opening up the road from Cambria to Carmel.

As an interesting juxtaposition, right across the road from the Carmel River State Beach, where minimally garbed vacationers cavort, is a Carmelite nunnery, home to a number of women who have vowed to spend a life in solitude and prayer.

of the mountains, twisting, turning, capable of making a flat-lander feel quite uncomfortable. We, the motorcycle and I, stop at Ragged Point, a small prominence high above the ocean, where an inn and a restaurant cater to the tourist; it is too early for the snack shop to be open and offer me cup of coffee. I wander out on the grass behind the inn and look down over 300 feet to a very rough sea. If your ship wrecked there, you might survive, but would have a dicey time trying to scale the cliffs; best to head down to the beach at San Carpoforo.

North of Ragged Point the stone-faced mountains drop directly into the sea, the road merely a cut-away on the surface sometimes closed due to the landslides I mentioned, especially in those rainy winter months. A right-hand curve is marked 15 miles and hour — best to heed these signs — and then the road drops down to Salmon Creek, where the waterfall is in full frolic. One car is parked, the occupants probably sleeping in a tent somewhere further up the canyon.

We climb up again and then wiggle down to where the road is only a few feet above the ocean, great granite walls looming high above. The road passes the tiny collection of businesses known as Gorda, with some of the highest-priced gas in the country should anyone be desperate. Nobody is around at this early hour; I have not seen a car on the road since passing Hearst Castle. A dirt road, Los Burros, goes off into the mountains and leads to the South Coast Ridge Road, a rough bit of work built in the years before 1900 to cater to the miners in the area. The minimal remains of a mining center called Manchester are up there in the Silver Peak wilderness. Silver was found along Alder Creek in the 1880s, followed by a brief flurry of activity until the lode ran out, and then Manchester fell into ghost-town status. Until all the buildings were destroyed in a forest fire in the 1970s.

But I'm on a road bike, not a dirt-road bike, and stay on Big Sur Highway. We cross Plaskett Creek and come into Pacific Valley, a small flatland where the mountains are set back a half-mile from the ocean and cattle graze. I could stop, park and climb over one of half a dozen stiles that allow travelers to cross the fence and wander close to the cliffs. But I am in it for the ride, not the walk.

Leaving Pacific Valley the road starts to undulate again, and we come to the turn for the Nacimiento-Fergusson Road, the only passage that crosses the Santa Lucia range between Carmel and Cambria. It is paved, but the seven miles to the top are a minor challenge, with more turns than a Slinky. At the top it connects with the north end of South Coast Ridge Road, or continues east into the Salinas River valley.

CA 1 goes past Kirk Creek Campground and on a few miles to Lucia, where a small old-fashioned motel and little restaurant have yet to waken. We drop out of the hills and back down close to the water's edge, looming cliffs above the road, and cross over Big Creek on a bridge made in 1937. It was the last of the major bridges built along the Big Sur, and it was the new-fangled concept of reinforced concrete arches that allowed these bridges to be constructed. The deep river canyons were too wide for a straight span, but engineering progress came along and mastered the problem.

Now the highway runs several hundred feet above the surf on a narrow flatness between ocean and mountain, past the Esalen Institute, a popular place for wealthy New Age types to come and get their souls cleansed in the hot springs. The coastal Indians knew of this as a healing place and pleasantly warm on a cold night.

Signs for the 4000-acre Julia Pfeiffer Burns State Park show up, the first of four state parks in the next 20 miles. It is worth a stop, especially in the spring, as Partington Creek ends with a waterfall crashing right onto the beach. Commercial businesses, tastefully done, of course, begin to appear, art galleries combined with restaurants. Past the Henry Miller Memorial Library, dedicated to the author who lived around these parts for the better part of 20 years, leaving in 1962; a dozen other writers and poets who lived in Big Sur are remembered here as well.. If it weren't so early I would stop at Nepenthe which is on the sea-side of the highway, offering the customer magnificent views while dining on a somewhat over-priced Ambrosia Burger. I take that over-priced statement back; considering the view, the cost is worth it. The business has thrived since 1949.

At the top of the hill the road goes away from the ocean and drops into the vale of the Big Sur River. A sign on the left indicates this is the way to the Post Ranch, where a fine room on the edge of a cliff will set you back about a thousand dollars a night. The road descends into the small town called Big Sur, catering to the year-round tourist industry. The Pfeiffer Big Sur State Park has a hotel and camping, followed by half a dozen small resorts in the heavily wooded valley. I like the Ripplewood myself, which has quiet cabins dating from the 1930s down by the river; these were originally used to house the road workers, and thankfully still do not have fixtures like television or telephones. It's not even nine in the morning, but I see the first cars on the road.

Hurricane Point, just north of the Little Sur River, can get right windy at times, but on a calm day the views north and south are unbeatable.

At the north end of the town is the Andrew Molera State Park, where the river meets the ocean and there is good access to the beaches. On the other side of CA 1 is the southern end of the Old Coast Road, which runs a rough ten miles of rarely graded dirt through the mountains to Bixby Landing on the coast. Before the building of the Bixby Creek bridge in 1932 this was the only way to get from Carmel to the Big Sur and its good grazing.

We blaze along as the road straightens out when passing the Point Sur Lighthouse State Historical Park, past fat cattle happily fattening on the grass, over a rise and then down in a gigantic U across the Little Sur River. The road climbs up to Hurricane Point, with its well-deserved name; on a blustery day this can be a pretty scary place. From the point I can look down and see Bixby Bridge a mile away. On the north side of the bridge the road straightens out, and the good ride is coming to an end.

I go by Garrapata State Park, Point Lobos State Reserve, and Carmel River State Beach. There are 150 miles on the tripmeter. Time to fill the tank. Should I go back down the coast? I think not, as the tourists and the motorhomes will soon be out in force. Best to take Carmel Valley Road down to the Salinas Valley, and then home.

There are many places in the world I would still like to get to, like Tasmania, or Chile, or riding up along Egypt's Nile River, but in the meantime, I am very happy in my back yard.

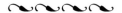

Bonneville Salt Flats Utah 2010

The author standing beside his 2006 Triumph Bonneville T100.

This is a book about roads, and places that roads take you, and this chapter is about a stretch of road that goes nowhere. It is not even a road, really, just a few miles of dead-straight, dead-flat track across a desert that has no end except in the mountains off in the far distance.

Most anybody who rides a motorcycle has heard about the Bonneville Salt Flats in northwest Utah, where speed trials are held every year. The flats cover about 40 square miles in the westernmost part of the Great Salt Lake Desert, which includes another 4000 square miles. Motorheads have cheerfully come here to try to go their fastest for nearly a century; in 1914 a

75

Blitzen-Benz automobile ripped across the desert at a claimed 141 mph. Back then there were no sophisticated timing devices, so that speed was probably computed by somebody with a stop-watch over a measured course.

If you aspire to go fast it is nice to have a large flat area with no obstructions. Like the flats. I thought it would be entertaining to go out with my eponymous Triumph Bonneville motorcycle, 2006 vintage, and see what the excitement was all about. Eponymous because in 1959 Triumph chose to name its fastest model a Bonneville since a Triumph-engined streamliner had broken records with a 214.47-mph sprint across the flats in 1956.

One could question this particular desire of many humans to go faster and faster. Airplanes broke the sound barrier in the late 1940s, and rocket-powered cars are now doing the same. But to go extremely fast, better than 200 mph, on two wheels? Which certainly lack any comforting sense of stability — that requires a different breed of rider. I'm an old-fashioned type, and merely wanted to see how fast my motorcycle would go, not set any record.

My accomplice and general instigator was friend, colleague, and neighbor Chris, a genial fellow, about as big as I am at six foot plus, old-fashioned enough to wear his baseball cap with the visor forward. He is an internal-combustion guru, and an avid proponent of motorcycling.

The flats are owned by us the public, through the U.S. Bureau of Land Management, and are listed as a recreation area. Anyone can go out there and open up the throttle, but it is far more interesting to do so when official speed trials are organized, with timing towers set up to make sure you know precisely how fast you were going, and not relying on your generally optimistic speedometer.

A number of go-fast organizations rent the flats each year, providing a small income to our government. Mostly these renters are car types, who generally and generously allow motorcycles to run, but the two-wheelers are sort of second-class citizens. Until 2004 when a fellow named Denis Manning organized the BUB Motorcycle Speed Trials, a week focused on motorcycles in which both the American Motorcyclist Association and the FIM International Federation of Motorcyclists — speed determinators would be on hand to verify records. Denis owns the BUB (Big Ugly Bastard) company that makes exhaust systems for motorcycles, and also the Lucky 7 streamliner which has several times held the record as the world's fastest motorcycle — 367.382 mph as of August, 2010. Records, after all, are made to be broken, and no one seems able to hold one for very long..

As a sop to those who weren't necessarily interested in going all that fast, he established a Run Watcha Brung class. RWB entrants are not going for records, just curious as to how fast their motorcycles actually are; AMA and FIM clocks do not lie.

Chris volunteered to provide his pickup and technical assistance. Not that we needed much, as I was planning on running stock. Even for the informality of RWB the bikes have to be properly prepped, which Chris did in delightful detail. Drain-bolts are safety-wired so the bike can't drop oil on the track. Axle bolts as well, so wheels won't fall off. The headlight is taped so that should there be an accident shards of glass do not end up on the runways. Mandatory number plates were put on, with 3120 an alphanumeric C A T — since cats bring me luck.

The rider's gear needs to be prepped as well. Leather suits, gloves and boots are required; apparently the man-made moto-clothing does not do nearly as well as leather when sliding along the salt at 200 mph. I have been easing myself into my Hein Gericke leather suit for the past 28 years, and by using a good deal of talcum powder I still managed to fit. Also, the helmet had to have the latest Snell safety rating, so a new Bell was in order.

It is roughly 800 miles from our town to the flats, and we would take two easy days to go out via the two-laners. Not having gone that distance inside a car or pickup since I don't know when, the road trip would be a test of my resolve. Chris showed up on a Thursday morning with the Bonnie strapped down in the back of his truck. He had also hooked up a trailer to carry our two Suzuki DR650 dual-purpose bikes, which we would use to play around on when we had free time. A kiss from The Wife and we were gone.

Wendover Willy greets visitors to West Wendover, Nevada.

Denis Manning, who runs this Bub speed week, is telling participants what to expect.

The pits were well organized and laid out with lots of space between the rows of canopies.

I've known Chris for 15 years, but never sat beside him for two days, nor shared a room. We would see how gracious our compatibility curve would be. Turned out he is good company, has good taste in music, put a good selection of nibbles and drinks in the cooler, and is quite happy just driving, not feeling the need to talk. That is important. He also prefers being behind the steering wheel to sitting in the passenger seat doing nothing, and I was okay with that.

Some eight hours later we rolled into Bishop, California, a town on the east side of the Sierra Nevada mountains well known for its many tourist facilities. A well-meaning friend had advised us that the best food in town was at the bowling alley; we stopped, got a motel room close by the alley, and went over for a reconnoiter. The menu was big on the fried foods and large steaks; after a day of merely sitting this heavyweight food was not for us. Just down the road was a Japanese restaurant, and Chris is knowledgeable concerning such fare. We ate well, ending up with a savory of flying-fish roe and quail eggs; don't knock it until you try it.

Next day US 6 took us all the way to Ely, Nevada, where, had we turned east we would eventually have ended up in Provincetown, Massachusetts, the Atlantic terminus of US 6, but instead went north on US 93 to Interstate 80 and Wendover.

Wendover, Utah, is a highway town, with a few motels, a couple of restaurants, several garages. West Wendover, Nevada, is quite another story, with three big casinos and hordes of Mormons coming in from Utah every weekend. Back in the days of the Conestoga wagon, 150 years ago, Wendover was known for its fresh water, much needed after crossing a hundred miles of the Great Salt Lake Desert. In 1910 the Western Pacific Railroad came through from Salt Lake City, and in 1940 the US Army built an airbase there for training pilots — very useful as there was lots of nice flat ground around should an emergency landing be required. Or a pilot be remarkably inept.

Chris and I had reservations at the Motel 6, where $35 paid for a rather small room, crowded with two beds, where compatibility was important. Fortunately we did not have to spend much time there — only to sleep. Unhitching the trailer with the DRs on board, we found we had lots of good company all around, as it seemed that just about everybody in the motel's 130 rooms was there for BUB week, and all manner of motorized two-wheelers were crammed into vans or towed in trailers. These people did not care about spacious bedrooms, they would rather spend their money on their machines.

The fraternity feeling was grand. Most everybody knew everybody else, and we were soon absorbed into the whole cheerful happening. These people were salt addicts running for records, which meant they would have five days to put in as many runs as they could and try to be the fastest. Granted, there are several hundred categories, from 50cc to unlimited size, vintage flatheads to the latest supercharged overhead camshaft designs, and, of course, the very expensive Big Boys going for the very top end.

One group of more than a dozen had T-shirts with SODIUM DISTORTION printed large. They had been coming out for nine years, and were well and truly addicted to the salt. This was their annual event, with fathers and children, mothers and grandchildren all taking part. Since we were newbies good advice was proffered, and we were told we should be out at the check-in site at six o'clock, even though check-in did not start until eight.

Eventually to bed, rising in the dark to drive four miles east on the Interstate, a sign indicating the exit to the Bonneville Salt Flats. Three miles of narrow asphalt led onto the flats, where BUB had set up the preliminary checkpoint. Already a couple of dozen vehicles were parked in front of us. For the next two hours it was schmoozing, unexpectedly seeing people I had not seen in years, meeting new people, generally fraternizing. It was a fine way to begin the salt-flats experience.

When an outfit like BUB rents the flats it has to get insurance, put out porta-potties (no ditches nor bushes to hide in or behind), and get everything organized. The check-in process is there so the staff can find your name on the list that proves you had paid your entry fee, and to sign waivers showing you are aware of the possible dangers. For me and the RWB status the cost was $150, for those who wanted to go for a record, $650; each entry also included a mechanic. Spectators paid $20. My RWB listing gave me two runs, although I could pay for more if I wished.

A temporary headquarters was being set up six or seven miles further out on the flats, with a large trailer housing the computers; there were also portable johns, several food vendors, and space for a hundred or more pit areas, which would all be protected from the sun by canopies that people brought along. Driving out towards the site gave us our first real view of the flats, and from the seat of our pickup we could not see where we were going, although orange cones were placed about every half mile. Since all the traffic was headed that way, we could follow the vehicle in front.

Eventually we saw the large boxy trailer on the horizon, and then more vehicles, and we were there. Three neat rows of canopies were sprouting up, and we selected a site in the middle, unloading the Bonnie. First order of this Saturday was to register at the trailer, which was rather more formal than the check-in. Paperwork all in order, health insurance documents viewed, good to go for scrutineering.

It was proving to be a beautiful day, with the temperature in the high 70s, the occasional puffy white cloud in the blue sky. At 4200 feet altitude, the flats can be scorchingly hot, but we had it nice. I rolled the Bonnie with my bag of personal gear draped across the saddle over to the scrutiny line. The old-time staffers were teaching some new scrutineers how the job is done. A mirror on a stick is the best way to determine that drain plugs are properly wired. Axle nuts okay. Doesn't he have to have a lanyard attached to the kill switch in case he falls off? No, the thumb-operated switch is okay. The Bonnie got a sticker on the fender. Chris looked on approvingly from the sidelines, glad his work had gone well.

My gear was spread out on a table. All okay. The Bell helmet got a sticker, too.

That was all for today. Chris and I cruised the pits for a couple of hours, looking, talking, asking, admiring. Some fellow had built a sidecar outfit using two Honda 175 twins. The Sodium

Bonneville Salt Flats, Utah 2010

Mildly bizarre motorcycles and sidecar outfits were very much in evidence.

This streamliner, powered by two Vincent engines from the 1950s, went over 200 mph.

The British journalist Alan Cathcart rode the new Norton 961 to a record.

82

Nitrate boys had two elongated, very low specimens, with the rider kneeling, almost lying prone, in front of the engine, one powered by a two-stroke 500 single, the other by a 900cc Buell V-twin. There was an old Indian, shades of Burt Munro's "Fastest Indian", and a flathead Harley WL. The new Norton Commando 961 was on hand, with Englishman Alan Cathcart set to ride. Hayabusas were common, all intent on getting into the 200 mph club. Next to our pit, four gents brought out a Honda 90 from a trailer; one of them had ridden it to a record back in 1969, and was back to retrieve his record — after a 41-year absence.

There was also a 2005 Bonneville, with a woman rider. She and her husband had come out from Chicago for the event, also doing RWB. So I did have informal competition, though she should be easy to beat, since she had the 790cc motor, while my 2006 had the 865cc. However, to my detriment I outweighed her by at least 100 pounds.

Mid-afternoon Chris and I drove back to the motel, unloaded our DRs and went for a ride in the Silver Island Mountains that border the flats to the west. We thumped along the dirt roads for awhile, chasing a herd of antelope along a narrow valley, climbing higher and higher, road turning to ruts. After an hour we stopped on a ridge, and far below we could just see an edge of the salt flats, with the way down looking pretty devious. Back? Or forward. Forward won, and we found ourselves scrabbling through steep, deep soft sand. The real pros could go down this slope on their back wheels, lofting the front, but not being pros we went slowly with our front wheels digging in. This was hard work, and could prove to be a challenge if a fence blocked our way and we had to climb back up.

Thank goodness, no fence! And we were back on the flats. Two very different approaches to motorcycling here, go fast on the smooth flats, or struggle with the soft stuff and steep slopes. Both are fun.

We rode out to the flats to see what was happening. Not much, as there were no speed runs that day. People were taking down canopies because of the wind that was reputed to be coming up that evening, but that was about all. When the wind blows out

Above: Lining up for scrutineering, with my riding gear in the bag on the back.

Scrutineers make sure that everything that should be secured is secured.

there, it can create a mischief, with canopies sailing literally for miles across the flats. On race days, all action is stopped if the wind exceeds 10 miles an hour, and the streamliners can't run it if is over 3.5 mph. Tricky little devils, those streamers, and expensive to crash.

Nobody is allowed to camp out there on the flats, but you could leave anything you wanted because BUB provided good security.

Motel 6 was like one big party that evening. The Sodium Distortion gang had brought along a big grill, filling it up with steaks and sausages. The pizza delivery car showed up regularly. Wendover, being in Mormon-controlled Utah, had no liquor store, but quantities of beer and wine and other libations were available on the Nevada side. Nobody was getting drunk, just having a good time. And we all turned in early because the riders' meeting was going to be at 7 a.m.

Dark and early we were driving across the flats, heading for the pits. A hundred or more riders gathered in front of the trailer for the briefing, holding cups of hot coffee; desert air can be downright chilly early in the morning. Denis opened the briefing, and allowed as to how he was not going to run Lucky 7 because, after all, he already held the record. And Lucky 7's closest competitor, Ack Attack, was not coming to this event. Then he turned the meeting over to the red-shirted staff, mostly volunteers who come just to be part of the action. They are an impressively enthusiastic lot, some traveling a thousand miles or more to get to Wendover, and they make this very complicated operation run very smoothly.

Ground rules were laid out, where to go, what to do, safety, emergencies, all that. The 11-mile long course was for record-attempts only. The parallel 5-mile short course was for record attempts and for the RWB crowd. The record runs would have the full five miles, the RWBs, three miles, starting at Mile 1 rather than Mile 0. With so many bikes running the idea was to get them through the traps as quickly as possible, and the RWBs did not really need the two-mile wind-up — one mile would be enough. Yellow flags are the mile-markers, red flags the quarter-mile markers, and the return track is off to the left.

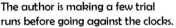

The author is making a few trial runs before going against the clocks.

All the new riders were asked to stay and get a secondary briefing. Two dozen or so of us remained to listen to a sensible counseling on how the operation works, what to do, what not to do, and what to do if you become hopelessly confused: Stop. Somebody will come and find you and lead you to where you should be. Do make sure that when your run is over you go left, not right, which might have you mistakenly crossing a track with someone approaching at 200 mph.

Time to go. I went back to our site, Chris helped me suit up and I rolled down to the preliminary staging — three rows, one for the 11-mile course, one for the 5-mile course, and one for RWB. Chris would spend the time hanging out with all the salt addicts, looking out across the tracks. The return run was right in front of the first pit row, with the five-mile course a quarter mile beyond that, and the long course over a half mile away.

The eerie thing about the Bonneville salt flats is exactly what makes them so good for high-speed runs — their flatness. Mountains loom hazily in the distance, but too far away to provide any sense of direction. I was sitting on the bike in the pre-staging area, very glad that I was the second bike in line, not the first, because I wasn't sure where we were supposed to go. The staff fellow waved five of us off and we headed across the salt. No signposts, just the occasional blue markings on the white salt. After a mile we saw three small canopies set up, with RWB written on the salt; that was our staging area, 60 yards from the 5-mile track.

We waited about 15 minutes, watching record-oriented bikes whiz past. Get ready, one of the staffers said, and another staffer

came around and secured our sidestands with zip-locks. The first rider went out 50 yards to where another red-shirt was standing with a green flag. A little discussion, green flag waved, the rider went forward 20 feet and turned right onto the track, just in front of the yellow one-mile flag. And then accelerated away.

My turn: Go out to the flagman. Track clear. Flagger told me to check that my visor is down, chin-strap tight and loose end secured, waved the green flag and I went forward to make a 90- degree turn onto the track, scraped smooth and flat. I was a bit over-enthusiastic, or nervous, and as I twisted the throttle the rear tire spun. Back off, get straight, and now I had a mile to accelerate to the max, red line in first, second, third, fourth   in this gear the engine peaked at 6800, not 7000, rpm. Fifth. The two-mile marker flashed by as the speedometer read 105. I held the throttle and hunkered down. Three-mile marker flashed past. I backed off, half a mile later I turned onto a well-beaten escape road, over to the return lane, and back to the pits.

Chris greeted me with a slip that read 105.705, thanks to the instancy factor of the computer world, the towers sending the results back to the trailer as soon as the speed is measured. I got back in line, back on the track, trying to crawl under the paint — and managed to eke out another quarter-mile an hour, to 105.957. My competition pulled 106.9 I've lost. Oh, the ignominy! Should I run away? Or congratulate her? Good manners won out.

That evening we talked about staying another day just as spectators, but the forecast was for rain, which can shut down the trials. At 3 a.m. we both awoke, hearing raindrops, and decided to leave. We could make this a one-day return run by sticking to the Interstates, with enough stops to allow me to cope with my vehicular claustrophobia. Chris did the entire 15 hours behind the wheel, while I contemplated mountain ranges, deserts, billboards, and the metropolises of Reno and Sacramento. In truth there is not much satisfactory voyeurism in a freeway trip, as these roads are designed with efficiency, not scenery, in mind.

And after four days of togetherness, Chris and I were pretty much talked out. Had we both had a great interest in and knowledge about quantum tunneling or swingarm-pivot placement, that might have filled the hours — but we didn't. Stopping at Donner Summit in the Sierra Nevadas for a stretch, we thought briefly about getting off the highway and taking the DRs for a spin but we had no idea where good riding might be. Also, it was quite apparent that, like sensible horses, we were headed for the barn.

Cellphones alerted our wives as to our arrival. Chris turned in at my mailbox, tires crunching on the long gravel drive. Sue greeted us with cold beers, which we drank as we unloaded my DR; tomorrow I would go to Chris's shop and retrieve my Bonnie.

And my two days on the flats — very satisfying. Nothing great was accomplished, but I derived a great feeling of pleasure from the event. Like a golfer shooting a round at St. Andrews in Scotland, the grail of the sport, even if he or she strokes over par. The only record set was my own personal one, and that was enough to make me feel happy.

Good trip; Chris and I both wonder if we will be tempted to go back to the flats. We have been told that salt addiction can take a while to show up. But it will have to be a pretty serious addiction if I'm to put up with those 1600 miles tucked inside a pickup truck or car . . .

Postscript: *Cathcart did set a record for Production Push-Rod on the Norton at 129.191, and the Sodium Distortion gang got two records. And three weeks after this event, at another speed meet, Ack Attack went 376.156 mph. And undoubtedly Denis was already planning his next record-breaking attempt.*

That is what 105.97 mph looks like on the Bonneville Salt Flats.

Inevitably a little salt would go home with all the participants.

Ahhhh. Home again and contemplating 'salt addictions'.

Brazil 2002

Illustration by Gary M. Brown

I had no idea where I was going, let alone how to get there; that's supposed to be humorous. I was in one of the biggest cities in the world, Sao Paolo, traffic was moving along steadily at about two miles an hour, the six-lane avenue hosting eight lanes of cars, vans, trucks, pushcarts and motorcycles. I could only hope that the road was going in the right direction, towards the coast, towards the city of Santos.

My sole usable phrase in Portuguese, the language of Brazilians, was, roughly, where is the road to Santos? I squeezed my BMW alongside a taxi driver and asked, in my wretched accent, *"Onde fica a rua a Santos?"*. All he needed to do was understand the last word, which he did, and pointed straight ahead. At a big intersection half the traffic was turning. I asked the driver of a van. He pointed left. I made the turn.

91

Through cunning use of sidewalks and grass median strips I finally managed to free myself from some of the worst congestion I have ever had the displeasure of riding in, finally getting on a toll road — motorcycles were free. And obviously Brazilians did not like to pay tolls, as there was minimal traffic.

North Americans really know very little about the continent to the south. We don't go there much, preferring the touristic delights of Italy or Ireland to Paraguay or Suriname. But if you are told, "Quick! Name me a country in South America!", most of us would probably come up with Brazil.

Home of Brazil nuts, one presumes. And the annual pre-Lenten carnival in Rio de Janeiro, what we call Mardi Gras, or Fat Tuesday; the uninhibited Brazilians put on a terrific show!

But who would want to go ride a motorcycle in Brazil? Myself, for one, though with no real idea of where I would be going. Cruising the world-famous beaches like Ipanema and Copacabana would be on the itinerary, of course, but other than that, where would Brazilian roads lead me?

One of these companies that sets up packaged motorcycle expeditions was doing a "scouting" tour and invited me along. The fun of one of these "scouting" trips is not knowing what to expect. The company needs to figure out whether or not it would be financially worthwhile — i.e. attract paying customers — to set up a real tour in this new venue, and wants the feed-back from some experienced travelers. Food, accommodations, will be pretty much catch as catch can, and especially the roads will be up for criticism.

What is the make-up of a good motorcycle tour? A number of essential parts include: The country has to be interesting. The roads have to be fun to ride. The accommodations should be pleasing. The food must be tasty.

Ah, the food! Touring should include pleasant, if not outstanding, gastronomical experiences, and I admit that in Brazil I ate so well, and so consistently, that I never once felt hungry while on the tour. The Brazilian staples are rice and beans and bread, accompanied by large amounts of savorily cooked beef, pork, poultry and seafood. Occasionally we ate at rather chi-chi restaurants, where quality was good but presentation was more important than quantity; mostly we enjoyed excellent trencherman fare.

The lunch I had at a roadhouse called, curiously, Charmin Country, somewhere in the Serra do Canastra, was so good I could have eaten there for the entire trip. It was a buffet, with a dozen cast-iron pots full of delicious stews and scrumptious simmering meats, another table with all manner of salad fixings, and a row of desserts — as much as you could eat for ten reales, less than $3. But I'm getting ahead of myself.

Ten experienced motorcyclists were due to arrive at the Sao Paolo airport to take part in this trip — six Germans, four from the United States. A Sao Paolo travel agency, admittedly unfamiliar with the ways of motorcyclists, had been tapped to provide an itinerary and hotel accommodations, as well as supplying motorcycles, a motorcycle-riding guide, and a chase vehicle to carry our baggage.

Thanks to airline incompetence I arrived at the Sao Paolo airport a day late. The others were understandably restless to leave so I said they should leave and I would get kitted up for the

ride, then follow the Mercedes chase van carrying our luggage, and meet them for lunch.

Except leaving Sao Paolo was no easy feat; some 16 million people call the place home and they all seemed to be on the road at the same time. After the first five frustrating minutes I waved goodbye to the van, figuring I could make far better time if I rode by myself. There was no lane-splitting, because there were no lanes to split, traffic was so tightly packed.

The toll-road I finally got on descended to the Atlantic Ocean, and just before Santos I turned north on a well-kept two-laner sweeping graciously along the shore, clean white beaches to my right, thick tropical vegetation to the left. There was very little traffic. I stopped at an isolated gas station to check my map and rendezvous instructions, and the attendant came over to see what I was up to. As I noted earlier, my Portuguese was pretty much non-existent, but communication could be accomplished by other means. The pump-jockey, having little to do but gaze out at the passing vehicles al day long, made clear that a group of motorcycles like my BMW had recently passed. A car pulled in, coming from the other direction, and I was informed that the driver had just seen the motorcycles pull into a resort area about 20 kilometers up the road. Eight colorful and large motorcycles (mine would be the ninth) were obviously not an everyday occurrence. Despite linguistic frustrations, I found the Brazilians consistently helpful and cheerful.

I was late for lunch, but came away with an excellent sandwich, essentially a grilled pork chop with all the fixings on what is called a "little loaf", a great improvement on the American bun. Brazilians take their bread seriously, and I never saw anything remotely like our own Wonder.

I had been to Brazil once before, back-packing through South America in 1969. Coming up from Uruguay, I had passed through Sao Paolo and Rio, taken a long bus-trip to Brazilia in the center of the country, then flown north to Manaus on the Amazon River, and finally gone up-river to Colombia. It was a big place, larger than our 48 contiguous states! Now in the 21st century the population was approaching 180 million, three-quarters of them living close to the Atlantic coast.

Brazil is the biggest country in South America and is, and should be, the dominant force in that continent, although it can't really seem to get its economic transmission out of second gear.

Here is the thumbnail history: the place was sparsely populated by Indians when a Portuguese ship arrived in 1500, and as empire-building Europeans were wont to do in those days, the captain declared everything in sight and well beyond sight as belonging to the king of Portugal. For the next 300 years the Europeans who immigrated here in South America were mostly searching for precious metals, rather than a plot of land to call their own. Some of these prospectors got very rich, as gold and silver was to be found, and when hard work was required they decided that using Indians, and later, Africans, as slave labor was preferable to raising their own calluses. In 1822 an ungrateful son of the Portuguese king declared the colony independent and crowned himself Emperor Pedro. His own son, Pedro II, was deposed peaceably in 1889 by a rabble of wealthy citizens who did not appreciate being dictated to, and the Republic of Brazil was created.

The Amazon River basin makes up the country's northern half, the southern half being more amenable to ranching, agriculture

The 200-foot statue of Christ the Redeemer sits on top of the 2000-foot Corcovado hill overlooking all of Rio de Janeiro — just wait until the Olympics get there.

Below:
We are beside Rio's Guanabara Bay with the Pao de Acucar (or Mount Sugarloaf) in the distance; yes, that is what a mound of processed Brazilian sugar does look like. There was time for a bit of beach lounging before heading off to take the aerial tram (barely visible on the peak) up to Mt. Sugarloaf.

and mining. As well as motorcycle riding. Our 1500-mile tour would stay in the southeast, starting at the Tropic of Capricorn and making a big four-sided foray, beginning by riding northeast from Sao Paolo along the coast to Rio, north towards Belo Horizonte, west to Araxa, and south back to Sao Paolo.

First night was in Ubatuba, a great name for a little resort town about half way between Sao Paolo and Rio. A dozen or so small beaches decorated this stretch of coast, and the place was considered an environmental asset, noted for its bird-life, with relatively minimal human intrusion. No high-rises. We stayed in a wonderful small hotel, about 20 rooms, opening right onto the sand. Dinner was on the patio, and the broiled seafood was excellent; to my wayward thinking, countries should be rated on their food, not their finances.

Our little group got to know each other, swapping stories of travel in Africa and Asia. Fortunately the Germans all spoke English.

In the morning we had a brief diversion, taking a boat out to Anchieta Island which used to house political prisoners; it is a lot more friendly than Alcatraz, I promise you, with a lot better climate. The place is so nice I imagine some prisoners chose not to escape. Brazil has not managed to avoid the South American propensity for dictatorships, as the military pretty much ran things from 1945 to 1985, but the army was less brutal than many such unelected governments. Since then elections have adhered to a viable democracy.

Then it was back to the motorcycles and off to Rio. As became the habit for most of the trip, our group broke into two components, fast and slow. Fast is fine in the countryside, where few roads and light traffic make the going easy, but coming into a sprawling city like Rio was a different matter, where everything was slow. Keep the ocean on your right, we had been told, and eventually you will get to your hotel.

We stayed for two nights at Le Meridien, a multi-star, 37-floor hotel right on Copacabana beach; one could not ask for better. As we strolled the beach, where all the lords and ladies in the most minuscule of bathing costumes taking the sun and sea seemed exceptionally attractive. One of our group commented that perhaps the police had standing orders to allow only beautiful people to go on the sand.

On our off-day, the temperature being very hot and humid and the traffic being horrendous, we saw the sights using our air-conditioned Mercedes van to get to the most viewable places. We all climbed into the steep funicular train that went up to the huge statue of Christ the Redeemer on top of the 2000-foot hill called Corcovado, and were delighted by the spectacular views of the city and the Bay of Guanabara. In the afternoon we used an aerial tram to get to the top of Pao de Acucar (or Mount Sugar Loaf, as it looks like a mound of processed sugar), which oversees the narrow opening to the huge bay, the best natural port on the 4600 miles of Brazilian coastline.

Late that afternoon I walked across the boulevard in front of the hotel to the beach and went for a swim. I had left my money locked in the safe in my room, as is appropriate, and had the key in the pocket of my trunks. The use of the safe was gratis, but I had signed a small piece of paper saying that if I lost the one-of-a-kind key, and the hotel had to drill the lock out, it would cost me $80. Guess what? I got rolled in the surf, lost the key, and spent $80 for the pleasure of a swim. One learns.

Next morning we threaded our way through Rio like a troop of nine elephants, over the bay bridge, and then headed north into the mountains that separate the coastal plain from the inland plateau. After a good twisty climb through the National Park of the Dos Orgaos Mountains, we arrived at the 19th century city of Petropolis, which was the summer home of the Emperor Peter II — hence the name. His palace is now a museum, with magnificent wood floors, and all visitors are required to wear soft slippers that fit over shoes and boots; this serves a dual purpose, both protecting the wood and helping to keep it shiny. Many touristed buildings could benefit from this creative way to keep the floors polished.

Running through the National Park of the Dos Orgaos Mountains , heading for Petropolis and the palace museum.

A day later, following the old Royal Road, a curvaceous stretch of new two-lane pavement from which trucks were banned, we arrived in Ouro Preto (Black Gold) which was home to 120,000 inhabitants back in 1700 — when New York City had only 40,000. Gold was the major attraction back then, but in recent years the mining has diminished, along with the population, which is now about 60,000. I was completely entranced; here was a place I had never heard about, a 300-year-old city tucked away in the mountains, with 21 churches sitting on the hilltops, steep cobblestoned streets leading every which-way. I was told that only half a dozen priests were in residence in the city, but they made sure that every church had a Sunday service. Such diligence kept them on the move, that is for sure, and I saw one cleric buzzing about on a motorscooter.

The city Ouro Preto is spread out over many hills; once a major gold-mining center it is now a tourist destination, and the tourist market, foreground, was right opposite our hotel.

Idle hands are the devil's workshop, so when the tourists aren't buying, this Ouro Preto vendor is creating more items that might sell another day.

Our crew was housed in the 18th-century building that was once headquarters to the region's administrator, and is now an elegant pousada (inn). Unfortunately the room that was assigned to me was down on the very bottom floor, with the only excuse for window a narrow firing slit that would have been useful 200 years before. My claustrophobia immediately got the better of me and I was moved to the attic, complete with skylight. Much better.

We had a free day there, during which I explored the cobblestone streets on my Beemer, admiring the colonial architecture which has withstood the ravages of time extremely well; those people knew how to build strong. I could easily have used three or four days, soaking up the history and the atmosphere. And contemplating the purchase of semi-precious stones. I felt that my visit to Ouro Preto was in itself worth the price of admission to this tour.

Leaving here our scouting tour skirted Belo Horizonte, the third largest city in the country, and headed off to Araxa, 300 miles west in the middle of a great plateau. Parts of the road were quite straight, while others, like the stretch near the town of Luz, in the Serra do Canastra, were sport-bike heaven, 75 blissful miles of fast sweepers. We found the roads to be well-maintained and generally lightly trafficked, with police presence only noticeable around the towns and cities. It was along here that we found the only gas station which did not have gas —although the attendant said there was a place 15 miles down the road where we could replenish the tanks. Truth.

At Araxa we stayed for two nights at the truly glorious Grand Hotel & Baths — along with some 300 members of the Brazilian BMW motorcycle club at their annual national gathering. The five-story hotel was completed in 1944, in the European grand style, with huge banquet rooms and corridors a hundred yards long; I wanted a bowling ball to scoot down the carpeted halls. At one end of the hotel were the hot springs and baths, with treatments in both "sulfuricated" and "radioactive" waters, depending on what ailed you. I opted for "sulfuricated" — a faint tinge of sulfur, but felt marvelous. Followed by a good massage.

The Grand Hotel & Baths in Araxa, where the Brazilian BMW club was having its annual get together, over 300 members showing up.

Once out of the cities and on the great central plateau there was really very little traffic to deal with, and none on the well-maintained back roads.

That is the main church in the town Tiradentes (Tooth Puller) where a dentist was hanged and quartered in 1792 for trying to free Brazil from Portuguese rule; the successful American Revolution had gotten a whole lot of people thinking.

From Araxa we headed south across mildly rolling countryside, and the valley of the Rio Grande River, to Ribeirao Preto, and finally to Sao Paolo. Which city, I believe, is the largest in the Western Hemisphere — but our indomitable guide managed to get us all safely back to the Hilton Hotel. And a flight home the next day.

We saw only a tiny fraction of Brazil, but I could easily spend more time in that country, as there is so much I have not seen, from the Iguazu Falls on the Parana River in the south to Belem at the mouth of the Amazon River in the north, maybe cross the Mato Grosso to Bolivia.

For that I would need more than a couple of weeks.

Along the way we saw this concrete, life-sized statue of a motorcycle and motorcyclist, but we never did find out why it had been commissioned.

Where to next? A moto-journalist can never be quite certain, but it's a thought to ponder — and best done fully relaxed.

British Isles 1960

When the motorcycle magazines in 1959 began heralding the arrival of a new machine from the Triumph company, advertised as the world's fastest production motorcycle. I had to have one. The excitement of speed was a primary motivator, normal in most young men. In truth the T120 Bonneville was not really all that new, but a Tiger 110 vertical twin whose proven engine had been pepped up with new camshafts and a second carburetor. Those 120 and 110 numbers were Triumph's way of saying how fast these models would go. My kindly Massachusetts dealer told me that by picking up the bike from the factory in England I could save enough money off the price to buy an Icelandic Airlines round-trip ticket to London — even better. The Brits were not into enforcing speed limits except in urban areas.

In June of 1960 I flew to London and headed for the Triumph motorcycle factory where my latest steed awaited me. Getting off the train in Coventry I walked outside the station and asked a blue-uniformed railroad employee where one could find the bus to Meriden. Looking at the Bell helmet in my hand he said, "You want the Triumph works," and pointed to a bus. A little later my bus stopped; a high wall was on one side of the road, a large drainage ditch and scrub growth on the other. "That's the place," said the conductor. A sign on the wall read: Triumph Motorcycles, Ltd.

Walking across the road and up the drive I went through old-fashioned metal gates and into a big courtyard. An elderly fellow in charge of the gate directed me over to the office building. A pleasant lady said that yes, I had been expected, and Mr. So'n'So would meet me in a moment, and would I like a cup of tea. Yes, please.

Mr. So'n'So came in, introduced himself, and asked if I would like a tour of the premises. That would be very nice. The buildings were long and reasonably well-lit, though most of the windows were grimy. Large open crates of parts were everywhere, and nothing like a conventional assembly line. In the sprawling engine shop two workers would build an entire engine, from crankshaft to tappets, rather than using the pass-along process. In the frame shop a man was heating up a section of tubing while his mate had a section of pipe over the end of the tube and was bending it to the correct angle to fit the steering head, precision techniques perfected in the 19th century.

Eventually we re-emerged in the courtyard, where stood my noble blue and silver T120, on the centerstand, engine warmed, with a small crowd of workers standing around. Mr. So'n'So turned to me and asked if I would like some instruction in how to ride this machine. "What!?" I expostulated; "here am I buying the fastest production motorcycle made and you're asking me if I want a lesson?" Mr. So'n'So calmed me and told a little story.

Illustration by Gary M. Brown

The year before, two Yanks had arrived to pick up a new Thunderbird, and, like me, they had tea and a quick trip around the factory, came out into the courtyard, and then while one was talking to Mr. So'n'So the other went over the the T'bird, turned the switch on, kick-started it, rolled it off the stand, put it in gear, let out the clutch, shot down the drive, across the road and into the ditch, breaking his leg. Since that time it was company policy to ask the question. I politely allowed as to how I was quite familiar with motorcycles, including Triumphs.

Another fellow, a mechanic, came up and asked if I had any questions. Break-in instructions? "Don't worry about the revs, mate, just don't lug the engine. Change the oil and check the tappets at five, six hundred." he said.

The Bonnie and I took the long way back to London, getting pleasantly lost in the quiet hills of central England, appreciating the narrow country lanes where one car took up most of the road. I had logged some miles on borrowed Triumph twins but this was all mine. I would wind the tach up to 5000 briefly, never lugged the engine, and was relishing the time when the throttle could really be twisted to the max.

Clement did not have much camera sense when he was 20 years old, and did not have one along on the trip; a cousin took this shot.

One horse is good, but the 46 ponies in a 1960 T120 Bonneville are better.

This column in Coventry, England, is dedicated to the memory of "Cyclists", presumably motorcyclists, who gave their lives in World War II.

Below: An all-too typical day in the Yorkshire Dales has a delightful road with spirited riding inhibited by rain.

In London I was staying with family friends, and next morning the boys at Pride & Clark, a large motorcycle and accessories shop, mounted a Craven luggage rack. My gear was not very motorcycle-worthy, using a waterproof aluminum suitcase strapped to the rack, and P&C sold me a pair of surplus army backpacks that I slung over the saddle. Plus the little rack on the gas tank held a small bag. The motorcyclist haberdasher Lewis Leathers fitted me out for a custom horsehide jacket; it would be ready in a week. I would do a quick lap around the islands and pick it up on my way back through to the continent.

First destination was John O'Groats up in Scotland; leaving London a rider might as well stick with the main road until north of Manchester and Leeds, out of the Midlands, but after that, take the byways. Secondary British roads were good, if rudimentary, and traffic was very light. Stay away from the truck routes and one had little to worry about. With a youth-hostel card, living was cheap.

I sliced through the Yorkshire Dales, stopped at Hadrian's Wall, and rode around the Cheviot Hills. In truth I was wondering if I would ever have the nerve to use all that throttle. I had already adapted to left-side riding, and breezing through the gearbox was a snickety delight.

Next morning I was up at the crack of dawn to make it through the highlands to John's place. Speeding out of town, a Rover police car came up behind me. Whoops, busted. Two constables got out, looked at my paperwork, and, more importantly, the Bonneville, which they had never seen, only heard of. The end result, "Looks like you won't be coming back this way, and you're a well-mannered lad, so we'll let you go with a little warning about city speed limits. Have fun."

Now there was full throttle capability, but I was righteously nervous; 46 horsepower may not sound like much in the 21st century, but it was more than this 20-year-old American was accustomed to. Shifting out of second at 6000 rpm, pushing 70 miles an hour, and if I held it in third, I was doing over 90. Unheard of speeds for the likes of me. The Dunlop K70 tires stuck well to the dry roads (in the wet it was quite unpleasantly different), the suspension worked fine, and even the brakes were pretty good . . . by the rather low standards of the day. Mostly I happily cruised in fourth gear, which pulled with no problems from 30 mph to — to wherever it might lead me.

In Scotland proper the riding was even better. In the center were the Grampian Mountains, separating the lowlands from the highlands, and then past Inverness and into the Northern Highlands. This part of the world was very sparsely populated, with sheep out-numbering humans by probably a hundred to one. Narrow roads crossed over old stone bridges, obviously built before World War I. But the pavement was good, and the Bonnie was running beautifully. What a wonderful summer lay ahead of me! John O'Groats had a few houses, couple of stores, a pub, and a hostel was down the road a few miles.

In the morning the road led south through charmingly desolate country. Sometimes the pavement was so narrow that pull-outs were provided every mile or so, should one meet on-coming traffic — though a motorcycle could always squeeze by. Coming around a right-hand bend, then left across a low stone bridge built over a little dip in the land, I found a sheep abruptly appearing in the center of the road at the far end of the bridge. Not wanting to hit a large woolly, I angled between the sheep and the end of the bridge, going off the road and into the gorse which

Livestock get to share the road on their way home, and here the border collie is trying to keep the cows on the left side of the road, as is proper in the British Isles.

looked smooth enough until my front wheel hit a small mound in the ground. The bike flipped, I landed on my back beside the motorcycle and lay there for a moment watching the rear wheel of the Bonneville slowly come to a stop. Dang blast it!

Two cars showed up and people came to offer help. No damage to me or the bike; we set the Bonnie to rights and found the baggage which had flown off. I was offered a cup of tea from a thermos, and all seemed right with the world. Which it was. After a quarter hour I felt quite revived, and thanked my benefactors for their kindness.

Continuing on to Loch Ness I hoped to get a glimpse of the monster. As I sat patiently on the shore an elderly local bicycled up and inspected the motorcycle. Then invited himself over for a bit of a chat. Had himself a little Ariel 250 before the war, but decided in his late age that he was better off on a bicycle, as most roads he used around the loch were quite flat. I asked him if he had ever seen the monster, and he said that was just some old-wives' tale to keep the tourists coming. What about all those supposed sightings of long-necked creatures breaking the surface and then disappearing? Ah, he said, there's a lot of water-logged trees down at the bottom of the loch, been there a long time, and occasionally one that has some air trapped in it breaks loose, shoots to the top, comes out of the water like a sea-serpent's head and neck, and then the air escapes and the log sinks back to the bottom. "But there's money in that monster story, so don't go spoiling it."

Skirting Glasgow by ferrying over the Firth of Clyde I kept going southwest to Stranraer to catch a big ferry that would take me to Northern Ireland, where cousins awaited over in County Fermanagh. Cousins are good, providing a place to do my laundry, feeding me well. They lived in the country, and one evening, after a fine meal accompanied by a bottle of wine, I said I would go put the bike in the old stables, a couple of hundred yards away.

Happiness for this Irish fly-fisherman is a tumbling stream and a trout willing to put up a good fight — before being released, of course.

On such a nice June evening I decided to take a little ride before turning in, with the local roads being one narrow lane wide and traffic-free. Rolling quietly along I saw a motorcycle coming towards me; I pulled over to the right to let him pass — and he did the same. I pulled further to the right, to the edge of the pavement, as did the on-coming rider. I went onto the grassy verge, and the Bonnie skidded and we slid together to the bottom of a shallow ditch. The other motorcycle pulled up on the road and the rider and passenger looked down at me quizzically and the rider asks, "Now, what'd you go and do that for?"

Because I'm American and forgot which side of the road I was supposed to be on. They helped me get the undamaged bike out of the ditch and back on the road, and for all I know are still telling the story in the Enniskillen pubs.

But time's a'wasting, and I was due to be in Spain in a week. Bidding farewell to the cousins I headed south to Dublin. This was before The Troubles began, and on the country road I first took the only way I knew that I had arrived at the limits of Northern Ireland was a simple barrier that I could have gone around. A sign said this was not an official crossing, and I should go back a mile, take my first right, that sort of commonplace explanation. Wanting an Irish stamp in my passport, I did just that.

After being stamped into the Republic of Ireland I found myself on a straight stretch of road, with no traffic, and thought it was time to see just what this vaunted machine could do in the way of top speed. I wound her up in third, shifted to fourth and, with head low, watched the speedometer needle climb past the 100 mark, creeping up past the 110, then hovering around 115 miles per hour. Wow!

And then the exhaust note changed, not drastically, just a little. Pulling over I inspected the situation. The American export model had little cone-shaped muting devices riveted in the ends of both mufflers, and one had blown out. The next garage was happy to remove the other one; no charge.

In Dublin I had a quick look at the tower that James Joyce made famous, then caught the night ferry out of Dun Laoghaire to Holyhead in Wales. Crack of dawn the ferry arrived in Wales and I began the 200 or so miles to London. North Wales was a delight, with hills and few cars, but after crossing into England and the Midlands the land flattened out and the traffic increased. I arrived on the London outskirts early evening, the M1 highway depositing me on the circular road that looped around the city.

I had been told that I must have a stop at one of London's biker cafes, either the Busy Bee or the Ace; the Busy Bee was right in my sights. Being a Friday evening the bikes were there in force, some stock, mostly mildly modified, with the riders all dressed in rocker uniform leather jackets, boots, and jeans.

I immediately collected a crowd, as Triumph was not even selling the Bonneville in England at that time; for export only. After a few cheerful "You bloody Yanks have it all!" I had a look at some of the hot-rodded bikes. Popular was a twin-carb conversion kit that some 500s and 650s had, with references to camshafts and compression ratios. But the Bonnie was the envy of the lot, and there were several offers to do some informal racing. Explaining that having a long summer ahead of me the last thing I wanted to do was to crash the bike, or blow the engine up. The rocker lads were a bit disappointed, but understood.

I went back to the friends' house and early next morning began sorting all my gear, and picked up my new jacket at Lewis. That afternoon I headed down to Dover to catch the ferry that would take me to the continent.

Here is the Bonneville badly loaded, with the trunk and the saddlebags aft of the rear axle — which could explain some of the accidents that summer.

114

Copper Canyon, Mexico 1980

It was my first foreign assignment: travel, romance, stimulation, expense accounts, the dream of journalists everywhere. I had been working at *Road Rider* magazine (R.I.P.) for only six months when the boss, Roger Hull, called me into his office. "Clem, do you have any objection to going to Mexico?" Not at all; I had lived there for a year and a half in the mid-seventies, and as Br'er Rabbit was noted for saying, "Please don't throw me in the brier patch."

"Good. There's a company that is putting together some sort of motorcycle tour, and I want you to do a story. It's a bit unconventional, as you'll be with a bunch of RVs. And you'll put the bike on a train at one point. Here's the info," he said, handing me a couple of brochures. "You're supposed to meet up with them in El Paso on November 13th. Take that new Suzuki 850."

I read the brochures. An outfit called Point South Caravans had been leading RV tours into Mexico for a few years and was thinking about expanding into motorcycles. A half dozen companies were offering guided tours for motorcyclists in Europe and North America, but none to Mexico. This would be a tortoise and hare kind of tour, with RVs and motorcycles combined. The interesting bit was that the tour included a 400-mile train trip on the Chihuahua al Pacifico Railroad, known locally as the "Chepe", from the city of Chihuahua westwards down to Los Mochis on the Gulf of California coast, with everybody aboard on flat cars.

A week and a thousand miles later I pulled into an El Paso campground. Some RVs were to be seen and five tents were set up, with motorcycles outside. But only one person was in evidence, Art, who came out of his tent with a white shirt and tie. "Everybody has gone into town for dinner," he said, "but I wasn't

Loading the bikes in the Chihuahua railroad yards on a snowy morning was not exactly what I would call a pleasurable time.

Here we are off-loading the motorcycles in Los Mochis after 400 miles on the Chihuahua al Pacific Railroad — not a trip I would care to repeat.

Ah, the pleasure of pitching a tent on a railroad flatcar is to be relished, and not forgotten. Not forgotten either is my lack of a zoom lens on the camera and the low quality of the film used at the time.

116

hungry. We're supposed to be on the road by five o'clock in the morning." Art, a very proper person when it came to attire, was reporting on the trip for *Rider* magazine. He was on an aged BMW R50/2. I saw two Harleys, a Gold Wing, and a newish Beemer, their riders having gone into town in an RV.

I met the rest when they came back from dinner several hours later. The caravan would consist of 14 motorhomes and six motorcycles. The fellow in charge chose to run the whole thing like a military operation. Our wake-up call the next morning was at four, on the road at five, a few miles on the streets through the city with the motorcycles following the RVs, and then the paperwork hassles at the border. The bikes got through with little problem, and we left the tortoises behind, making the 250 miles across the arid northern Mexico landscape to Chihuahua in good time. Where we found our accommodations at the Victoria Hotel, which obviously had been built in better times and had since run a bit to seed. Though the water in the swimming pool had probably not been changed in several years, the bar did serve all the beer and tequila we could wish for.

We spent the next day sightseeing in the vicinity, including the Pancho Villa museum, which had a large photo of the man himself standing next to a 1914 Indian motorcycle. Nobody knows where that particular Indian ended up, although historians and Indian buffs have made many searches. Locating that would be a journalistic coup.

Late in the afternoon black clouds appeared and it began to rain. After I had gone to bed I heard the rain stop — and in the early morning realized that the precipitation had turned to snow. No matter; we were due in the railroad yards to load the RVs and bikes. The RVs made wide tracks in the inch or two of snow, and we avoided the missing manhole covers, which regularly got stolen by locals and sold as scrap. Dropping a wheel into one of those holes could certainly put a crimp in your chassis.

Our leader supposedly had arranged with the Chepe to have a special train waiting for us — but there was none. We stood around in the snow for six hours waiting. Eventually a train did arrive, the RVs slowly went on and were properly secured, then

On the 250 miles from El Paso to Chihuahua we passed many post-Columbian ruins, business enterprises that had failed out there in what is mostly desert.

After taking the train past Copper Canyon and arriving on the coast, I decided to take the Topolobambo ferry to La Paz, on the Baja California peninsula.

six bikes were strapped down on one flatcar, and another one held our tents. The deal had included a comfortable, heated passenger car for the motorcyclists, but the carriage that was hooked up had broken windows and no heater.

Late in the afternoon, while waiting for the train to leave, I went to a nearby cantina to warm up and have some supper and were it not for a local noticing that my train was moving, I would have been left behind. Which might have been better than the cold, miserable night I spent in my sleeping bag.

Next day about noon we pulled into a siding near a small town, where repairs had to be done to the engine, and we motorcyclists were promised a better passenger car. The station master said this would take at least an hour, probably more, so Greg, one of the other motorcyclists, and I hiked up to the town half a mile away to get to some sustenance. Half an hour later I looked out the door and the train was gone.

The only person who would know we were not on the train was Greg's wife, but she might think we were visiting people in an RV. We ran down to the station where the station master was apologetic, saying he had not been able to get another passenger car, and the repair to the engine had taken much less time than expected, and he did not know two of us had gone to town. But he did have a radio, and he radioed to the engineer on the train to stop. Moments later a taxi pulled up, we piled in, and set out on the dirt road alongside the tracks. When the dirt road ran out the taxista cheerfully set off across the fields, crashing through the dry grass, bumps and ruts, until finally we could see the stopped train. A handsome tip, and we were back on board.

Our caravan guide had had no idea why the engine had stopped, but when he saw us coming knew who the culprits were and was fuming. We were given strict orders to never, ever leave the vicinity of the train again without his express permission. Donna was quite relieved to have her husband back.

Next stop was Creel, which sits at about 8000 feet, the town where those interested in going down into the Copper Canyon would generally start. Copper Canyon could easily swallow our Grand Canyon without even a burp, and is actually made up

Poking around in abandoned Mexican mineshafts is not really an advisable pastime — but as long as I can see the light I am okay.

of six canyons, with the six rivers joining as the Rio Fuerte and flowing into the Gulf of California. The name comes not from the presence of copper in the canyon, but from the copper/green color of the walls. Prospectors did find silver in the canyon, and mines were operating until the early part of the 20th century, but eventually the lodes all played out.

Several dirt roads go into the canyon, and a couple of small towns exist along the rivers, but we were not going there. We were staying with the train, and would get our lofty appreciation of the canyon from a place called El Divisadero, which does offer a grand view. Along with an elegant hotel — at which we were not staying — and several dozen Tarahumara Indians selling handmade tourist trinkets. As I stood on the edge of the canyon and gaped at the magnificent vistas, all I could think of was how wonderful it must be to ride down to the bottom.

The train tooted, the guide made sure I was aboard, and then it was down, down, down to the coast, through 86 tunnels.

We arrived in Los Mochis, the flatcars were vacated, and decisions were made. Several bikers went south with the RVs to Mazatlan, several headed north, and I went to Topolobambo to catch the ferry to La Paz and Baja California.

Point South Caravans sensibly chose not to continue including motorcycles on their tours.

* * * * *

A new opportunity awaited me at the magazine. While I was on the road BMW had dropped off their brand-new dual-purpose machine, the R80G/S a new concept in the motorcycle world, big enough to handle long stretches of highway, agile enough to cope with bad dirt roads. And Roger was trying to figure out how to give it a proper test. "I'll take it to the bottom of Copper Canyon," I said. "That'll be a damn good story." Ah, the life of a wandering moto-journalist.

I did my laundry, packed the single saddlebag the G/S offered, strapped on a big duffle bag, and I was off. Feeling that it might be better to have two people on such an adventure I had called a dual-sport riding friend in New Mexico to join me on her Yamaha 500 Enduro. We met up in Nogales, Arizona, and in the morning headed south 175 miles to Hermosillo, the capital of Sonora state.

Mexican road maps back then tended to be pretty sketchy affairs, but the one I had folded and in my jacket pocket showed a road of sorts heading east from Hermosillo over the Continental Divide and eventually going through Creel. Seemed like a good idea to me, and it even had a highway number,16. A short stretch of pavement soon turned to good dirt road, which turned into a bad dirt road, and occasionally detoured along creek bottoms and the like. Late on the wintery afternoon we got to a village called Yecora, about 5000 feet above sea level, found a room in a very basic sort of lodging, and went looking for gas. This we found at the only store in town, which was in the small square where the church was located.

As we were filling up from the big 55-gallon drum a gent in civvies came along and asked us, in English, where we might be headed. I told him Maycoba, the next town on my map, connected by a dotted line. He said that when we were done gassing up we should come and talk with him, and he indicated his house next to the church. Which we did.

Turned out that Father Jose was the local priest, from Spain. The civilian attire was due to the fact that a long time ago the Catholic Church backed the losing side in some Mexican fracas, and since then the clergy has not been allowed to wear clerical

Copper Canyon, Mexico 1980

Gassing up in the Mexican hinterlands takes a bit longer than at your average Ameican gas station, transferring the fuel from a 55-gallon drum into the bike's tank.

As we crossed Mexico's Continental Divide near Yacopa, we appreciated just how high we were — over a mile up in December.

garb outside of church property. He was going to Chihuahua in the morning, via Maycoba, and said that few people traveled that intermediate stretch, as for shopping the Yecorans went to Hermosillo, Maycobans to Chihuahua, with the middle section of road being very little used and very hard to follow. He would be going slowly, but it would be worth our while to follow him. We agreed, thanked him much, and said we would see him in the morning.

It was a cold night, and thin bedding covers meant that we got into our sleeping bags. Come morning Karen and I had a rudimentary breakfast — coffee and sweet rolls — and went out to start the bikes. Knowing I had the benefit of the electric starter, I amusedly watched Karen jump on the Yamaha's kickstarter a few times until it eventually fired. At which point I turned the key on the G/S and touched the button. All I got was a weak ka-chunk, ka-chunk as the engine turned over reluctantly a couple of times and quit. My battery was too small, the oil too thick. And the short-throw kickstarter was not very useful, giving only a revolution and a half. Ah, well. I parked the bike over the hot coals of a campfire, the day warmed up, and eventually the motor did start.

Father Jose was a patient man and waited for us in his elderly VW, and I am glad he did. Not long after leaving Yecora the minimal road went onto a sheet of flattish rock that stretched for several miles, with no visible path to follow, nothing to be seen — nothing. If you knew where you were going, as Father Jose did, fine, but newbies like us could have searched for the road continuing on the far side for hours. The exit road was not even very noticeable, just two thin tire tracks disappearing into the brush. After a few more miles we arrived at the dozen or so houses that made up Maycoba, and Father Jose stopped. He told us we would not get lost from here, and that we should definitely stop to see the Basaseachic waterfall — the 11th highest in the world, he said.

We got to a village, which had at least two dozen houses, and locals directed us towards the waterfall. It was a bit of a hike from the parking area, but well worth the effort, as we stood on

Here I am in Yacopa, trying to warm up my engine on a cold morning. The hot coals of a small open fire go a long way in accomplishing that — provided one uses a little caution of course.

End of the road — at least for us that day, still some 20 miles short of our goal of reaching Batopilas in Copper Canyon.

the rim of a canyon and looked across at water cascading down some 800 feet, originating in a spring high in the Sierra Madre mountains. It is always a bit of a wonderment to me that water chooses to go to the remarkable effort of pushing itself out of the earth thousands of feet above sea level, but that is what makes for great waterfalls.

It was getting dark when we returned to the bikes, but a local farmer had turned his house into a rudimentary hotel for the occasional waterfall visitors. It was another cold night, but we had more bedding than back at Yacopa. Morning came, and we ate a leisurely breakfast while waiting for the day to warm so that the BMW would start. Karen thought this was almighty funny; I couldn't say I blamed her.

Arriving in Creel we got a room at the Hotel Nuevo, and I went to find some lighter oil to put in the crankcase. Our hotel's host had lived in Creel since 1949, making his living as a schoolteacher, and when the Chepe was finally finished in 1961 he opened this hotel. And was a wealth of information about Copper Canyon, from the Tarahumaras who called it home, to the first Spanish mines in the 17th century, to the American entrepreneurs who tried their hand at getting rich less than a hundred years ago.

He advised us to go to Batopilas, a small town that had begun to understand that tourists would be the next big thing. It was a hundred miles away, although more than 5000 feet lower than Creel. Since I like doing dirt roads without baggage, I told the professor that we would leave our gear behind and be back that evening.

With the lighter oil the G/S did start early next chilly morning. Wearing many layers of clothing the two of us headed south. The first 50 miles were considered a main road, but very wash boarded. Washboard is one of those irritations which offers two choices — very slow or very fast. We chose the former. At a minscule collection of houses called Napuchi a rough sign reading "Barranca del Cobre" pointed to the right, while the main road went straight. The lone store sold some foodstuffs and had gasoline in the standard rural container, the ubiquitous 55-gallon drum.

By comparison to the washboard, the dirt road down into the canyon was smooth and wonderful, but much attention was needed. We idled through another tiny village, Quirare, dodging curious dogs, and at the next corner we were stunned by an absolutely splendid view of the canyon, and we could see the river thousands of feet below. And the road winding down and down and down, and even a little bridge at the bottom. It was nigh on as perfect a shot as I could imagine. After ten minutes of gawping we decided we should continue on.

It was a great ride, as long as we stopped to admire the scenery rather than do the viewing while moving; no Armco barriers were at the edge of the road. Riding down a steep hairpinned road, especially on dirt, gave me thoughts of a motorcycling Icarus. Wouldn't it be immensely cool if I just accelerated to the next corner and went straight, riding out into the sky? Fortunately, better sense prevailed.

The temperature got warmer and warmer as we descended in the bright sunshine, and we dispensed with several layers. Finally we were at the bridge at La Bufa, crossing over the river, just 20 miles from our destination. Cheerful thought as we maintained a good clip paralleling the river — until we rounded a curve and found the road blocked by a landslide. The steep hillside, dirt and rocks, had come straight down covering the road completely and continuing on into the river. Obviously we were the first people on the scene, as there weren't any footprints to be seen. I did not even dare try to walk around the slide, for fear it would give way, or more would come, and I would end up in the fast-flowing river.

I looked at Karen. "Game's over." We hustled back up the canyon wall to Quirare and Napuchi, which I must admit was more fun than going down. Then on to Creel. At supper our host talked about the canyon, and that there were many trails passable by horses, crossing several rivers, and it was possible to go to Batopilas and make a big loop via Urique and end up back in Creel not in the rainy season, of course. Sounded interesting, for some future excursion.

The next day Karen and I took off for the north, and at Janos we split, she headed back to New Mexico, me to California. Despite the frustration of the landslide it had been a good ride.

As the Italians say, it doesn't happen twice without a third time. Fourteen years later, to the month, I found myself again in Creel with six other dual-sport riders, all of us on single-cylinder bikes. With me on yet another journalistic assignment, this time for *Rider* magazine. Down through Napuchi and Quirare to Batopilas we went, where we had rooms in an old hacienda and a great dinner. Since this was the dry season, the next day we planned to ford rivers and get to Urique. Unfortunately, the weather gods had decided to play games with us, and that evening it began to rain, and rain, and rain. Next morning the river was in full flood. Not a chance of getting to Urique through the canyons. We went back to Creel the way we had come.

Maybe a fourth time is in order.

On my way home from Copper Canyon I thought to take a short-cut across the Sonoran Desert — but prairie dogs thwarted me.

Europe, Grand Tour 1957

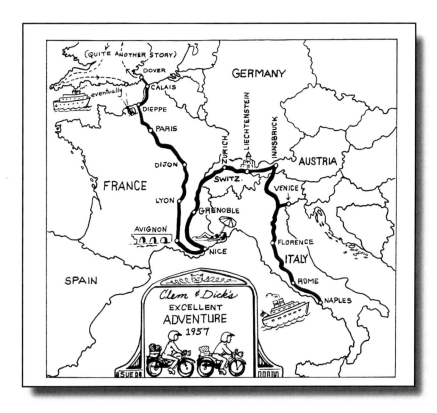

"Where are the tent pegs?" asked Dick. The tent was unrolled, lying on the ground, the poles that held it up were there, but no pegs. This was long before the age of free-standing tents, back when eight pegs had to be strategically placed in order to tension the poles and keep the sides spread out. Obviously we had forgotten to pack them that morning, and here we were, over 100 miles away.

We could have blamed each other, but sensibly we did not. This was the fourth night of a two-month trip, and to squabble about whose fault it was would not have been wise. Although neither of us thought that way. In clearing up the rain-soaked mess of the previous night's campsite, the pegs had been forgotten. Looking up at the sky, we could see no clouds. Perhaps it wouldn't rain, and we could just roll out our sleeping bags.

It was a summer of teenager adventure, two American 17-year-olds tearing around Europe on two motorcycles. In this overly cautious 21st century people might cringe and ask, "How on earth did their parents ever allow them to do that?" Simple; they trusted us.

This is the tale of a trip, not of a place, of two friends riding together for over 2000 miles, seeing places, meeting people, getting to know each other better. Travel is enlightening, informing, and should be a lot of fun.

Dick and I had known each other since we were six, his father a doctor, mine a professor, living across the street from each other. I might blame him for my passion for motorcycling, as before we were even old enough to have drivers licenses he had bought an old Harley 125, on which we crashed around in the nearby woods.

When I was 16 my father took a sabbatical leave from his college in Massachusetts to live in Rome, Italy. Knowing the 'rents wanted me to come

Clement with the 1954 NSU 250 Max on which he toured Europe in 1957. He had little appreciation for its sophistication, with an overhead-camshaft engine and mono-shock rear suspension.

along — although they did give me the option of staying behind at boarding school — I had a little bargaining power. "I'll come if I can have a motorcycle."

"You earn the money, you can buy a motorcycle," they replied.

My 16th summer was spent stripping wallpaper off of dormitory walls, under the auspices of the college's maintenance department, standard entry into the laboring world for many faculty brats. Saving every dollar, there were enough to buy a used NSU Max 250 when I got to Rome. Dick and I kept in touch the old-fashioned way, putting a letter in an envelope and affixing a stamp. In the spring we decided that he should come to Italy and we would tool around on motorcycles for the summer. He would send me some money, and I would buy him a suitable motorcycle — which I did, a BMW R26 250.

His ship was due in Naples in June and I took a train down to meet him; this was back when travel by ship was the norm. We trained back to Rome, and next morning fired up both bikes for a trial run through the hills south of the city.

Having already had the better part of a year to practice my riding skills, I was proceeding briskly through the curves until at one point I heard a BANG! CRUNCH! SCRAPE!, looked over my shoulder, and Dick was sliding along the road on his butt, while his bike fetched up against a large stone kilometer-marker.

He was unscathed, but picking up the bike we realized that the front forks had been severely bent, rendering it unrideable. In a nearby village we found a blacksmith who had not only a forge and an anvil, but a set of tools as well. Of course he was familiar with straightening-out motorcycles, as it happened all the time.

Organizing a flatbed truck and a couple of layabouts, he picked up the BMW and brought it back to the smithy. "I'll give you a call when it's done", he said.

Two days later the call came. We rode back to the village and stopped in front of the blacksmith's shop. No sign of him. A local sitting on bench informed us that the smith had gone on a little ride just to make sure the work was done right. He reappeared an hour later, obviously having stopped by a bar or two, announcing that the motorcycle handled better than when it was new. We headed back to Rome to get ready for our trip.

This was to be done on the cheap, with camping gear, youth-hostel cards, and advice that we should never eat at any place which had clean, white table-clothes — too expensive. The only date to be minded was that of the departure of a ship from Southampton, England, at the end of August, which would get us home in time to start our senior year in high school.

Our gear, clothes in suitcases, tent and sleeping bags wherever, was lashed in a rudimentary fashion to the back of the seats and small luggage racks both bikes had, using five-foot long rubber ropes — this was the pre-bungie cord era. Secure one end of the rope, wrap it around and around, secure the other end somewhere, and away we went.

Florence had one of the most magnificent youth hostels in Europe, in a villa with gardens, a swimming pool, restaurant with inexpensive food, and a bar, a very nice cosmopolitan touch. Being our first hostel, we thought this whole hosteling idea was pretty fine — until a seasoned hosteler informed us that the average hostel was pretty basic. Here an individual's stay was limited to three days, being strictly enforced in order to prevent people who had reason to be in the city for a long time from becoming permanent residents.

From Florence the road swooped north through the Apennine Mountains over the Passo della Futa and Passo della Raticosa our first real taste of mountain riding. Exhilaration! Dick allowed as to how he might sometimes fall behind, as he was not quite as exuberant as I in rounding the curves. Crossing the flat Po River valley we found a campsite east of Padova, set up our tent for the first time, and headed off to Venice for an evening on the town. The city was too expensive for our budget, but a visit was in order. We strolled around for hours, eating slices of pizza when we were hungry, and then back to the municipal garage to retrieve our motorcycles. Just as we pulled out the skies opened up; we donned our ponchos, our rudimentary raingear. A three-mile bridge connects Venice with the mainland, and in less than a mile deep water was flowing along the roadway. Lifting the bikes onto the broad sidewalk we covered the rest of the distance to land — and the rain stopped.

Back at the campground we found we had not raised the entrance lip of our tent properly, and the little habitation was flooded, including sleeping bags. The proprietor was sympathetic, and said she had a room for rent — but declined to tell us there were no screens on the windows and mosquitoes abounded. It was not a good night. The morning sun served to dry most of our gear, and was followed by a late start for the Alps.

The afternoon sun was not far in the west when we got to Merano, where a campground in an orchard offered accommodation. The early stop would allow a final drying out of any still-damp gear. Dick went to the little store to see what could be had for supper, while I was preparing to set up the tent. I looked around for the pegs; no where to be found.

"Do not worry," said our camping neighbors, "the radio says it will be a nice night." And it was. Dick appeared with salami and bread, apples for dessert, and a bar of chocolate. He took the problem of the missing tent pegs with great equanimity; I was a little more frazzled.

Next day it was over the Passo di Monte Giovo — a dirt road at that time, with a deep drainage ditch on the mountainside, a 45-degree descent on the other. A bus came barreling down towards me, taking up most of the road, as I rounded a curve. The bus passed, and I waited for Dick to appear. Which he did not. Turning around and going back to the far side of the curve I found Dick and motorcycle safely in the ditch, unharmed, having sensibly gotten out of the way. A little push and we had his Beemer back on the road.

Our days were quite leisurely, with no real rush; a local grocery would provide an excellent sandwich and we could happily spend an hour in a field contemplating the valley in front of us, talking idly about where we might spend the night. Plummeting north into Austria from the Brenner Pass we came across a very nice patch of woods close to the Inn River, and decided that a little free-camping was in order. After all, we were traveling cheap. And if the trees were all in precisely the right position, maybe we could set up the tent. They weren't, and we couldn't, but it was a clear, rainless night. Note to self: Buy some sort of tent pegs tomorrow.

In the morning, over instant coffee — disgusting stuff, but all one needed to do was boil water — we contemplated a map and decided we could make it to Zurich, Switzerland, where a large hostel awaited us. The road led over the Arlberg Pass, where we stopped to admire the view; not having thought to bring a camera along, visual memories would have to do. Today most travelers take the nine-mile tunnel that goes under the Arlberg, but they miss the mountains and valleys, the thick green forests, their loss.

Dick, being an organized fellow, decided to make sure his passport was in his pocket since we would be crossing into Switzerland soon. It wasn't. Nor any other pocket. We took the kit off of his bike and searched through it; not there. Then the kit from my bike, just in case; not there. We headed back the way we had come, found our camping spot and looked; not there. A desperate search of all places again; found!

Time's a'wasting; back on the road, over the Arlberg, heading for Feldkirch on the Swiss border. Also close to the border with the tiny principality of Liechtenstein. Dusk was gathering as the Liechtensteinian official stamped our passports, providing proof that we had actually been there. We were hoping for a pleasantly wooded spot where we could perhaps string up the tent, having been too concerned with passports to worry about pegs, but it appeared that all the land in the 60 square miles of the country was spoken for, with fences to remind us not to trespass.

Arriving at the Rhine River an old-fashioned covered bridge

went across to Switzerland, with dikes on both banks to prevent flooding. For the record we wanted to spend a night in one of the smallest countries in the world, and rode along the top of the dike for a hundred yards. A bit of a moon showed, and clouds were moving about as we rolled out our sleeping bags. And soon fell into the arms of Morpheus.

Awaking to a light rain splattering down on my face, I reached around to pull my poncho over me and went back to sleep. Only to awaken again as I heard muttered oaths from Dick, who is not a person prone to swearing. He had made himself comfortable in a depression on top of the dike, and the depression had filled with water, and his sleeping bag was soaked. The rain stopped.

136

Dick blamed his sodden condition on poor Prince Franz Josef II, who was probably comfortably asleep in his castle in Vaduz. In a moment of quiet rage, Dick decided that the prince should pay for this indignity. It was about 4 a.m. Taking his toolkit out, and with the help of a flashlight Dick unbolted and removed the muffler and went for a ride. For half an hour I could hear his every gear shift as he did the grand tour of Liechtenstein, as probably did many inhabitants of the little country. What prompted my otherwise mild-mannered friend to do this remains a minor mystery.

The first glimmer of dawn was in the sky when he returned, put the muffler back on the motorcycle, and we packed and left Liechtenstein via the covered bridge.

Vaduz Castle, where Prince Franz Josef II may have been sleeping when Dick decided to wake up the entire country.

The roads were damp, though it was not raining, and we rode circumspectly. In a small town the road split; with no traffic in sight, and being in the lead I stopped at the intersection to read the signs better. There was the screech of a locked-up brake, then the crash/scrape/tinkle of a bike falling and skidding along the asphalt. Damn, I thought, Dick's down. Crash/crunch, the noise of a bike hitting another bike — Damn, he's hit me. Except I was sitting happily on my NSU as I watched Dick's BMW skid past me on its side. Looking over my shoulder I saw Dick standing there, left foot on the pavement, right foot in the air, as if his bike had been knocked out from under him while he was stopped.

Which it had. Right behind him was a Swiss fellow extricating himself from under his own motorcycle, being the one who had locked up his rear wheel, fallen down, and slid into Dick. No real damage done, except Dick's suitcase had burst open and all his clothes were scattered on the road. We picked up the bikes, and Dick's clothes, the Swiss apologized profusely, stuffed a few francs in Dick's hand, and rode away. We continued on to Zurich.

Several days later, with large metal spikes rather than wooden tent pegs in hand, we left Switzerland and headed south for the warm beaches of the French Riviera. We set up the tent near Grenoble, and it did rain. My bright red and white Italian helmet was left out, and in the morning it was a strange sight — it seemed to have been made of layers of cardboard glued together, and the glue had come unstuck. In Grenoble a shop had a French-made Geno half-helmet, that being the only style available in those halcyon days, a much more sophisticated item than my Italian hat, with a thin aluminum outer shell, much padding inside, and a leather harness around my skull.

Being the principal navigator for the trip I looked at a map and saw that the most direct way to the beach was via "La Route Napoleon", the route taken by Nappie when he came back from his exile on the Mediterranean island of Elba to meet his Waterloo. Superb road this was, endlessly curving around the Maritime Alps, occasionally tunneling through them. A 250 single with a four-speed gearbox was all one needed to have fun. Dick's Beemer put out about 15 horses, my NSU, 18, plenty of power for the likes of us. Mostly the road was a narrow two-laner with a low stone wall on the outside to prevent a motorcycle, but not the rider, from going over the edge and into an abyss.

Riding rather too rapidly into one dark tunnel I was blinded by the transition from bright sunlight to near-total darkness and aimed for the light at the far end, presuming it was the exit. Only to realize almost too late that the light came from a big window cut in the side of the mountain to illuminate a curve in the tunnel. From then on I slowed considerably when approaching such a passageway.

This was not the high road, as our highest point was the Col de Bayard at a little over 4000 feet. Some 40 years later I was some 40 eagle-flying miles southeast of Bayard at the Cime de la

Bonnette, at a heady 9200 feet the highest paved road in all the Alps. Anyone thinking that is not very high should be aware that la Bonnette is less than 50 miles from the sea — the Alps do rise abruptly.

In Nice we set up camp and spent two days gawking at the bikinied women on the beach. Being relatively penniless 17-year-olds that was really all that was possible in that rather expensive city.

We headed west to Avignon, where for some forgotten reason I wanted to see the bridge where the French children's song said people danced:

> *Sur le pont d'Avignon,*
> *On y dance, on y dance.*

Nobody was dancing on the broken bridge. Dick was not impressed. Nor, in truth, was I.

Aiming our 250s north along the Rhone River we headed for Dijon, where another home-town friend was spending the summer learning French. We ate lots of good mustard smeared on excellent sausages cushioned in fresh baguettes. The French do take their food seriously, whether one is eating at a truck-stop or a Michelin-rated restaurant; Dick and I were definitely not the Michelin sort. Our main meal was in the middle of the day, and we were quite happy being at a roadside cafe, sitting under wisteria, with half a roast chicken and a plate of pommes frites.

Unfortunately the Dijon youth hostel was the worst we ever stayed at, with plumbing that made even teenagers balk.

The construction of Notre Dame de Paris, the Gothic cathedral on an island in the Seine River in the middle of the city, was begun in 1163 and more or less completed in 1345 — and stands to this day as a marvel of architectural beauty.

Off to Paris, where a hostel hosted us for four nights. Other than for a trip to Versailles we left the bikes at the hostel and used the Metro — one of the most usable subway systems in the world. We did museums like the Louvre and Les Invalides, strolled along the bookstalls on the banks of the Seine River, and sat at the once-famed Les Deux Magots cafe drinking *citron presse*. Pressed lemons = lemonade.

I like Paris, and Parisians. Tourists in that city are often too sensitive, complaining about bad service and insolent waiters, expecting too much for the small amount of money they spend. Paris is like any large city, the inhabitants struggling to survive, snapping at any stranger who comes along, be it an American or some hapless fellow-countryman. Especially in August, traditional vacation-time, when the tourist-industry employees would all rather be in the country.

Time was pressing as our ship would wait for no laggard. Heading northwest towards the English Channel we stopped in Rouen to see the statue of Joan of Arc. She was only 15 when she was leading armies, and we thought we were pretty brave riding motorcycles around Europe at 17. The bravery was actually on the part of our parents, while Dick and I suffered only mild bedevilments such as left-behind tent pegs and a misplaced passport. Joan, unfortunately, got burned at the stake in 1431 for her efforts, and we hoped to avoid such a fate.

My directions led us to the village of Cleres, near to there being the Ecole des Roches, a boarding school I had attended when I was 12. That year my father worked for the United Nations in Paris, and the parents had relegated me to this countryside school, feeling it provided a better environment and education than the city could offer. The ecole was a well-respected institution, built on the grounds of an 18th century chateau, and the entrance was via a broad avenue lined with tall trees. In 1945 the Germans had placed a V2 rocket launcher under the canopy and cut a hole in the branches to allow the rocket to pass through;12 years later one could still see where the hole had been. The Allies did learn that something was up on the estate, but a bombing raid failed to take out the launcher, though it did flatten the castle that had been the focus of the school.

My clearest memory of the place was of the cold showers we were made to take every morning, including winter — shiver, shiver. Maybe that is why I don't remember ever getting sick. The students ranged in age from six to 19, and in the older boys'

The village of Cleres was near Clement's boarding school in France, and where he would go with his parents for lunch when they came to visit him. Clement sent this postcard to his mother during that era.

dining room, where I belonged, at every lunch and supper every table was adorned with a bottle of wine and a bottle of hard cider which we would drink mixed with water. I do not remember ever seeing any of my classmates even the slightest bit tipsy.

The place being on vacation nobody I could remember was around, and we rode on the coast just south of Dieppe. This place had been immensely fortified during the German occupation in World War II, and following the war barbed wire and unexploded ordinance had been removed, we trusted, and anything movable taken away, but nobody had seen the need to go through the tremendous, and expensive, work of demolishing the defenses that rimmed the cliffs above the beaches.

Heading down a dirt track towards the channel we came out on a billiard-table smooth grassy area, perfect for parking motorcycles and pitching a tent. This was actually the top of a large bunker, the crafty Germans having spread dirt on the flat surface and sown it with seed, so that from the air it looked just like a field. It was late, bread and cheese for supper, and to bed.

The next day was spent wandering through these remnants of modern war, a war both our fathers had participated in.

Much preferable in my romantic mind are medieval fortresses with crenellated ramparts, towers, and a portcullis, but the use of gunpowder did not do much to enhance the architectural qualities of defense structures. Bombs from airplanes and 16-inch shells from battleships did even less. The construction of our bunker was impressive, with five-foot thick walls of reinforced concrete and narrow slits for the guns. The chance of a naval shell getting through an artillery opening was small, and probably bombardment from the air would have merely given the occupants headaches.

That evening we cooked our last meal on the continent, sumptuous by our standards on the one-burner stove. Soup from a package, boiled eggs, cheese, bread, and fruit for dessert. We looked out to the Channel and tried to imagine a thousand ships and landing craft, and were glad that the nuclear stalemate between the US and USSR would probably mean we would never have to face the kind of battle these fortifications had prepared for. In 1957 the draft was on the mind of every young American male, but no wars seemed to be on the horizon.

We slept well, untroubled by dreams of war. At dawn we awoke, packed up, kickstarted our bikes, and headed north the hundred miles to Calais, where a ferry would take us to Dover, England, followed by a quick ride to Southampton. And then our ship, the *S.S. Castel Felice*, would take us and our motorcycles to New York City.

Where one story ends, another usually begins.

Guatamala 1975

YOU CAN'T GET TO THERE FROM HERE

We were ten miles down the road when I reached back, behind my passenger, to check that the tent and two skinny duffles were still stacked on the luggage rack. Ohmygod, they're gone!

I braked, made a quick U-turn and started to head back the way we had come, hoping to find them before some local picked them up. And this 20 minutes into a 30-day trip.

"Stop," said Sonora, loudly, getting through my helmet, "they're still there, except they're under the rack." I stopped, looked behind, and sure enough, the three bags had slipped backwards from the big Craven luggage rack, but the bungies still held them on upside-down. Arranging the packing for a month-long, two-up road trip on a motorcycle takes a bit of doing, and obviously I had been lax. I restacked the load, reinforcing the tie-downs with two non-elastic straps. The BMW R75/5 was kitted out for camping, with proper sleeping and cooking gear, including Sonora's supply of spices.

Sonora put a finger under each of the straps and lifted, making sure they were tight. "Just checking," she said. We redonned our helmets and were back on the road.

This particular road began in San Miguel de Allende in central Mexico, where I was studying for a Master of Fine Arts at the US-accredited Instituto Allende. And teaching English to cover my fees. Uncle Sam's GI bill for the Vietnam-era soldier was giving me enough to live a rather splendid life in that town, with a large house, a twice-weekly maid, and invitations to all the best social events. Xmas break was a long one, to allow American kids to return home for the holidays, and I had an equal break.

Since I derive great pleasure from wandering around architectural relics of times long past, Sonora and I were on our way to visit a dozen or more pre-Columbian sites in Mexico and Guatemala.

Sonora was a California lass who had come to San Miguel to expand her consciousness, as the saying went in the seventies. She was bright, cheerful, articulate, and with a large mop of brilliant red hair drawing attention wherever she went. She was a good companion for such a trip, as she loved passengering on a motorcycle, loved camping, and loved seeing new places.

Our first night would be in a hotel, as I wanted to show her, and see for myself, the pre-Aztec pyramids at Teotihuacan, northeast of Mexico City. Tourists to the site usually took day trips from Mexico City, and at that time the small town of 5000 or so inhabitants had only a couple of inexpensive little hotels, one of which provided us with a room. We spent a few hours

This shot of yours truly was taken at San Miguel de Allende, the Mexican town where I was living in 1975 and 1976, from where the Guatemala trip began.

walking around the much-restored archeological site that was once the center of a city of 200,000 or more inhabitants. The antiquities covered several hundred acres, smaller buildings lining a long Avenue of the Dead anchored by the Pyramid of the Moon at one end. A half-mile away was the main temple, the Pyramid of the Sun, the third largest pyramid in the world. New World pyramids have a stepped, or layered, structure, with a flat area around the top of each layer, and stairs to help in getting to the top, where religious ceremonies would be held.

Except these stairs are usually almost a foot high, as opposed to the seven-inch rise on your household stairs. A visit to a Mexican archeological site does demand a lot of climbing. We climbed the Sun, and then the Moon, and from the top watched a quarter moon rise in the sky. After returning to the Avenue of the Dead - so named because it was lined with tombs - we felt as though we had climbed mountains, returning to the hotel tired but satisfied.

On the way to Guatemala, we passed a dozen sites around Mexico's Yucatan peninsula; Chichen Itza was probably the most restored, as it is near the tourist base of Merida.

The Mayan ruins at Palenque, Mexico, were the most fun, as they were the least developed and the least supervised; nobody cared where we went.

After a pleasantly quiet evening we retired. In the morning we went down to the hotel's restaurant for breakfast, with the only other customers being a few locals. The waitress gave us menus, in Spanish, and I noticed "Huevos de tortugas". Never having had turtle eggs, this was an opportunity for something new. I presumed they were prepared in their own special way, so I did not ask for fried or scrambled. What I got was a tall, thin glass with two raw turtle eggs inside, the yolks intact and the whites translucent. Sonora looked at me. The waitress looked at me. "You do not cook these eggs?" I asked in my rudimentary Spanish. "No, you eat them like this," she replied, "and they are good for your manhood." Everybody was looking at me, and Sonora was beginning to giggle.

What the hell! I upended the glass and swallowed one without breaking the yolk, then the second one. A small round of applause from the locals. It was consumption without taste, and I decided from then on that I would prefer chicken eggs, scrambled, with chorizo sausage.

We moved on to the coast along the Gulf of Mexico, into the Yucatan peninsula, camping at Mayan sites like Palenque and Uxmal and Chichen Itza. Long before the Europeans developed the architectural knack of vaulted arches, essential in building cathedrals, the inhabitants of the New World built their far simpler pyramids, starting some 2500 years ago. Impressive structures, they were built to honor, or to appease, the local gods, who on occasion apparently appreciated a human sacrifice.

Now the ruins were sensibly being used to attract tourists. These sites were generally lightly supervised; a care-taker would have a booth at the entrance, sell us tickets for a nominal sum, and nobody minded where we walked or climbed. At Palenque we could wander into the thick jungle backing the ruin site and find the walls of still more buildings, waiting to be cleared when more money was available.

The jungle, or rain-forest, is really a moving force. Leave a large stone pyramid alone and untended in the forest for several hundred years and Mother Nature will take it back. Winds come, dirt blows up, trees take root, and the roots themselves

Tulum, on the Caribbean coast not far south of Cancun is undoubtedly the most romantic of the Mayan ruins, being right on the sea — and has survived a thousand years of hurricanes.

Camping is the best way to travel inexpensively, especially when your campsite is on the balmy shores of the Caribbean Sea.

will dismantle, in time, what humans have so laboriously put together. It wasn't until the late 19th century that the spirit of archeological reconstruction began making itself felt, and much effort and money has been spent in the last century to make these ruins look as they once were.

We stopped for half an hour at Cancun, which at that time was a sandspit just getting developed, with two operating mid-sized hotels, half a dozen more under construction. This was to be a purpose-built tourist destination, most money coming from the Mexican government. Now in the 21st century over 150 hotels have thousands of rooms, and with four million vacationers arriving every year the place has become a genuine money-maker.

Sipping a fruity alcoholic drink at a beachside cafe, Sonora commented on the difference between tourism and travel. "I imagine that it would be nice to stay at a hotel on the beach, and not have to worry about a single thing, food, drink, bed, all right there. But I am afraid I would get bored very quickly. I do like the way we are traveling."

Some 40 miles south of Cancun was the small Mayan site of Tulum, one of the nicest collections of ruins I have ever had the pleasure of wandering through. It resembled a medieval fortress, with a castle built right on the top of a 40 foot cliff rising from a Caribbean beach. This was apparently a major trading site, and easily defensible, as a great wall surrounded the three landward sides, 15 feet tall and 25 feet thick; it would take a serious army to try to capture the place. On top of the castle was a chamber which served as a lighthouse, should trading canoes be out at night.

"I wonder how they felt when they saw those great Spanish sailing ships approaching," observed Sonora as we stood on the castle's roof. "Did they know immediately it was an enemy? Or did their curiosity get the better of them? I read somewhere that they may have thought these great winged vessels were carrying gods."

We found a campsite on a beach just a few miles south of Tulum. Sonora prided herself on her camp-cooking, with a single

A hammock, a couple of appropriately placed trees, and you have a fine spot for a brief snooze; I never did master the art of sleeping all night in one of these contraptions.

Traveling is tiring work, and taking the occasional nap along the way is essential to a happy trip — about that I am religious.

pot and a one-burner stove. We would stop in the nearest village and get the evening's supplies for a bang-up supper. Shopping was easy, as a village would have only one or two stores, selling local produce, bread and canned goods, usually with prices well-marked. Mexico is not really a bartering culture, like the Middle East, except when it comes to tourist trinkets.

If there was a fresh-killed chicken, she might buy a quarter to put in the pot, along with a sweet potato and tomatoes, and the ubiquitous chilies. The vendors, always women, were always fascinated by her hair — which would expand gloriously as soon as she took off her helmet — while the menfolk would stare discreetly. Her smile could make anyone's day.

Then it was down into Belize, a semi-independent ex-British colony, where the population was mainly of African descent and the language was a rough English. Belize City was a delightful place, as close to a scene from a Joseph Conrad novel as I have ever appreciated, with rusty tramp steamers anchored in the harbor, lighters carrying goods to the old wooden docks. The Belize River flowed through the middle of town, and many houses were built on stilts to avoid rainy-season flooding. The only fire station, with two antiquated engines, was on the north side of the river, and twice a day the swing-bridge slowly pivoted to allow boats through. A siren announced the event, and one of the fire trucks would start up, cross over the bridge, and sit on the south side, just in case it was needed. Backing onto the south side of the river were a whole series of bars with small porches at the back, and all manner of illicit commodities were easily available.

Sitting on one of these little balconies on a hot afternoon, Sonora took the cold bottle of beer and rolled it against her temples. "I never imagined what the tropics might be like, but I rather like the temperature. Very pleasant."

Leaving the BMW tethered to a post under the guesthouse where we were staying, we took a boat to one of the off-shore islands. Our landlady had given us the name of a place to stay on the island, with a four-poster bed and mosquito netting. All there was to eat was lobster cooked in coconut butter and home-made bread; what a shame. I would have liked to stay more than two nights.

Off to Guatemala. At the border the Belizean officials were quite cheerful and laid back, whilst the Guatemalans tried hard to look ferocious and efficient. A full-fledged territorial dispute was then raging between Belize and Guatemala, as the latter wanted to annex the former. This did not happen, namely because the British armed forces continued to provide protection to the ex-colony.

Guatamala 1975

The temple complex at Tikal was pleasantly rustic, with trees still left in the open space which the buildings surround. Just climbing to the top of one of the Tikal temples was precarious and a lot of exercise, the angle being so steep. On some of the temples a chain strung down the middle of the stairway was a helpful aid in pulling oneself up the incline.

The northeastern third of Guatemala, known as the Peten, was remote from the rest of that country, and my next goal was the Mayan temple complex at Tikal — those of you who viewed the first "Star Wars" movie would have seen the three great temples rising above the jungle canopy. A well-used dirt road ran from the border west towards Lake Peten, and midway was the turn to Tikal, another few miles north. The setting at the park entrance was rustic, with a basic campground, a store selling souvenirs and food, a small restaurant. We set up camp and then strolled over to the gate, as a flimsy fence surrounded the large site. A couple of quetzel, the local currency, and we were in.

Tikal was quite different from Teotihuacan, with smaller but steeper stepped pyramids. The Pyramid of the Sun had had about a 30 degree slope, whereas the Tikal temples were closer to 60 degrees. With much steeper stairs; nervous tourists could be seen coming down backwards, not wishing to look at the possibility of a hundred-foot tumble. The tallest of the temples was 230 feet, and from the top I could look out over a veritable sea of green, the jungle going as far as my eye could see. Nearby were the tops of other structures; the area around the five main temples has been cleared by the archeologists, revealing the Great Plaza and many smaller structures.

All this work was originally done over a thousand years ago, and then abandoned — probably due to lack of water. There was no river here, no wells, the tens of thousands who lived in the area having to rely on catching and keeping the rain-water both for themselves and their crops. Which is probably why the campground had no showers. The temples were made of quarried local limestone, and the quarries themselves were turned into reservoirs to catch the 80 inches of rain that fall each year — unless there was a drought.

A small airstrip had been built near the ruins, and the next morning we heard a plane come in, with a dozen or so freshly dressed tourists from Guatemala City arriving, poking around for four or five hours, and then leaving. Along with several buses that picked up tourists in the island town of Flores, on Lake Peten. At night the ruins were pretty much left to the campers.

The Tikal complex shining above the trees in the late afternoon sun.

At Tikal we met a Canadian motorcyclist, and he and I decided to see if we could get to the ruins at Uaxactun, about 15 miles north of Tikal.

The gate was officially closed at dusk, but the guard was easily bribable, and Sonora and I, and a Canadian motorcyclist at the campground, had a delightful moonlit stroll. Mystical. Lying on top of one of the pyramids, with stars and a waxing moon, I could dream a pleasant fiction of what life might have been like here 1000 years ago; of course I imagined myself a lord, not a laborer.

We learned that there was another unexcavated complex of ruins, Uaxactun, about 15 miles north, with a very primitive road headed that way; it was not a through road, and we would have to come back the same way. The Canadian and I decided to take a look, while Sonora had the good sense to stay at Tikal. Within a couple of miles it became obvious that the road had not been used in quite a while, and not maintained at all. Trees had fallen across it, and we couldn't go around because of the thick jungle, so we would have to hoist the bikes over. After the third tree we discussed the fact that we were going to have to repeat all this arduous nonsense a second time, on the way back, and gave up the notion.

Sonora and I headed for Flores. Along the way the Beemer suffered a flat tire. I took off the wheel, pulled out the inner tube, got the patch ready, opened the tube of glue — dry. Being a bright sort, I had brought along a second supply of glue. Also dry. What to do? With the rear wheel detached, it was quite obvious what the problem was. A car stopped to see if help was needed. Sorry, no glue, but they could give me a ride into town. I was a bit concerned about leaving Sonora on this lonely road. "Go ahead," she said, "I'll be fine; these are friendly people here. And I have this . . ." as she patted the machete I had brought along. I unchivalrously left her and the bike beside the road.

After being dropped off at a tire repair shop I got the tube patched, but nobody had little containers of glue for sale. I decided I wanted a second tube as a backup, but there was no one selling motorcycle inner tubes in town. The shop inflated the tube to make sure the patch was holding, and I put it around my waist like a skinny Michelin man. While I was walking back out to the road a motorcycle appeared, and I waved the rider down;

Guatamala 1975

The road from Tikal to Uaxactun was not exactly in good condition, and obviously no vehicle had gone this way in months, if not years.

It is one thing to hoist a motorcycle over a fallen tree, or trees, another to know that this is not a thru road, and all the hoisting will have to be repeated again on the way back.

his was a dual-purpose bike with a tire the same size as mine. And he had a spare tube at home which he would sell me. And for a small consideration take me back to the BMW. Done deal.

Sonora said only half a dozen vehicles had gone by, and all had stopped to see if they could be of help. Nothing unpleasant. A compliment to the Mayan culture.

In Flores we put up at a lakeside back-packer's hotel, with a room over-looking the water. After cleaning up — remember, no showers at Tikal — we went down to the patio below to have a cold beer and discuss the next step. My teaching job meant time was a factor, and we were half way into our 30 days. From Flores there was150 miles of bad road going south to connect with Guatemala's main, and only, east-west highway. I would rather ride that stretch alone, and Sonora would be happy to fly to Guatemala City. The next morning I put her on the plane, saying I'd see her in three days, and took off.

It was a bad road, even by Central American standards, with mud, ruts, corrugation, soft sand, stream crossings, and forest debris covering the single lane. But I only fell down once, and that was in a flooded spot a hundred feet wide, which wasn't very deep, but was extremely slippery; resulting in baptismal-quality full-body immersion. A ferry took me across the Rio Dulce, and 15 miles later I was back on pavement.

I spent a night at the Quirigua ruins, where minor archeological excavations had begun back in the 19th century. This place was settled in the valley of the Motoagua River by an offshoot of the Tikal kingdom; perhaps they were tired at not having showers. Their problem was not too little water, but too much, and the place occasionally flooded. The United Fruit Company bought up the whole area in 1910 for banana planting, but kept the 75 acres where the ruins are as a major historical site, and eventually gave the place to the government.

Next day I detoured into Honduras to see the ruins at Copan, one of the farthest reaches of the Tikal culture. I do enjoy clambering over ruins, which may have begun when I was six years old and my English grandmother would take me on picnics to the crumbling remains of Corfe Castle, not far from her house in Dorset. For me there is a fascination about ruins, whether they are Greek temples in Sicily, ancient Buddhist wats in Cambodia, or crusader castles in Turkey; show me a ruin and I want to have a look-see and feel the centuries beneath my boots. By the standards of the universe my time on earth is very limited, but I do like to get a feel for those who have passed this way before. For a thousand years the Mayans held sway over this part of the Americas, and then their time was past. It is common knowledge that great civilizations only last for so long, and then vanish.

The border crossing into Honduras was quite basic, along a little-used dirt road. A bored soldier was sitting in a shack on one side of a shallow river, helped himself to a proffered cigarette, and waved me through. I splashed through the water, and an equally bored official on the other side took a cursory look at my passport, accepted a cigarette, and sent me on my way. Ah, the traveling was good back then. The Copan ruins covered some 40 acres, with a central section featuring an acropolis, a huge plaza, and a ball court — where the losing side, it is said, would be executed. If we played by those rules, that would bring a whole new interest in American basketball.

Nobody minded if I brought the motorcycle up close to some of the temples back in 1975; nowadays I am sure the parking area is a good deal further away.

Next afternoon I was in Guatemala City where Sonora had been staying at an inexpensive hotel, popular among the low-cost travelers. She was sitting on the front verandah when I pulled up, and happily greeted me with a hug and a kiss. It was obvious that a number of would-be swains had been pursuing her ardently, and several were sitting with her on the front porch when I arrived. There were introductions, with Sonora saying how sweet they had been to her, but they greeted me with a certain chilliness and even a bit of hostility, exacerbated by the affectionate response that I received from the lady. Lone gringas were not often found on the Central American hippie tour, and she had thoroughly enjoyed all the attention. Allowing that she much preferred the motorcycle to planes and buses.

The following day was Xmas Eve, and an artist friend in Antigua had invited us to stay for the Holy Days. Antigua had been the old Spanish capitol beginning in 1543, but unfortunately the valley where it was located had proved to be prone to earthquakes, and after 250 years the government was moved to the site of the present Guatamala City. The mountains in that part of Guatemala are very volcanic, and three tall volcanoes, all over 12,000 feet, provide a backdrop to Antigua's valley, being both very picturesque and a bit scary. The Volcan de Fuego rarely erupts, but emits smoke every day.

Antigua was beautiful, very well kept with cobbled streets, mansions and churches dating from the colonial era. The Cathedral of Saint Joseph, built in the vaulted style of Spanish churches, has two towers dating back to the 17th century, but the rest of the building, destroyed in the earthquake of 1773, has been rebuilt. A more sensible construction is the rather baroque La Merced church, built six years before the great quake of 1773 and still standing, because its architect had understood that in this region of shifting tectonic plates low and solid is better than that high and mighty. Everyone was dressed in their Holy Days best, and the cathedral and churches were all spic and span. The parque central was the meeting place, and one could see the eligible young ladies, with chaperones, doing a clockwise circuit, while the young men, nattily attired in black pants and white shirts, and trying to look very sophisticated, went counterclockwise. Sonora and I did several circuits, arm in arm.

A dozen people showed up for Xmas dinner, and toasting was done with local wines, probably derived from the vines that the friars had brought over from Europe in the 16th century. Christ's blood, as the Bible says. The guests were resident, or semi-resident, Americans, some in the jade business, as jade is mined in the valley, others selling real estate. Or retired folk who came south during the cold months. But they all thought of Antigua as being a peaceable kingdom.

On the third day we left, heading home. We spent that night at Lake Atitlan, a beautiful volcanic lake where the locals still spoke one of the Mayan dialects and dressed in the traditional brightly colored woven clothing. I had been to the little lakeside town of Panajachel in 1968, when it was barely a glimmer in the traveler's eye. Now half a dozen small hotels were catering to the back-packing crowd, and little restaurants provided scrumptious food, some of the cooking being done by hippie types who wanted to prolong their stay. Ten villages dotted the shores of the lake, which has a depth of a thousand feet or more, but no road connected them all — just the daily mailboat.

"Oh, this is wonderful!," said my companion. "Can't we stay here a few more days?"

Sorry, it was way more than a thousand miles to get back to San Miguel, and my devious route would take us almost a week. We'd go up to Oaxaca, Mexico, to see the Zapotec ruins at Monte Alban, then over to the Pacific coast and roll up from Puerto Angel to Acapulco, and then north. Three nights at Panajachel and we had to move along, as I had to meet my teaching commitments.

"Well, we can always come back," she said. We never did.

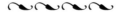

Japan 1972 and 1984

Travel by a Westerner in the land of the rising sun in the 21st century can be a lesson in financial humility, downright embarrassing to a bank account to have to pay for simple food and lodging.

In the 1980s I took two trips to that island nation under the auspices of Japanese motorcycle manufacturers, wherein we, a small group of moto-journalists, were greeted, guarded, transported, shuffled, fed, conveyed, looked after, cared for, wined, dined, and finally bused back to the Narita airport with our arms full of gifts, our pockets full of exposed film, and our notebooks full of information. And we would have been in the saddle for a few precious miles on the latest models.

But we learned very little about Japan. Which may have been the intent of our hosts.

My own estimation of that island nation is that it has a remarkably homogeneous society which doesn't much want to integrate with foreigners, whether they are Americans or Koreans or anyone else. Thanks to excellent managerial techniques and creative production concepts and great cooperation between government and industry they enjoyed an economic boom in the 1960s and '70s which left much of the developed world stunned. And sometimes in awe.

But the Japanese are not miracle workers, they are only human beings, and since then they have suffered some serious economic reversals.

My first trip to that country was in January of 1972, when the dollar was strong and the yen weak. After 18 months in Vietnam I was on the way back to the United States, with an American friend, and though I was on government orders to proceed as fast as possible (sounds intriguing, but all it meant was that I was supposed to be filling a vacancy somewhere else), I shuffled the paperwork so that I could spend a couple of days having a quick look around that oriental constitutional democracy. I have never had a great urge to see Japan, the way I have other places, but as my Aunt Agatha would say, "The time to take the tarts is in the passing."

I don't speak a word of Japanese, and while the history and culture of the island is fascinating to some, I much prefer the chaos of India to the organization-state that is Japan.

On that first trip my friend and I checked into a hermetically sealed hotel in downtown Tokyo and quickly decided the city was not for us. The next morning we took a train 100 miles southwest to Fuji-Hakone National Park. Being so close to the great metropolis, it was a goal for many urban Japanese, especially honeymooners.

Fuji Mountain and Hakone Lake are the centerpieces of Japan's Fuji-Hakone National Park, with the mountain top some 12,000 feet above the water.

The first Western-style hotel in Japan, the Fujiya, built in the 1870s, was in the park, which sprawled over hundreds of miles. It was not a national park as we think of one, with no inhabitants, but instead a large area incorporating all the existing villages and towns. Growth was controlled by the government, and what development was allowed served to enhance the recreational qualities of the area.

This old postcard is of the Fujiya Hotel, back when it opened in the 1870s; it was considerably changed following World War II, when American servicemen frequented the place.

The hotel was discreetly decadent, a single-storied wooden structure with large, comfortable rooms. And hot mineral baths. The staff was effectively bi-lingual, though the clientele was mainly Japanese. Mostly they were blushing brides and nervous grooms. I could see only one other Western couple in the dining room. The dollar was all-powerful then, so what was a middling price for us was a hell of a whack for the locals.

"We need more American tourists," said the manager, "because we Japanese do not have enough money ourselves to stay at this hotel." Times have changed, and prices have, too, as evinced by looking up the hotel on the Internet. I wonder how many Yanks can afford to stay at the Fujiya these days?

In the morning Sally and I went off on a long self-guided tour through the huge park, well-known to many Japanese. The hotel staff was most helpful in describing the route, glad that we Westerners wanted to appreciate the same things that natives did.

A very small train took us to an outdoor sculpture park, full of mostly rather modern Western three-dimensional forms, from Henry Moore to Giacometti. It was a cold January day, but the visitors oohed and aahed over everything, including us Western visitors. I was tall and bearded, my lady friend sartorially New Age in jeans and a woolen cape.

A short walk led to a funicular railway, which took us part way up Sounzan Mountain; Mount Fuji was way off in the distance, a very perfect, very Japanese mountain. The crowds were out to see this white-capped cone, as just the view of it is supposed

In the Fuji-Hakone park is a famous outdoor sculpture display, from English Henry Moore to Italian Giacometti — and whoever designed these semi-swimming sculptures.

to enhance the quality of ones life. Anyone wanting to go for the full reward could climb the 12,389 feet to the top of Fuji, the Shinto version of a Muslim trip to Mecca. We declined.

Leaving the funicular we found a small eatery full of chilled visitors slurping hot soup and tea. No English translation to the menu was available, nor any translator, so the middle-aged, white-capped ladies who ran the show ushered us into the kitchen and began lifting the tops off the pots. I had no idea what it was we ordered, but it was good and warming, and we provided an excellent sideshow for the customers and staff alike, using slick lacquered chopsticks on slippery noodles.

A young man, looking studentish in white shirt and black pants, came over and asked, "Is velly good?" Excellent, we replied, at which point he turned around and informed the cafe of what we had said. Many smiles and nodding heads turned our way.

After lunch we took a cable car over the steaming fissures of the mountain and down to Lake Ashi, which was the real center of the tourist trade. A large amusement park catered to the youth, and arcades full of minor gambling machines kept the adults occupied. I am sure it has long been surpassed by the Tokyo Disneyland, but in its day it was chock-a-block with happy, healthy families. A boat took us across the lake, and then a bus trip completed the loop back to the hotel.

At the hotel the staff enquired as to our day. It was a most excellent adventure, we said. They beamed.

The beaming attitude seemed to change in a dozen years.

* * * *

As Japan grew into an economic super-power they began to act like nervous parvenus, sure of their wealth but unsure of their status. And whether or not they would be asked to join the best clubs.

They commanded the American motorcycle market, and would at times try to ingratiate themselves with the round-eye motorcycle press by inviting them to come, all expenses paid, to this land of industrial excellence.

These trips were like a child's nightmare, being rushed through a toy store without opportunity to touch and play. Our hosts were determined that every waking moment would be crammed with activity — to what end I was never sure. But we never saw much that we couldn't have seen in the United States.

The manpower and expense that went into these brief five or six day jaunts was stupendous. In the summer of 1984 the yen went through the roof while the dollar sank to the basement, U.S. motorcycle sales had collapsed, and Yamaha would have been wise to have cancelled the invitations. Too late. The inexorable oriental wheels were in motion, and we would go forth.

A small group of us met at Los Angeles International Airport, along with an American representative of Yamaha. We shuffled onto the plane and some 12 hours later disembarked at Narita Airport, followed by a two-hour bus ride into Tokyo and then a late-night dinner at the penthouse restaurant. As we drank our brandies, thinking of nothing but bed, an earthquake occurred and put the elevator out of commission for several hours. It was a long walk down to our rooms.

Our host company had assigned a junior executive to watch over us, and god forbid that anything would botch a schedule. Ours was a pleasant fellow who simplified names by using the

Western handle of Dick. He was about 30, lived in a company hostel and had his entire career figured out. He was locked into a good company, and he would keep his nose clean, make his way part-way up the corporate ladder, retire and die. He was not a dreamer. But since less than a third of the Japanese workforce were in this coveted "salaryman" position, a womb-to-tomb job with all benefits, he was not willing to rock the boat at all.

Formality demanded that the higher executives meet with us at least once, but those evenings were always painful, generally done with overweening good taste in a terribly expensive locale. They had nothing to say to us, nor we to them, as they were moneymen, not motorcyclists. And our junior exec would stand in a corner, looking nervous, too lowly to be acknowledged by the powers that were, but terrified that we heathens would do something that would reflect badly on him.

So much involved just getting around. Along with our junior exec we would have a travel guide whenever we ventured forth, whose job it was to make sure that all connections were made, train tickets had been bought, buses were in place, and food

Clement was always out there wielding his weapon of choice, a Japanese Canon camera loaded with American Kodak film. That was when photojournalists used film sparingly so as to save the magazine's film-processing costs.

supplied when necessary. A press toot was a labor-intensive effort for our hosts, hustling bored and weary scribblers from hotel to bullet train to bus, rushing north to Sendai, south to Nagoya, seeing racetracks and factories and resorts, making sure we had no time to ourselves.

We were in a bus as we passed through a small village having some sort of harvest festival, with cheerfully decorated ox-carts and villagers looking very traditional. We asked our junior exec to stop. We can't, he said, we will be late.

We must take pictures, we pointed out, background for our articles we will write on your magnificent company.

Five minutes, Dick allowed; no more. And he sat, looking distressed, as we rushed forth to raise the Kodak stock at least two points.

He wanted us to see motorcycles being built by robots, computers designing new engines, workers working hard, efficiency and wealth . . . not farmers. Obviously our hosts' desire was that we be impressed, but the high-tech tours we were subjected to could have been done a lot more cheaply in Marysville, Ohio, or Lincoln, Nebraska — both home to

We American moto-journalists had a happy day at Yamaha's Fukuroi test track, trying out the latest models; fortunately, nobody fell down and so no face was lost.

Japanese-owned motorcycle plants.

We had a day at Yamaha's Fukuroi test track with an array of new motorcycles. Our hosts loved the occasion because they were totally in control. We were in a confined area, doing what they wanted us to do. It was an impressive track, so spotless that it was hard to imagine hundreds of vehicles going thousands of miles every year. At the entrance even our bus ran slowly through a bath that washed the tires so that no dirt or grime would sully the premises. The well-groomed grass, as good as on a first-rate golf course, grew right down to the asphalt on the track; there was not a speck of actual dirt in evidence. Which is all to the good when it comes to racetracks, but the degree of neatness bordered on the obsessive.

We cheerfully hurtled round and round all day; it was about 3.5 miles done in a very, very narrow figure 8, with an arched cross-over in the middle, tight 180s at each end. One nifty aspect

of the track was that the more serious corners had spring-loaded nets to catch anyone foolish enough to wander off course. Some tracks have what is called run-out, acres of grass bordering the racecourse which gives the rider who runs off the pavement time to get back under control. That requires space. Or they might have gravel traps, slowing an off-track bike rapidly, but even those need a bit of room. Space is at a premium in Japan, and run-out had been sacrificed, replaced by these nets.

Fortunately, none of us tried them. But they looked as though they should work.

The next day was a road ride, and we could see at breakfast that our handlers were nervous; their control would be lessened. We would get on the machines, ride a ways on a toll road, then get off and ride in the hills not far from Mount Fuji. Under tight supervision.

The hosts were a bit concerned over our coping with the left-side driving pattern in Japan. To keep us under corporate control we would break into two small groups, each one with a Yamaha employee riding in front, another behind. Once in the mountains we would stop, and a segment of road be marked out, and we would then be allowed to ride back and forth on this two-mile stretch, with corporate minions posted at each end to make sure we did not wander off and get thoroughly lost. By the time one counted up the Yamaha personnel versus the journalists, there were far fewer of us than them.

But it was a nice day, if a bit hazy, and Fuji was obscured. I did get an adrenalin boost when I came around a curve at a high rate of speed to find a fellow journalist approaching — on the wrong side of the narrow two-lane road. Would he go left or right? Serendipitously he understood what was happening and veered off to his correct lane. Nobody fell down, and after we all returned safely we could almost hear the collective sigh of relief from the hosts.

At times I felt that the gastronomical delights we were occasionally presented with were almost a quiet joke perpetrated by our hosts. Not all Americans are delighted at the thought of broiled eel, uncooked squid, or fried bean curd with a raw egg on top. The hangup is definitely cultural.

We were taken one evening to a very elegant, very expensive sashimi restaurant, where we divested ourselves of our shoes and entered a low, paneled room. The main course was already on the table, trying to crawl off the platter. One journalist said to no one in particular, "I know I'm going to hurt somebody's feelings, but I'd much rather have a hamburger."

He did not get his hamburger. But nor did he have much to eat that evening, although the kitchen did provide a platter of thoroughly, albeit recently, dead fish fried in tempura batter.

Each morning at whatever hotel we were at a very Western buffet breakfast would be laid out, with scrambled eggs and bacon and the rest at one serving table, more indigenous foods at another. Our junior exec manfully would join us in our high-cholesterol diet in an obvious effort to be one of the boys.

On the last morning I noticed him sitting off to the side, with a plate of cold rice and tofu and fish. Joining him, I asked why he had gone through a week of denying himself if this is what he really liked to have at seven o'clock in the morning.

"I am your host," said Dick. "I think that a host should eat what his guests eat. I hope you will not think my manners bad, but I very much missed my Japanese breakfast."

As we left Tokyo that morning, our bus drove by an automobile showroom with BMW and Mercedes cars. I asked our Dick what a bottom-of-the-line Mercedes would cost.

"I don't know. I'll never be able to own one, so it does not matter." He seemed a bit young to be so fatalistic. And infinitely relieved to see us go.

Kashmir, India 1973

Four of us were strolling around the lake and thru the buildings of the beautiful Golden Temple — the Vatican of the Sikh religion. This is in the city of Amritsar, in the northwest of India. We, Kenny from Detroit, Barry from New Zealand, and Carolina Cass on behind me, were headed for Delhi, but I thought a little detour up to Kashmir would be in order.

When you are traveling there is always a choice to be made: to get to your destination as quickly as possible, or to take as many side-trips as possible. Who knows when I would have the next opportunity to see Kashmir. And what is an extra week?

I succeeded in convincing the others that to venture into the Himalayas would be well worth while. Some say that Kashmir may have been the inspiration for Shangri-la, but that was all a long, long time ago, and recent history is more of strife than of peaceable kingdoms.

However, if you could slip in between the riots, tear-gas and occasional bullets, it still promised to be a most wondrous place, especially the valley with the city of Srinigar and Dal Lake.

The trip up there was mildly eventful. The newspapers told us that Moslems and Hindus were cheerlessly bashing each other over the head in the area, and when we got to the outskirts of Jammu we were stopped by the Indian army. Jammu, it should be noted, is called "The City of Temples", and was once famous for attracting Hindu, Muslim, and Sikh tourists. But at this point an imposing army major, with a Sikh turban on his head, said there were riots ahead, and the rioters had erected barricades which the army was busily tearing down. After spending several hours sitting by the side of the road, come evening we ventured in to town, sniffing lachrymating compounds and admiring

The inevitable flat tire occurred as we neared the Banihal Tunnel, at 7000 feet, and this was the only convenient place to do the work along the narrow road. A nasty, necessary job always goes better with brilliant scenery as a background.

Coming down from the Banihal Tunnel in the Pir Panjal Range in the Himalayas, we stop beside the Jhelum River for a break.

rubble-strewn streets. We put up at a small hotel owned by a nervous-looking Moslem and spent a restless night.

Next morning we departed early, figuring that the rioters had had a hard day and would probably sleep in. A few miles out of town the road was running through harvested fields, away from the masses of humanity. I came over a rise and headed into an empty valley, except for a school compound ahead on my right. A truck was coming in my direction which stopped in front of the school and dozens of teenagers leaped off, while scores more poured out of the school gates, greeting each other with great camaraderie, effectively blocking the road. High-school high jinks.

Okay, we were merely a couple of innocent tourists, and these schoolboys would surely let us by. I edged into the seething mass of fresh-faced, bright-eyed juveniles, saying, excuse me, excuse me. They grudgingly parted, then closed in all behind us as I crept forward. A small shriek came from my passenger. I wound the throttle, dropped the clutch, the front wheel lifted, and I powered through the mass of humanity, feeling my passenger's arms practically breaking my ribcage. My gloved hands at the ends of the handlebars struck bodies, but I was not worried about bruising these little monsters, just about getting free of them.

We broke clear of the mob, and I turned to see Kenny and Barry coming down the rise behind. They barely broke stride, shooting right through the crowd at speed, revolting children spinning off of Kenny's fairing like so many bowling balls, Barry following right behind.

Kenny said later, "I saw what happened to you, and figured if we didn't hammer on through, we'd never get past." He was probably right. Cass's shriek had come as a result of nasty little fingers trying to get at her erogenous zones. We sped off into the mountains.

We rode up into the Pir Panjal Range, through the rough, rocky Banihal Tunnel carved beneath the mountains, and down into the Vale of Kashmir. The three motorcycles arrived on the edge of Dal Lake that fine September afternoon, looking for a place to stay. A houseboat, of course.

That is our houseboat, officially known as the *New Golden Hind*, which slept six people for a week with no problem.

The British, in the days of the Raj, escaped the torrid summer heat of the Indian plains by coming to the mountains, developing the idea of floating houses as being suitable vacation homes. If one were so inclined, one could leisurely drift through the various lakes and their connecting canals, looking up friends and mooring alongside for a night or more. It was an excellent way of solving the problem of being a guest without being a burden. But that was long past.

Looking across the water we could see the houseboats all tethered on the far shore of the lake, looking like nothing so much as a flooded trailer-park. Forty or fifty of them were lined up, long boxy things with a small verandah at the lake end. It was post-season, but a few stalwart owners immediately surrounded us, each one extolling the excellence of his particular craft.

The proprietor of the *Golden Hind*, one presumes named in honor of the vessel of the Elizabethan seaman Sir Francis Drake, was remarkably persuasive, and advised us to come just look. I doubt if there was much difference among the houseboats, but the *Golden Hind* had a large living room with a wood stove, small dining room, three bedrooms and two baths. The place was a trifle on the decrepit side, but what could one expect a quarter century after the departure of the Empire?

Dickering with the owner established the price, on the Modified American Plan — breakfast and dinner included. The parking area where we would leave the motorcycles was guarded 24 hours a day. The deal was done.

Life on the lake was as sybaritic as one could hope for. The days were still sunny and warm, though the nights were quite cool. We could lie on the verandah and read, or go into Srinigar, with hordes of children caterwauling behind the bikes as we idled down the dirty streets. Indian troops in riot gear were obvious by their presence.

A picnic in the mountains; we went with some other late-season travelers on another houseboat for a day trip in the hills north of Dal Lake.

Kashmir offered no real cultural or intellectual inspiration to the visitor. It had no architectural delights like the Taj Mahal, or stunning ruins as dot the plains of central India, or impressive museums such as in Bombay, but it was a very nice place. The climate and the scenery had attracted many people, the beauty of the mountains and the lakes created a general loveliness, rather than anything specific. I was impressed.

Another motorcycle appeared, with a French couple intent on seeing as much of the world as possible before settling down to raise a family. We invited them to join us; Barry and Ken could bunk in together. We were an odd collection of motorcycling drifters.

Cass and Barry were both on dissimilar spiritual quests, which was the fashion in the 1970s. In these years India was a great magnet to Westerners, much to the amusement, and occasional consternation, of their hosts. Religion was one of India's few exportable commodities, and a number of swamis and gurus were making money hand over fist, preaching to the pale-skins.

Kenny, on the other hand, was quite down-to-earth, and was having an adventure. Achieving higher consciousness was not on his list of things to do. Nor mine. I was happily seeing much of the world, and would do so until the money ran out.

Evenings were spent in a suitably besotten manner. The dining room was cold and unheated, so dinner would take place in the warm carpeted and upholstered luxury of the livingroom. Mustafa, the son of the houseboat owner, would light the fire in the stove, bring a large curry and a pot of rice, chapatis, plates of fruit and sweetmeats, and we would dig in. After clearing the table he would bring in a hookah, and then we would spend the rest of the evening puffing on the pipe of tranquillity and discussing matters of consequence.

Usually it ended up in a head-to-head debate between Cass and Barry as to the correctness of their respective chosen paths. Barry was more ecumenical, and felt that the road was equally important as the destination, whereas Cass was an advocate of the big bang theory, of instant revelation.

Barry, twice the age of Cass, was far more effective in

marshaling arguments, and would usually reduce her to tears by the end of the evening by virtue of hard-nosed, if devious, logic. "How can you be so mean to me?!" she would cry out before dissolving into tears; "nobody who has seen the light would want to be so cruel!" And she would rush off to bed.

Barry would shake his head sadly, saying that the poor girl was going to have to learn that finding God was a long, difficult process, and you had to be prepared to defend yourself at every turn. It was like watching a bout between Pollyanna and Torquemada. The French couple, sober, clean-living folk, were absolutely enthralled, and more convinced than ever of the moral and cultural superiority of the Gallic way.

One morning we were sprawled on the verandah as the local merchants came by in their shallow-draft boats. The fruit and veggie man could always make a sale, whereas the butcher knew he had to deal with the houseboat owner. Being an essentially Moslem community with Hindu overtones, pork and beef were out, but there was a lot of fly-specked mutton and scrawny chicken lying in the bottom of the boat, very small amounts of which would end up in the evening meal. This morning the local drugstore paddled up, offering soap, razor blades, toothbrushes, aspirin — and a full range of pharmaceutical products that in some countries were considered illegal.

The pharmacist was a pleasant-looking fellow, with a white turban, white shirt and white trousers, all equally dirty. Barry was fascinated, the fellow unfolding pieces of paper and opening pots to reveal ganja, hashish, opium, and an assortment of chemical entertainments.

"LSD," the chemist said, showing a jar of small capsules. "Very good."

"Anybody want any acid?" asked Barry.

We declined; chemically based drugs were dangerous enough, but pharmaceuticals without an FDA approval on the label were a bit like a trip into the unknown. Or eating wild mushrooms without the help an expert to determine what might kill you.

Barry bought a hit. "You're crazy," we said.

Kenny, an amateur expert on mind-altering substances looked

at the pill. "You got no idea what's in this thing," he said. "It could be junk, worthless, a no-go. Or it could fry every circuit in your brain. If you don't know the producer, you're way better off staying away from the stuff."

Barry pondered; "I'll think about it."

Next morning Barry was still thinking. Kenny and Cass and I wanted to go up to Gulmarg, which claimed to be the home of the highest golf course in Asia, if not the world. The French couple would come along. Barry didn't want to go up to Gulmarg. He was going to try the lysergic diethylamide acid.

Kenny shook his head; "You're crazy. Absolutely crazy. I'd rather eat food out of a garbage can." He had been seeing a lot of that lately, and he absolutely could not comprehend it; why the hell didn't the people get food stamps?

Three of the bikes roared off, heading into the mountains. A good paved road, uncluttered by traffic, led up to Gulmarg. None of us had the slightest interest in smacking golf balls, but the clubhouse was a perfect remnant of colonialism, a wooden building that could have been in England. It was such a beautiful day we sat outside at a white-clothed table and a white-jacketed steward brought tea and lemonade and scones and mounds of sandwiches.

Nanga Parbit, standing a modest 26,660 feet tall, was on the northern horizon, reasonably well-kept greens all around us. Not a plus-four nor a seven iron to be seen. Obviously the locals had other things to do besides hit little white balls with long sticks. Somewhere west and north of us Indian troops faced off the Pakistanis.

We returned as dusk turned to darkness. We got to Srinigar, but somewhere I misplaced the road to the lake. We stopped and with a flashlight looked over the pulp-paper map of "Srinigar & Vicinity"; an elderly man appeared.

"May I help you?" he asked. We described our problem, and he pointed down the road, "I know exactly where you want to go. Just go down there one half-mile, and the road will turn left or right. Turn right, and you will be at the lake in less than five minutes. And would you like to come and see my shop? It is close by. My name is Mohammed."

The inevitable business slant. In South Asia the three major professions are the all-encompassing businessman, the desirable bureaucrat, or the omni-present beggar. He presented us with his card, which promoted fine rugs, antiquities, and objects of art. We explained that being on motorcycles we had no room to pack purchases.

"No, no. I do not expect you to buy. Just to come and see. I am proud of my wares and like to show them to people. I offer you hot tea and pleasant conversation. And certainly no need to buy."

It was a very good low-key approach. We went. The shop was a small warehouse stacked high with carpets and carved furniture, sheepskins, beaten copper, blankets, but it all seemed well outside of the traditional tourist trap. Hot sweet tea was brought, and we sat and listened to the old man as he directed two boys, grandsons, he said, as they showed us rugs and robes and an endless supply of truly lovely things.

We oohed and aahed, and were impressed. But I was not going to buy anything. Until a robe appeared, a beautiful long black robe, embroidered from hem to collar with wonderful patterns. The old man could see my interest aroused, and put it in my arms.

"Try it on," I said to Cass, who had been in a remarkably foul mood all day. She had suffered another loss the night before in the theological boxing match with Barry, and was bearing a grudge. She was capable of being an attractive person, but when her disposition was ugly, so was her appearance. All day she had been striding around like some scary Halloween creature.

Sulking, she put the robe on over her shirt and jeans. Like a miracle, her ugliness disappeared.

What an astounding robe, I thought; I must have it. Obviously Mohammed could read my mind. We entered the intricate bargaining *pas de deux*, in which nothing can be too definite, nothing too final. Since there had never been a figure mentioned, I was starting from a disadvantage. I bid in at $100. He responded with $500. The dickering went on for a good half hour.

We eventually agreed upon a price that was obviously acceptable by Kashmiri standards, a giveaway by any Western shop. I asked him to pack it up and send it to my parents for safekeeping. He had the presence of an honorable man, and I felt I could trust him. Three months on I heard from my mother that this most gorgeous robe had appeared; 15 years later it was the gown in which my bride was wed.

KASHMIRI WEDDING CLOAK

1973 VISION   1989 REALITY

As we left Mohammed came out with us, and we admired the starlit sky while zipping up our motorcycling jackets. "Be aware," he said, "that by the end of the month great changes can come in the weather. I would not wish to have to cross the mountains after the first storm has arrived."

Upon returning to the parking area we beeped our horns and flashed our lights and Mustafa came to pick us up. All was well, and dinner would be served right after we got on board. Inside the livingroom we found Barry, deep in an overstuffed chair, looking quite self-satisfied.

"How was the trip?" he asked.

"More's the question, how was yours?"

"Bully," he said, "I've found the way to God."

"You've what?"

"I found the way to God. Mustafa will be my guide."

That provided some interesting dinnertime conversation. Mustafa brought the food and Barry smiled eloquently at him. There was nothing as sordid as sex in all this, but while blazing through the universe that afternoon, Barry had had a long conversation with our boat owner's son, and was absolutely sure that all he needed to do was hang out with him for a few weeks, and he'd be right on that yellow brick road.

His mind was made up. We told him we were bailing two days hence, and if he were smart, he'd come along. Nope, not a chance.

Cass was irate. It was a confusion of emotions. On one side she had been frivolously wasting her day with us and missed the spiritual bus that Barry had got on. On the other, she knew that Barry was merely suffering acid-induced hallucinations, and that Mustafa could not possibly be on a direct link-up to God. But there was that sneaking suspicion that maybe Barry did know.

We mere mortals retired, leaving Barry in the armchair contemplating the perfect universe. He was still there in the morning.

"Must have been a heavy hit," observed Kenny.

"Do you think we should take him to a doctor?" asked the Frenchman. No, there was nothing wrong with him other than he had expanded his consciousness a bit more than any of us cared to.

Finding God is a nice idea, perhaps even better than the pot of gold at the end of the rainbow. And once somebody is convinced that God is just around the corner, it is hard to hold him back. Barry went through the day smiling beatifically, Mustafa went about his labors.

The next day we all went off to some mogul gardens, acres and acres of reasonably well-tended lawns and flowerbeds that the local mafia had built some centuries before. Nothing was blooming in this season, and it looked quite bleak; but it held the promise of a stunning springtime gala. The borders were neatly defined, the rosebushes well pruned, all in order, merely waiting. It would be a cold damn wait.

Late that afternoon I went to town to get a bottle of overpriced claret. As soon as my motorcycle appeared in the narrow alleys, I was again followed by a screaming horde of children. They had nothing better to do, I am sure, and I could not blame them for creating a small amount of excitement for themselves. But I am sure the Hindu merchant would have been happier not to have 30 or 40 snotty-faced delinquents swarming in front of his shop, as he immediately sent out his clerks with switches to keep them at bay.

Dinner was a curious time, as Barry was bubbling over with happiness, and declined even a puff on the hookah. Cass was again in a foul mood, prompted by the thought that this earthy Kiwi was going to get there, wherever there was, first. A good deal of competition exists in the spiritual world I was finding out.

Late that night, standing shivering on the verandah, I once again told Barry that he was nuts.

"Maybe," he allowed, "but I've got to do it. You've got to grab the opportunity, and this is mine."

We left him standing by his motorcycle, with the promise that he would keep enough money aside to pay for gas to get to New Delhi.

By the time we got up to the 11,570-foot tunnel we could feel the winter chill in our bones. Nice as Kashmir was, we were glad we weren't wintering there. Even if it meant we wouldn't get to meet God.

Mountains of the Moon
Italy 1991

My new bride and I had arrived in Italy in May of 1990, taking up residence in the old family farmhouse in the province of Fermo, in the Marche region. Being old, quite old, a lot of things needed to be fixed. For more than a year we had been coping with the passive resistance of the local construction industry, which seemed to reason that the sooner the repairs were done, the less work they would have in the future.

Yes, the fixer of walls would be there next Tuesday morning, but "next" has a vaguer connotation in Italian terms. It might possibly be next Tuesday, but more likely the next one, or perhaps the one after that. Same with the plumber and the electrician and the chimney man and the roofer and the fellow who cleans the black holes, as the old-fashioned septic systems were called, and the glass-man and the carpenter and the painter and the tile-layer. I am sure they all meant well, they just had a rather different view of time.

Which meant that we, or I should say Sue as I had other work to do, spent a good deal of time waiting in vain for Vesprini and Marinozzi and Silenzi and Raffaele, et cetera. Occasionally, when in need of a break, we would go off on a ride. She had bought me a 1981 Moto Guzzi SP1000, and I had responded with a 1978 Honda CB400F — with only 15,000 km. on the odometer.

They made an interesting pair, the two 475cc OHV cylinders of the Guzzi against the four 99cc OHC cylinders of the Honda. Mine had a workmanlike two-into-two exhaust, hers had a sexy four-into-one. The Goose was demurely dressed in dull blue-grey with matte alloy wheels, while the Honda shone with canary-yellow paint and shiny chromed spokes and wheels. While mine got 200 or more miles to a tank of gas, her range was about half that, but her four Mikunis consumed 30 percent less than my two Dell'Ortos — no mean statistic in this land of $5 a gallon gasoline.

Our remaining time in Italy was growing short, and summer was passing into fall, and the whole Death of Communism bit

This is the old family house at San Tommaso, and I'm prepping the bikes; I did take the box off the back of Sue's Honda, which she used when grocery shopping.

was so insufferably boring that Sue announced that we should take a little trip next weekend. Perhaps I should add that I had been glued to CNN news — aired inconveniently at 4 a.m. — ever since the attempted coup in Moscow, and Sue was getting fed up with all this to-do about not much.

"Sure, sure," I agreed abstractedly, watching the latest horrors going on in Yugoslavia. I figured the trip would be a Sunday morning jaunt 20 miles up to Cousin Franca's place in the hills, where we would lay around the swimming pool for a bit, have a seven-course lunch, and ride home.

"We're going to Pennabilli," she said.

That got my attention; "Where is Pennabilli?"

"It's up by the Alpe della Luna." She had me there; the only Mountains of the Moon I was aware of were somewhere along the equator in Africa.

"The Alps are too far away for an overnighter," I replied distractedly.

"These aren't in the Alps, these are part of the Apennines." For those who flunked geography, the Apennines are that long chain of mountains which run down the length of the Italian boot, viewable from the house.

"Alps is Alps and Apennines is Apennines," I retorted, by now in bad humor as I never like to admit there is a place I have never been to, much less heard of.

"These Alps are in the Apennines, if you would care to trust your Touring Club Italiano maps," she replied in dulcet tones, knowing she had won this little battle. Truth, the word "alpe" in Italian translates to "high mountain."

"Where in the Apennines?" I asked sullenly.

"On the far side of the Marche, way east of Fano, on the border with Tuscany."

"Oh," I replied off-handedly, and watched yet another statue of some Leninist/Stalinist stalwart come down off its pedestal.

Friday evening we were eating roast rabbit and Sue said that Cousin Minnie would take care of The Cat. "Why does The Cat need taking care of?" ask I, having already forgotten our earlier conversation.

"Because we are going to Pennabilli, and we'll take a tent so you won't have to fret about spending money at a hotel." Worrying about cash-flow was one of my more passionate pastimes.

"Okay, okay. Where is this Pennabilli place?" I asked. She unfolded a map and showed me a tiny town stuck in the very northwest corner of the Marche, somewhat to the east of Monte Penna. "It's a bit far," I allowed; "won't you be rather uncomfortable on the back of the Guzzi?" Guzzi's SP model has always given the passenger short thrift, and a very small bit of the saddle, especially when the rider is 6 foot 3.

"Yes. Which is why I am taking my own bike."

"All that way on the Honda? It's never been that far from home before. What if it breaks down?" Hers was a very nice little beast, but in its 13 years of existence before she bought it, it had never been out of town, so to speak. We had been on a couple of short trips, but never anything of this longitude.

"That's what my bike is for, to take trips. And since the cretinous Croats and stupid Serbs snookered our trip to Yugoslavia, we're going to Pennabilli. And if you just want to stay here and feed your face, fatso, I'm going alone!" She did not really say that bit about feeding my face, but I knew she was thinking it. I must admit I had put on about half an ounce a day since we had been been in Italy, which adds up after a year.

A couple of motorcycles, a beautiful weekend, and Sue and I were off on a minor adventure.

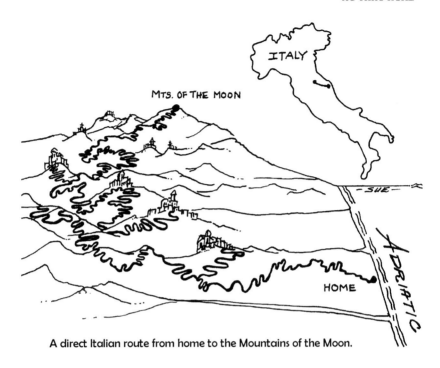

A direct Italian route from home to the Mountains of the Moon.

Bright and early we got on the road, tire pressures checked, oil levels leveled, chain (hers) tensioned, gas tanks filled with liquid gold, wallet stuffed with lire. I might have opted for a straight, fast shot up the autostrada to Urbino, then a brief bit of twisties to Pennabilli, but that was not to be. She had the map of the Marche all marked up, with a green hi-liter going through every blessed hilltown and village on the west side of the region. Not a McDonald's, Holiday Inn, nor video-rental shop along those roads. — Torre San Patrizio, Monte San Pietrangeli, Francavilla d'Ete, Macina, San Grisogono, Mogliano — after an hour we were at the Abbey of Fiastre, a Cistercian hangout whose construction was begun some 900 years ago. Along with the abbey, which covers a fair number of acres, there was a nature preserve and other ecological embellishments. It was all quite pleasant, even the souvenir shop which sold genuinely old brass things, cooking ceramics, and lovely wooden plates. The monks must pick up a pretty penny from the concessions.

This is a somewhat more recent section of the Abbey of Fiastre, where construction was begun in the 12th century; Cistercian monks live here.

Back on the road, heading towards Tolentino, a largish place where I got totally lost, we ended up circumnavigating the ancient walls several times before I found the road going to San Severino Marche. We rode up along the Potenza River, over Gagliole, down to Matelica, up to Cerreto, through San Michele to Fabriano (Paper-Making Capitol of Italy), through the canyon of the Sentino River, past the Umbrian villages of Casacce and Isola Fossara, and hang a right at Valdorbia. On a dirt road we stopped, spread a cloth on the side and ate cold rabbit, prosciutto and grapes, washed down with a glass of red wine.

"Golly," I admitted, "I'm actually having a good time. I've never been on these roads before."

"Trust your wife," she said, and we took a nap.

And so it went, one painfully charming village after another, some with crenellated castles, every one with a church or two, a piazza, outdoor cafes, the whole Disney approach. Around five o'clock we were in Borgo Pace, an unwalled village with a pleasant tree-shaded square, the Stagecoach Inn, and the omni-present church. On the village bulletin board we saw an announcement that Borgo Pace is part of the communities of the Alps of the Moon. Almost arrived.

Back in the Middle Ages, just about every Italian town or farmhouse was built to be defensible.

Above us was the Spugna Pass, at a mildly lofty 2500 feet, crossing between the Marche and Tuscany, paved on the Marche side, dirt on the Tuscan. I was expecting to find a wonderful west-facing flowery meadow at the top where we could pitch our tent, but all we found were scrub woods and fences, and steep ploughed fields. I became depressed, thinking we should go back to that inn in Borgo Pace.

Roughly every ten kilometers is another hilltown, so spaced centuries ago to allow the farmers and their oxen to get to their fields in the morning, and be home before dark.

Up in the Apennine Mountains there are long stretches of good gravel roads, easily traversable in summer, not plowed in winter.

"None of that," said The Wife, "we press on." Down towards the valley of the Foglia River we went, my negative state of mind figuring we would end up in some ditch somewhere, with rabid dogs and scorpions and mosquitoes for company. My capability for finding the rain in any cloud is unmatchable.

We came to the hamlet of Valenzano, part of the community of Sestino, province of Arezzo, region of Tuscany. I doubt that the place would be found on any map with a scale of less than 1:100,000, as it consisted of six houses, 12 dogs, 36 cats, and a few humans. I was looking at a map when one of the locals, a middle-aged gent, came out of the closest house and walked over. "Do you know of any place to camp?" I asked.

For several minutes he sized the pair of us up, and came to the conclusion that we were neither looters nor pillagers. "Up there on that hill," he said, pointing to an unused dirt track. "Nice place for a tent. If you need anything come knock on the door."

As I folded the map Sue shot up the steep, rutted path. "Your wife can ride well," he observed, coming from a culture where women don't usually ride motorcycles of more than 50cc.

It was a perfect place, with a 360-degree view, the austere Alpe della Luna to the west, Monte della Scura to the north, Monte della Rocca to the east, and the Spugna Pass to the south. We had ham and cheese and whole-wheat bread, a bag of potato chips, with flan (packaged like yogurt) and grapes for dessert. Our hosts came up to visit at dusk, and told us about life on these slopes for the past three generations.

Life was hard, work was hard, some farms still using ox-carts and ox-pulled ploughs, eking a small living from the long-used soil. In the 1950s there had been a genuine community here, with festivities, marriages, dances, fun things to do. Then the young folk were enticed away to work in factories, where they could earn money and buy cars. The children came back to visit the parents and grandparents maybe once or twice a year. In truth, they said, life was very lonely and our visit was as exciting as things got around these parts.

Sue, coming from a small farming community in northern Minnesota, could identify with what was happening. After our hosts left, tears welled up in her eyes. The stars were out. We went to bed.

Chivalrous to the end, I gave my sleeping bag to my beloved wife while I wrapped up in a large Tunisian blanket. Unfortunately it was cotton, not wool, and by dawn I had all my clothes back on.

In the morning we packed up and rode down to Sestino for some *latte macchiato*, which is hot milk with a smattering of caffeine, a very warming drink without the diuretic effect of lots of coffee. Then it was over the mountains and back to the Marche, to Pennabilli, a charming spot with a 12th century castle and a reputedly famous antique fair every summer. People were pouring out of church and into the cafes for an espresso and a *pasta* - a baked sweet roll, not a plate of spaghetti.

For the run home we ambled along the hilltops one ridge to the east of the way we had come up. Being a Sunday morning all the sport bikes were tearing along the winding bits of asphalt, scraping pegs and scuffing sidewalls. No fear of hot pursuit by police in this tolerant nation.

A town with a view.

We made it back for supper, and our neighbor, Ida, had thoughtfully left us some homemade tagliatelli and roast chicken. I immediately turned on the television and learned that the Congress of People's Deputies was convening in Moscow, that President Bush was about to recognize the Baltic states, and that the CIA was grousing that it had no one to play with any more.

Nothing changed. And I had a great weekend to remember.

Naples, Italy 1972

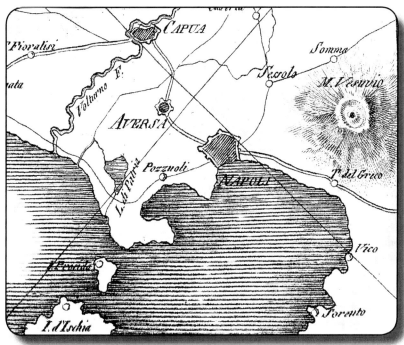

— 1814 French book-map engraving —

There is good reason that Italians have long been known for their motorcycle and motor scooter expertise — most of their cities were founded back when nobody gave much thought to the invention of the internal-combustion engine. Naples, as an example, began as a Greek colony over 2500 years ago and is now Italy's most important port city, and two-wheels are the only sensible way to get around.

On the north side of the Bay of Naples is the city of Naples, where traffic always seems to be one car removed from a permanent road-jam. On the east side of the bay are the ancient towns of Pompeii and Herculaneum, as well as a mildly active

Salvadori Is Named To Foreign Service

President Nixon has commissioned Clement Lawrence Salvadori, son of Mr. and Mrs. Max W. Salvadori, of 36 Ward Avenue, Northampton, a Foreign Service Officer of the United States. The oath of office was taken at a ceremony in the Department of State, in the presence of William B. Macomber Jr., Deputy Under Secretary of State for Administration.

The Foreign Service of the United States is a career professional corps of men and women who are selected and trained to carry out our country's foreign policy. Salvadori received this appointment after successfully completing highly competitive written and oral examinations.

Within a few weeks, he will be assigned either to a United States Embassy or Consulate in one of the more than 100 countries with which the United States maintains diplomatic relations, or to the Department of State headquarters here.

Salvadori was graduated from Williston Academy in Easthampton, Massachusetts.

CLEMENT L. SALVADORI

He received a B.A. in 1962 from Harvard University, and an M.A. in 1968 from the Monterey Institute of Foreign Studies, Monterey, Calif.

This is the self-confident pose of a newly-minted American diplomat on a corduroy-clad weekend, rightiously upstaged by the insolent cat at his feet.

On Clement's way back from Germany in February on his new BMW, it did get a mite frosty on occasion; actually this was just a look-see detour onto a road not taken — or he might not have made it to Naples before spring thaw.

If one gets beyond the always expanding city of Naples, country roads wander off into delightful valleys and small towns.

volcano, Mount Vesuvius, with a narrow road leading up to the edge of the crater. Too much fun! On the south side is the Amalfi peninsula, where driving is remarkably hazardous, due to the fact that the road around the edge was built when ox-carts were in fashion, and paved in the era of the Fiat Topolino, tiny cars barely five feet wide. By 1972 huge tourist buses would careen around the curves, forcing me on my motorcycle to duck into the little pull-outs. The peninsula is one of the more spectacular rides I know, and romantic, with a spine of mountains running steeply down to the sea. The occasional fishing village along this Amalfi coast are now equally attuned to catching tourists as fish, with excellent restaurants and infinitely charming little hotels.

I had arrived from Vietnam to take up my post at the U.S. consulate late in January, 1972, and on my first free day strolled through town — where sitting in the window of the Moto Guzzi agency was that stunning V7 Sport, with light green gas tank and red frame, the first one I had ever seen. Marvelous! I got on the phone to Moto Guzzi headquarters and asked what the diplomatic discount on the V7 would be. Manufacturers love to have their vehicles seen with CD (Corpus Diplomaticus) license plates, and usually offer sizable cuts in the price to such clients.

Unfortunately, it seemed that no diplomat had ever wanted to buy a Guzzi, and the company was not willing to give me a discount. Second choice was a BMW R75/5, and a call to Munich got an immediate 35 percent reduction in price. Since BMW had no motorcycle dealer in Naples I flew to Germany and had a chilly ride back. And entered the fray of Neopolitan driving manners with great abandon.

Italians tend to be good drivers, more competent than their American counterparts, if a bit reckless. And the Neopolitani are more reckless than most, as Naples is a fearfully proud place. Pride is the basic principle of life, and death; eating, sleeping, sex are mere also-rans.

The natives seem to have extracted and capitalized on the "proudful" gene from 2500 years of antecedents, Greeks and Romans and Moors and Spanish and French. While a certain amount of pride is normal in the human race, an excess can

Photo by Steve Bergren

Narrow roads wind past hillside villas and medieval fortresses built on steep cliffsides. Strategically positioned fortresses (usually on high promontories) were built centuries ago to repel invaders. Considering the area's numerous rugged dropoffs to the bay waters below, it was an effective defense.

Photo by Steve Bergren

In the old part of Naples the streets are narrow and laundry is hung out to dry; clothes dryers and electricity are expensive.

create rather a comical character. However, the Neopolitan has transcended the comic and taken the excess of pride to an art form, to a religion, where it has become the governing quality of everyday life.

To make a Neopolitan lose face, to give him *"la bruta figura"*, can be worth your life. It used to be knives, now more often it is guns which serve to dignify the situation.

In such a society structure is extremely important. Etiquette takes on a light never imagined by Emily Post or Ms. Manners. There is a proper way of doing everything, whether it is attending a baptism or a funeral, a dinner party or a game of bocci. It is presumed that anybody who sways from the precise line is doing it on purpose, with the intention of rendering a message. The rules and regulations covering behavior are known to all, except to benighted foreigners like myself.

Most Neopolitans really had very little to do, as the Camorra, a local version of the Mafia, ran the economy, and the bourgoisie and minor aristocracy who were forced to actually live in the city busied themselves with parties and theater goings and suchlike.

This city by the bay can be lovely, a curve stretching from the Posillipo along the Mergellina to Santa Lucia to the heart of Naples, a narrow seaside backed by steep hills. In the up-scale Posillipo gardeners diligently raised roses around the modest villas along the shore, while further up the hillside and along the Vomero respectable apartment buildings were homes to middle-class families. Everybody had a car, few people walked. I had a little-used Fiat Spyder convertible, and the new Beemer.

Down behind Santa Lucia it was quite the opposite. You couldn't squeeze a car into most of the alleyways, and bicycles, motor scooters and motorcycles predominated as transportation. And shoe leather. This was the home of the true Neopolitan, the old men in black serge suits playing cards, the old women in black dresses hanging clothes to dry on the laundry lines that ran from house to house across the narrow streets, the dark-eyed young women in skin-tight dresses trying to provoke the black-haired young men in silk shirts and butt-hugging trousers. Youth spent a lot of money on ensuring *"la bella figura."*

Naples, Italy 1972

Where once fisherfolk eked a living out of the sea, now the views from the villages are immensely valuable.

The Bay of Naples, home to the island of Capri and having Mt. Vesuvius in view across the water, can be one of the more romantic places in the world.

The most usedful transportation in Naples is the ubiquitous scooter, which can squeeze through most traffic and can park anywhere.

The houses were small, the living room was the alley. During the day every door had a chair or two outside, and of an evening the cobblestones were thronged. The ragged *scugnizzi*, the local young delinquents, never preyed on their own, but would go up to the Vomero or over to the Palazzo Reale to see what the pickings were.

When I first arrived the newspapers were full of the daring-do of a young (presumed) delinquent, who would ride his motorbike full tilt into the Piazza Municipio, daring the police to give chase. The grapevine would know when he was to put in an appearance, and throngs of people (an early version of the flash mob) would converge on the square to watch the hero dance with his motorcycle, doing lots of wheelies.

The police would converge as well, but the crowd was such that the cars of the Polizia and Carabinieri found themselves jammed in amongst the hordes. Waiting for the arrival of the maestro, the noise level would be high, people talking, yelling, until a sudden silence would manifest itself from one of the streets approaching the square. And the howl of a barely muffled two-stroke engine. From a vantage point you could see the crowd parting, until it spewed forth a shiny red machine with a helmeted rider, giving him the look of "The Man in the Iron Mask." The helmet was to conceal his identity, rather than to make his pastime safer.

He would then run back and forth through the square, balancing the motorcycle on its rear wheel, while the police struggled to get through to him. The crowd would cheer and ignore the pushing law officers, until the moment when the masked motorcyclist would head into the crowd, the mass of people stepping aside for a moment to let him pass, and he would disappear down a street, the crowd closing behind him, police wallowing in futile pursuit.

Sad to say, after several months of this entertainment, the cops finally got him by organizing several hundred officers and sealing off all streets a block from the piazza. He turned out to be the scion of a local family of some importance, and was much lauded in the press for his demonstration of masculine prowess and pride. The judge slapped his wrist and let him go.

Naples, Italy 1972

Having a morning coffee at a sidewalk cafe is part of the job of a U.S. consular officer in Naples.

Photo by Steve Bergren

If a nation is rated on its food rather than its finances, Italy would be one of the first in the world. A glance through a shop window can make your mouth water.

Naples has an excellent opera house, the Teatro San Carlo, and being an opera buff I attended frequently. One of my first visits was in the company of a Neopolitan maiden, Catarina, heiress to a very minor coffee-importing fortune, and afterwards she took me across the Via Toledo into the lower-class warren and introduced me to one of the true delicacies of Naples, the stuffed pizza (*pizza ripieno*), more commonly known as calzone. This has now been popularized in the United States, but the American rendition does not even qualify as a poor imitation of Neopolitan calzone, a round of pizza crust loaded with fresh ricotta (the key ingredient) and mozzarella made from buffalo milk, and perhaps some sausage and onions, the crust is folded over, a smearing of tomato sauce is put on top, the fat thing slipped into a wood-fired oven, and in ten minutes food fit for the gods is in front of you.

For my second, or main, course I ordered a second calzone, rather than fish or beef. Catarina was not amused. It wasn't done. The waiters were amused, and the owner came over to congratulate me on my good choice. Catarina was mildly mollified.

She lived with her widowed mother, and spent most of her time in the local whirl of trendy youth and down-at-the-heels aristocrats, drinking heavily. She called me very late one night not long after we had met, thoroughly drunk, and asked if she could come over. A taxi deposited her at my door, and minutes later she had passed out. In the morning I left her sleeping in the guest room and went to work.

That evening I returned to find her still there, still suffering from her excesses. Demurely she asked what had happened between us. Nothing, I said.

"Why not!?" she raged, "aren't I beautiful enough for you? Or do you like men!?" Naples had no fury like a woman scorned, and pride was considerably more important than chastity. She preferred the Fiat to the motorcycle, so that relationship did not last long.

My job within the consulate was anything but tedious. I issued the non-immigrant visas, in those days when Italians and 170 other nationalities had to have visas to enter the United States.

Photo by Steve Bergren

Tourists flock to the Sorrentine peninsula and Almalfi coast, as evidenced here by the big buses parked on the waterfront at Positano. It is a popular alternative to white-knuckling it around blind, tight cliffside roads in your own vehicle, unless that vehicle is a more suitable motorcycle that won't rub mirrors with the buses.

Photo by Steve Bergren

These boats are all part of the mysterious economy of the Bay of Naples, although whether they are used to catch fish or smuggle cigarettes, etc. is moot.

Most of my clients were up-standing types, tourists, businessmen, students, who wanted to go to America for their own reasons, and intended on returning. But I had a fair share of people who were trying to bypass the immigrant maze.

Getting an immigrant visa took time — often lots and lots of time and mountains of paperwork. If you could get a tourist visa, get into the States, hire an immigration lawyer to get your status changed, you had about a two-year lead on those who patiently stood in the official immigration lines. The appeal was great.

I had a large ante-chamber, where my clerk, Gianni, sat, and a small office with me and my secretary, Anna. The secretary's presence was doubly useful, as she could be a witness if any rejected visa applicant decided to make mischief.

Gianni would greet the applicant, take down the particulars, and then give him a date some three days hence to return for the interview with me. It was up to me to determine the moral, political and financial qualities of the applicant. The US Congress had seen fit to give every US consular officer almost infinite power in his authority to issue or deny a visa.

I did not have to have a reason to deny a visa. If I got out of bed the wrong side that morning, the Pope wouldn't get a visa. Also, if the applicant had put down that he had ever belonged to a Communist organization, or had a criminal record, I was required to seek dispensation from headquarters. That could take years. We were not supposed to have access to Italian police files, but of course we did. My clerk would run the names through the back channels, and we would get copies of any arrest sheet.

One morning Gianni came in with a folder, saying that I would enjoy this one. The lady applicant in question had an arrest sheet for prostitution as long as the proverbial arm. It was popular for Italo-Americans with connections to houses of ill repute to bring over some old-country talent, and the girls would often stay on. This meant that at the very least she should have applied for a visa to work, and she had marked TOURIST. Right there were grounds to reject her.

Show her in. She was extremely demure, and rather petite. There was no flamboyance, no revealed bosom, no overly painted

Naples, Italy 1972

Photos by Steve Bergren

Naples loves statues.
Above: Alighieri
Dante, Italy's most
famous poet, was
born in Florence but
is revered throughout
Italy, here in Naples'
Piazza Dante — the
seagull, on the other
hand, seems to have
less respect for poetry.

The wood carving at
a seaside restaurant
commemorates a
street urchin enjoying
finger food. What else
but a big plate of
pasta!

face. She had obviously been well-prepped for this occasion, with just a touch of light lipstick and hair drawn discreetly back. Her loose white blouse went to the throat, and her full skirt revealed only a pair of well-turned ankles. Not your average hooker. You would be tempted to take this one home to meet your mother.

She said she worked with her mother at home, doing piece-work for a clothing factory, and before she got married and settled down she had a wish to go and see that wonderful place called America. The only flaw in the story was that she was 28, which was a bit on the spinsterish for a Neopolitan lass. But even that could be explained away.

I went down my list of questions: Have you ever been arrested?

She looked shocked! How could I even ask such a thing sort of look. Never, she said. It was an impressive performance.

I could see that Anna was having a hard time keeping a straight face. I lifted the arrest sheet off my desk, handed it to the putative tourist, and asked her to explain it.

It was glorious; she took one look at the rap sheet and exploded. She made no attempt to lie, no attempt to deny it, just got to her feet and called me every filthy name in the book. The transformation was almost miraculous, from Biblical purity to the most foul-mouthed shrew. Her face, from being that of a Madonna instantly became bitter, twisted, whorish. She did not enjoy being caught out. She had gone to a lot of work, and probably could have done quite well on the stage. As it was she stormed out of my office and through the crowded ante-chamber, screaming imprecations upon all Americans.

Gianni could sometimes not resist giving his own personal evaluation of an applicant, though I never asked him to. Usually he was correct, though I adhered to my own counsel.

One day he brought in a folder and merely shook his head as he put it on my desk. The applicant was a 33-year-old mechanic, had his own one-man repair shop, and said he wanted to go have a look-see at America. The American-government thinking was that if an applicant could display sufficient economic status, then he was probably not going to the US to seek a better life, and could be given a tourist visa.

Economically speaking, Giorgio was on the weak side. Anybody could be a self-employed mechanic, and you could fix an Alfa equally well in Los Angeles as in Naples.

Giorgio came in. He was certainly no figure of sartorial splendor, though he had tried. His suit jacket did not match his trousers, and while his shirt was buttoned to the neck, he had no tie. His hands were clean, but his fingers had a good layer of permanent grease under the nails. He was definitely a working man.

He was nervous. Did he own his shop? No, he rented. What kind of mechanicking did he do? Fiats? Ferraris?

"Motorcycles."

"What kind of motorcycles?" I asked.

"I can fix anything," he said, "I can fix Guzzis and Ducatis and Laverdas, but mostly I work on scooters and motorini." These were the little mopeds that half of Naples rode. We got intimate real quick, and spent a while talking bikes. Then I remembered my job.

"Giorgio," I asked , "what do you want with a visa to the United States? I know you can't earn much in your shop, and you say you don't have any relations in America to stay with, so this trip will cost a lot. And you don't speak a word of English. Visa aside, I don't think you have the money for a round-trip ticket."

"I don't even want to go to America," he replied. "The truth is I was at my local bar a while back, and people, people much better off than I am, were talking about how hard it is to get a visa to the United States. And I said I could get one. They all laughed. We made a bet. I got my passport, and now I want to get a visa in it and go back and show them. That will give me *'la bella figura.'*

He got his visa and his prestige at the bar was considerably elevated. I got a good mechanic for my motorcycle. As far as I know, he never did go to the United States.

Nepal 1973

Lumbini Gardens is the birthplace of the Buddha in 561 B.C., and the only accomodation in 1973 was the government-run guesthouse seen beyond the motorcycle.

There was a genuine lack of road. Detroit Kenny and I were in Lumbini Gardens, a very small Nepalese community on the Nepali/Indian border, and we wanted to get further into the country. However, at the police station the officers told us there was no road beyond Lumbini, just a track with several rivers and no bridges, and we would be advised to return to India, go east a few miles, and then enter Nepal at Bhairahawa.

Kenny and I had no desire to go back to India and then back into Nepal, as each border crossing tended to be an exercise in minor frustrations. We asked the police if motorcycles could make it along the track. "Big river, the Kanchan," they said; "no bridge; only high trucks get through."

"Crocodiles?" Kenny asked. No, no crocodiles. We'd give it a try, we told the police.

Fording this river between Lumbini and Bhairahawa was easy because the ford was actually demarcated and the cement surface was laid when the river was dry; Kenny is staying within the markers.

Crossing this stream barely counted on the trip from Lumbini to Bhairahawa.

The views in Nepal are absolutely marveloous, with the not-so far-off Himalayan mountains presenting a formidable barrier

We loaded up. The track was lightly traveled, with a few pedestrians and bicyclists riding or pushing their well-laden bikes along. This was the terai, the Nepalese lowland jungle, and old tire tracks showed that wheeled vehicles did occasionally venture this way. Bamboo and thick vegetation closed the track on both sides, but after several miles we were approaching a bright open area — the sandy banks of a wide river. There wasn't much current, and people were wading through the waist-deep water, holding precious bicycles and parcels above their heads. A bit deep for the likes of us, on a pair of BMW boxers, since the air intake on the carburetors was less than two feet above where the wheels touched the ground.

We stopped and surveyed the situation. There were a few people around, including some fellows who appeared to work for tips after helping people get across with their purchases. I looked around for a truck that we could load the bikes onto. Nope. Maybe an elephant? Nope.

This was definitely not a thru road.

* * * *

How did we get here? Back in India my occasional traveling mate Kenny and I had gone to Agra to have a look at the Taj Mahal, and then planned to ride on to Nepal.

The Taj was superb, a reminder that true love does exist. Unfortunately, the morning we planned on leaving for Nepal I was doing a little maintenance outside the hostel and realized my rear wheel bearing had developed some slop, and I was worried. Why I hadn't noticed this in Delhi beats the heck our to me, but having had one near-catastrophic bearing failure two months before, I did not want to repeat that scenario. I thought I might have to put the bike on a train and go back to Delhi and wait for parts.

On the questionable road maps available in India I had planned a route entering Nepal via Lumbini Gardens, the place where the Buddha was born, just to see the place. Because of the bearing problem Kenny and I decided to split up, as this could take me a while. We said our goodbyes because we didn't know if we would meet up again.

Every year
Tibetans gather
in Bodh Gaya,
in northeast
India, where the
Buddha received
his enlightenment;
Kenny and
Clement were
invited to attend.

Nepalese
engineers figured
it was easier to let
water flow over
the road than to
route it under, this
being on the way
from Kathmandu
to the Tibetan
border at the
Botakoshi bridge.

In Agra I was riding down to the railroad station to see about getting the Beemer on a train when I happened to pass mechanics' row, a stretch of palm-fronded huts with loin-clothed mechanics under the hoods of everything from a Tata truck to a Mercedes-Benz. I stopped to look.

A well-dressed gent strolled over, introduced himself, and asked if I were there because perhaps something was wrong with my motorcycle. I told him about the bearing problem.

"Well," my new friend said, pointing, "there is the best wheel-bearing expert in the city; perhaps he can fix your problem." The expert had a pair of greasy shorts on, sandals, and was doing something under the hood of a taxi. Not quite like Mr. Goodwrench. I grimaced.

My friend noticed. "Ah, I understand you Westerners. You do not trust the mechanical ability of us Indians. That is understandable. Though not justified. I think that perhaps this man can help you." Okay. I rolled the bike over to the shanty, took the wheel off, uncovered the bearings, and the mechanic inspected them closely, moved them with his fingers, and then said something to my host.

"The bearings merely need to be tightened," translated my friend, "and he can do the job easily." I agreed, and then my host, who was having his Mercedes worked on, and I sat down on chairs in the shade and a small boy brought over cups of tea. The job was done right, the bill so minimal that I added a large tip, and my host invited me to dinner that night.

All in all it was an extremely pleasurable experience, and I learned a good deal about Indian life. And I was just a day behind Kenny, who was headed for Lumbini. I followed, some roads crowded, others not, crossing the major Ganges and Gogra rivers; lots of rivers flow out of the Himalayas. The road soon went from two paved lanes to one and a half. At the town of Bansi I crossed the Rapti River, and when I got to Tetri Bazar the road went to one lane. And then unmaintained, with more potholes than pavement, and finally to dirt. Obviously the Indian Department of Transportation did not wish to spend money on roads going to other countries.

This overlook is in the Indian Himalayas not far from the Dalai Lama's residence in exile at Dharamshala.

A group of unladen equines is coming back from delivering goods to villages far up in the mountains. Little human supervision was necessary as they knew the routine well and kept to the track.

As I approached the border the road was lined on both sides with vendors' stalls selling tourist trinkets, sweets, and canned sodas. The border itself was merely a pivoted pole across the road which, after a few bureaucratic formalities, a bored Indian soldier raised for me. On the vendorless Nepalese side I was greeted with a great swath of green grass covering five or six acres. In the distance was a large tree, with a Buddhist monastary to one side, and beyond that the low profile of the Annapurna range of the Himalayas. To my left was a small police station. To my right a government-run guest house looking like something out of a Clint Eastwood western, with Kenny sitting on the upstairs verandah.

Lumbini Gardens, birthplace of the Buddha some 2500 years before. This was a holy place, and the Nepalese government had decided to keep all commerce, other than the rather austere guest house, on the Indian side. There was one other guest in the guest house, an Australian pack-backer, but the house had few amenities. The restaurant was out of food, except for tins of fish and rice that a group of Japanese tourists had left behind. Back then Lumbini was hard to get to, as the occasional bus would have to come up from the Indian side. Our hotelier allowed as to how occupancy was sparse, as most visitors came as day-trippers, carrying their own lunches, and his last overnighters had eaten all the eggs.

But I found the place delightful. And entirely calm. After the hustle and crowds of India, this was an oasis of peace. I walked over the sala tree that claims to be the descendant of the one the Buddha's mother held on to when she gave birth. A stone-lined bathing pool was in front, where the baby Buddha was immersed temporarily, of course. Everything was quiet, well-kempt. Very meditative.

That evening the three of us walked back into India to see what sort of sumptuous feast we could avail ourselves of. Sorry, no restaurants, only those candy stores which sold the boiled milk and sugar concoctions, which were very, very sweet indeed. Canned fish and rice it would have to be.

In the morning Kenny and I walked over to the police station

The bikes are all packed up and ready to leave after crossing the Kanchan River which was wide and deep enough to stall the engines, so they had to be pushed through.

Nepal has a thin strip of lowlands bordering India, called the terai, but 85 percent of the country is mountainous, with marvelous roads winding through valleys and around mountains.

to ask about getting further into Nepal. And several hours later we ended up on the shore of the Kanchan River. I unloaded my gear and gave it to two of the porter fellows, who set across the river on what they felt was the shallowest route. Still waist deep and maybe 50 yards wide. They dropped the panniers and duffle on the far side and began to return. In the middle I signaled them to stop, fired up the R75, put it in gear, and rode into the river. About half way across the engine quit and the three of us quickly pushed the bike to the far side. Where it fired up right away.

Then it was Kenny's turn. Unfortunately, when his engine quit he sort of forgot that the intake was under water and decided to see if it would restart. No, but it did suck up a whole bunch of water. We pushed it out, Kenny pulled his plugs, ran the starter for a while, and water gushed out of the holes. Plugs back in, hit the starter, Vrooom! We gave the porters a couple of hundred rupees and everybody was happy.

We were between rivers here, and no jungle, just a well-marked track. The next, wider, shallower river had a demarcated crossing which we happily splashed through. Then we were up on a low dike, with a narrow strip of asphalt down the middle, cluttered with pedestrians, animals, bicyclists and three-wheeled bicycle trishaws.

A trishaw was coming towards me, so I politely turned to my right to let him pass — unfortunately forgetting that Nepalis drove, and bicycled, on the left. The trishaw did the same; we had a small collision, nobody even falling over, but I bent one of the wheels on the trishaw. I immediately offered to pay for a new wheel, but the trishaw operator, obviously seeing a chance to make some money off of this beleaguered tourist, began raising a ruckus. And attracting a crowd. I was the show that day. Arbitration went on for a little while until a scholarly looking fellow appeared and announced that he was the local school-master, and he would decide the issue.

He obviously had some clout, because everybody was quiet while he found out what had happened, and then asked several on-lookers what they thought the cost of repair or replacement

Clement and Kenny went for a little stroll in the Himalayas south of the Annapurna range, but not having a trekking permit were eventually turned back.

In Pokhara BMW-mounted Clement and Kenny meet two other travelers on Indian-made Enfield Bullets.

North of Pokhara, the BMW R75/5 posed in front of the Annapurna Range of the Himalayan mountains; that is Annapurna I, at 26,500 feet, over the gas tank.

would be. He then announced his decision, and everybody, trishaw man included, agreed that it was fair and just. I handed over the cash, we shook hands, and there was a round of applause.

Kenny, sensibly not wishing to be part of this event, was waiting up at the end of the dike, where it joined with a road that would lead us to Pokhara. Great ride, up to Phewa Lake and Pokhara, about 3000 feet above sea level, then a modest town of maybe 15,000 inhabitants. The most dramatic sight was the Annapurna peak that back-dropped the town, soaring to some 26,500 feet. On a moonlit night the mountain seemed to be right on top of the town.

We thought we would take a little hike up towards Annapurna, and rode our bikes to the very end of the road north of Pokhara. There we left them with a Tibetan shepherd, and went trekking, planning to be gone less than a week. That very evening we arrived in a village which offered several simple restaurants and houses where we could roll out our sleeping bags. It also had a trekking checkpoint, and we did not have trekking permits; such permissions were charged for, giving a small supply of cash to the country's coffers, but the source of the permits was in the capital, Kathmandu. We were politely told we could not continue without permits.

Next day we retrieved the bikes, giving the shepherd some financial gratitude, and headed east on a reasonably good paved road towards Kathmandu. That city, in a well-forested valley, was a sybarite's delight, with inexpensive lodging and good food. Having lost interest in trekking, since we did not want to go all the way back to Pokhara, we decided to see about riding to Tibet, which the Chinese had laid claim to 25 years before. A visit to the Chinese consulate was quite unproductive, as the clerk said that any such visa would have to be issued in Peking.

We would ride up to the border just for the fun of it, and see what happens. The road was dirt, in good condition, and the only traffic was an occasional truck. Stopping at the bridge crossing the Bhotokoshi River, which divided Nepal from Tibet, the Nepalese officer in charge was quite amused at our thinking we might get into China this way. We did give him our particulars, in case the Chinese border guards might choose to hustle us away, so that he could inform the American consulate when and where we had last been seen.

On the Chinese side of the bridge was a simple pivoted barrier, backed up by a dozen soldiers. No one seemed to speak English, and the fellow seemingly in charge wanted nothing to do with us. He just kept on pointing back the way we had come. So we did his bidding. Our Nepali friend gave us a cup of tea and wished us a good journey back to Kathmandu.

What next? Back to India.

When Kenny and Clement went trekking for a couple of days, they left their bikes in the care of a Tibetan shepherd who lived at the very, very end of a dirt track.

New Zealand: 1974 and 2000

Gazing out at the Tasman Sea at dawn, two miles of deserted beach between the headlands with white sand and a gentle surf, behind me semi-tropical vegetation with sweeps of giant ferns and palm trees, backed by abrupt limestone cliffs that soar straight up into to the sky — picture-postcard perfect. Only flaw is that it would be difficult to earn a living way out here, as we are a long way from any urban hustle and bustle. Maybe an Internet business . . . ?

This brief travelogue is about the beauties of New Zealand's South Island, the little incidents along the way, and lots of strange nomenclature, as many towns are using the old names from the Maori language.

New Zealand is much like home; I'm on the west coast of the South Island, at a place called Punakaiko, and it is similar to California's Big Sur coast, near where I live. Only this is actually a bit better, being lusher and having far less traffic — until I remind myself that this stretch of real estate gets over 200 inches of rain a year. We have been lucky with the weather.

I've never talked with anyone who has not loved taking a motorcycle trip through New Zealand, but there have been two consistent complaints — it is too far away, and can be too wet. Not much can be done about that 12+ hour flight from California, but in the 15 days Sue and I have been there it has rained only twice — and that was between midnight and six o'clock, as things should be in Camelot.

Touring this distant South Pacific island by bike is not really an adventure, no grizzlies to eat you, no unexploded land mines unless you count riding on the left as being adventurous. What it is is a very beautiful place, with delicious roads. Which is really what these organized motorcycle tours are all about, taking you to a new place and cramming a great deal of excellent riding into a couple of weeks.

Our group did not travel in a pack, but since the lunch stops recommended by our guides were so good, we would often meet up at lunchtime.

Twelve days before, 28 of us — 26 Yanks, one Brit, one Ozzie — had convened in Christchurch, the major city on the South Island, where we were wined and dined and told by our guides what to expect on the trip: stunning scenery, curvaceous roads, great people, and maybe a bit of rain now and then. The first three were spot-on, while the fourth, gladly, never really came about.

Our route would follow a very squiggly 2000-mile figure-8 around the island. We rode out of town as a group, 18 bikes including those ridden by two guides, plus the baggage-carrying chase vehicle, but within an hour or two the group had splintered into individuals and pairs traveling at their own chosen speeds. As it should be. With no language problems, and little chance of getting lost, nobody felt any need to follow a guide. Though we would often find ourselves together at recommended lunch spots.

Leaving the fertile plains of the east coast, we headed over Burke Pass to the central valleys where flocks of Romney sheep hold sway. And the snow-capped peaks of the Southern Alps were glimpsed on the distant horizon.

Look at your map of the world; the South Island lies roughly 40 to 46 degrees south, and from Cape Farewell in the north to southernmost Bluff is less than 500 kiwi-flying (except the kiwi bird cannot fly. Ha, ha!) miles; that puts it on a similar northern latitude with New England or Oregon. And the island is never more than 150 miles wide, an oblong of some 58,000 square miles lying between the Pacific Ocean and the Tasman Sea.

The terrain is spectacular; think of a slab of central Colorado surrounded by ocean. Mt. Cook, the highest peak in the Alps at over 12,300 feet, is a mere 20 miles from the sea. The inland valleys tend to be dry, while the coasts are almost tropical. And with only a million people on the island, the place ain't crowded — compare that to Illinois, roughly the same size with 15 million people. The island has hundreds of miles of good two-lane asphalt, no traffic lights except in the odd city, and the biggest hazard seems to be herds of cattle or flocks of woollies blocking the road as they move from pasture to pasture.

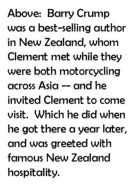

Above: Barry Crump was a best-selling author in New Zealand, whom Clement met while they were both motorcycling across Asia -- and he invited Clement to come visit. Which he did when he got there a year later, and was greeted with famous New Zealand hospitality.

Middle: Sheep are moved around according to the grass, and this was a sheepherders cottage on the South Island, no lock on the door, food in the cupboard, and a note to please leave the place as one found it.

Left: Even though Clement is not ready yet for a permanent resting place, graveyards are nice places to have a nap, as they tend to be quiet and peaceful.

* * * *

This was my second trip to Kiwiland.

In '74 I had come by ship from Australia, my motorcycle in the hold, and a friend, a Kiwi raconteur, fellow motorcyclist and writer named Barry Crump, had met me on the dock in Auckland, on the North Island. I spent a month with Crumpy and his mates, visiting all the good spots on that island, then bade my goodbyes and ferried over the Cook Strait to the South Island. If the North was good, the South was twice as good, the people even friendlier, the riding more dramatic.

Back then I was traveling on the cheap, and the New Zealanders had a very good hostel system, with many hostels being simply empty houses in small towns that had no resident in charge. A note on the door would tell the traveler where to go to get the key, and I might be the only one there. I stopped one evening in the village of Livingstone, close to Dansey's Pass, and had the hostel all to myself. The local shop sold me some hoggett — sheep meat half way between lamb and mutton — and I made myself a nice supper in the hostel's kitchen, then went for a walk. A local gent soon chose to walk along with me, and he allowed that it would be nice to get some fresh blood in town, and could fix me up with a job at a nearby boy's school. And he just happened to have a daughter whom I would probably find quite attractive. New Zealanders are wonderfully direct.

Opportunities missed.

* * * *

Now I was back, along with my wife, Sue. Accommodations were somewhat more elegant than in my hosteling days, with comfortable hotels that usually had a big open fireplace in the main room. Food was cheerfully rugged, none of that frou-frou nouvelle cuisine in this hard-working country, with eggs, bacon and sausages in the morning, generally roast beef or lamb or hogget in the evening accompanied by potatoes and three veg. For lunch Sue and I would might head to a bakery, myself being a great fan of the local meat pies and sausage rolls. Or get some scrumptiously fresh seafood while sitting on the deck of a cafe on the coast.

Clement actually rode one of these high-wheelers — once. Way too dangerous, he thought, and sticks to the chain-driven "safety" bikes when he has to pedal. One nut-case rode a high-wheeler around the world in the 1880s.

The two-night home-stay was a very nice aspect of this trip, with the farmer describing how sheep-herding works — the dogs do most of the work. Occasionally, the farmers hold sheepherding trials with a serious hillside course that tests just how good each dog and master is at the job.

If you think that Norway is the only place with fjords — defined as a narrow inlet of the sea between steep cliffs — think again. We are on the good ship Milford Wanderer sailing through Milford Sound in Fjordland National Park. It is a spectacular sight, and one wonders what the first Europeans thought when they came upon this marvel.

After a night at Twizel, south of Mt. Cook, we returned to the east (Pacific) coast — the Tasman Sea lies to the west. And the little roads the guides could point us to were certainly the frosting on this two-wheeled cake. For sheer riding joy the Ngapara road to Oamaru (Ocean to Alps Scenic Highway) provided unparalleled motorcycling bliss, wending and weaving its way through the valleys, over hills, with green fields, small farms — such a ride cannot really be described, it has to be ridden to do it justice.

Dunedin, the Scottish capital of the southern hemisphere, was our second small urban foray, tucked into the hills at the south end of Otago Harbor, a long bay protected by the Otago Peninsula. The Victorian buildings attract the architectural eye, but the motorcyclist heads towards Baldwin Street, reputed to be the steepest paved road in the world with its 3:1 slope, a 2.86 gradient at its most severe. Ever ride your motorcycle up the initial hill on a roller-coaster? I stopped half way up, and with the front brake locked the bike slowly skidded backwards — until I let out the clutch and moved upwards. That is steep!

We were staying the night in pseudo-aristocratic elegance, at Larnach Castle, a few miles out of town, on the peninsula, with views of the bay to die, or pay dearly, for. The "castle" was built in the 1870s by one William Larnach, a banker and politician; unfortunately the gent had rather a dysfunctional family, and ended up shooting himself after his third wife ran off with his son from his first marriage. There is nothing new on "Oprah".

I could write this whole story on the Larnach experience, but I have to move on. We rode over the west side of the island where the group was broken up and assigned to various hospitable farmhouses for two nights. This provided for home-cooking and some genuine interaction with the locals, and Sue, a farmer's daughter from Minnesota, appreciated the Kiwi take on making a living from the land. It was an excellent experience.

In between we ran our bikes along the superb road to Milford Sound, the centerpiece of Fjiordland National Park, and spent an afternoon aboard the good ship "Milford Wanderer", sailing under waterfalls and watching dolphins play. Remarkable.

Then it was off to Queenstown, headquarters for New Zealand's

Oh boy, that is Clement at the world's first official Bungie Jump, at the bridge over the Kawarau River near Queenstown; fools have been bungieing there since 1988. He had to decide whether to jump like a paratrooper or dive like he was going six feet into a swimming pool, and chose the latter. Proper tensioning of the elastic bungie cords made sure his head just missed by a non-existent hair in touching the water a hundred feet below.
What they failed to tell Bungie Boy before he jumped is that he would have to hike back up the steep cliffside afterwards. A major adrenalin rush comes in handy.

Somewhere in the clouds behind Clement is Mount Cook, at over 12,000 feet the centerpiece of the huge Mount Cook National Park, with more than 140 peaks of over 6,600 feet and 70 glaciers — all this within a few miles from the beaches of the Tasman Sea.

"adventure" sports. In and around Q'town you can raise your adrenalin levels in any number of ways, from jet-boating to sky-diving, flying in a P-51 Mustang or bungie-jumping. That last caught my attention; the idea of jumping off a bridge with a big rubber band attached to my ankles somehow appealed to me.

A fellow named A.J. Hackett set up the world's first commercial bungie site in 1988, at an abandoned bridge over Q'town's Kawarau River, and has become a rich man since then. If you go to Paris, you have to go to the top of the Eiffel Tower; if you go to Q'town, you have to do the Kawarau bungie jump. Even though it is the most unnatural thing in the world for your neural synapses to cope with, making parachuting look like a romp in the sandbox. The five M.D.s along on the trip all counseled against the jump, saying my back would suffer, my eyeballs would fill with blood, et cetera. Sue elected not to jump and to go down below the bridge and take pictures of my leap into space — perhaps her last memory of me.

I walked out on the bridge, got on a scale, and the facilitators asked if I would like to get my hair wet, or stop just short of the water, 130 feet below. Just short, please. The elastic bungies were tied around my ankles, I hobbled to the edge of the platform, and had to decide whether I was going to go off like a paratrooper or a high-diver. The latter, as I put my hands together and tilted forward. Smooth, graceful, fun. My balding head did not get wet, a boat came along and collected me as I dangled in the air, and a rapturous kiss from the wife. A man's gotta do what a man's gotta do . Been there, done that.

Then it was over the Haas Pass and up the West Coast, which is usually wet, but for us was sunny. Some riders stopped along the way to helicopter up to the glaciers in the Alps so that they could throw snowballs at one another; others of us continued to the beach and our night's lodging.

The next day we rode north along the coast to Greymouth (mouth of the Grey River), and then turned and headed eastish. First we followed the fertile valley of the Grey River, with ploughed fields and sheepy meadows (apologies to Dylan Thomas), then into the forest covering the Victoria range of mountains, over

This is the Keokohe Beach on the east coast of the South Island, and these are the Moeroki Boulders. In case you are curious about these round rocks, geologists have them all figured out, calling these septarian concretions, formed millions of years ago on an ancient seabed.

Lewis Pass and down to the lowlands to spend the night at a place called Hanmer Springs. Here gouts of hot water burst out of the ground, and many people come for a good soak.

From Hanmer Springs we went along to Kaikoura on the coast and up along the South Pacific Ocean to Picton, with surf on our right hand, the occasional farm on the left. From Picton the Queen Charlotte Drive took us to Nelson, sitting at the head of Tasman Bay, and that stretch of pavement cannot be beat with a stick; good road, great riding.

At Nelson, with a free day, I abandoned a temporarily ailing wife and shot north around Abel Tasman National Park and up to Cape Farewell. Tasman was the first European to make comment about the existence of New Zealand, back in 1642, and the Maoris tried to dissuade further exploration by killing four of his sailors. It worked for 200 years, but the enterprising British set up the New Zealand Company and came to land at Nelson in 1841, dropping off a bunch of settlers that would, the investors hoped, make the company rich. I don't know how the stockholders did, but the immigrants loved the place, and many more followed.

Then we had to finish our very squishy figure-8, going over the island divide at Hope Saddle and down along the Tasman Sea to Westport and Paparoa National Park. Which is where I began this little dissertation, sitting on the beach levee at Punakaiki. Forgive me all those Maori names, but they will come back to you, dear reader, should you ever have the opportunity to ride in this part of the world.

Fly-or-die tickets said we would have to leave on the morrow. We scaled 3025-foot Arthur's Pass and returned to Christchurch, handed in the bikes, bought all the souvenirs and sheepskins we could fit in our bags, had a farewell dinner — and left the next day.

Now, if Boeing could just build faster airplanes . . .

When I left New Zealand in 1974, this was the sight of the R75/5 being hoisted aboard a Chandris line ship in the harbor of the capital city of Wellington. We both arrived in Panama safely two weeks later.

Back in 1974 New Zealand was just changing over to the metric system, and sharp eyes might note the changes from feet and miles to meters and kilometers.

Spain, Pamplona 1960

No room at the inn. Or anywhere else in the city of Pamplona for that matter. What else could I expect, arriving as the festival of San Fermin began in early July, 1960. I was riding my newly acquired Triumph Bonneville, having just come down from England for this very occasion of running with the bulls. This was the time when most every college student was influenced by reading Hemingway's *The Sun Also Rises*, as well as seeing the

233

1957 movie version starring Ava Garner and Tyrone Power. I was going to live the fiction, following some bizarre hormonal rite of passage.

This was Pamplona's annual opportunity to shine in the Navarre sun, and the city took advantage of it. The festival dates back hundreds of years, combining respect for the patron saint of the city with an annual cattle market, but in the 19th century the religious aspects began to take second place to the general carousing. Following World War II the event had grown from being a provincial holiday to becoming a huge affair that had taken on international proportions, thanks of course to Hemingway and others. In the 21st century the festival hosts around a million people.

Granted, it was not nearly that large in 1960, but 50,000 visitors would certainly add to the local coffers. The city fathers loved the money that rolled in, and they knew that they could only rely on the tourist swarms for at most two weeks out of the year. Enough rooms to accommodate them all just did not exist.

What to do with the overflow, which were mostly young and relatively impecunious? Despite their limited traveling budgets it would be financially unsound to turn them away. Pitch army tents on the soccer field, have them pay a few pesos, get a tent number, and let them worry about comfort. The white canvas tents were set up with military precision in long neat rows, dozens and dozens of them.

I eased the motorcycle down the narrow passageway to #2E. It was a tent, alright, just a tent, no cots, sitting on a plot of grass. By army standards it would have been a six-man tent, by Pamplonan standards it could fit a dozen of the college-age tourists who had come to see the running of, or to run with, the bulls. Inside a half-dozen backpacks were laying about, and an industrious fellow was busy scribbling a letter. It does seem that a traveler spends an inordinate amount of time writing home to tell the folks and friends what a good time he is having.

Alan said he had been there two nights, and that sleeping arrangements were pretty disorganized. I unstrapped my gear from the bike, threw it into the heap and headed into town on foot. It was mid-afternoon.

The central square was only moderately crowded, as the crowds had either gone off to the bullfights or were still waking from a long afternoon's nap. Sitting at a cafe table I scribbled my own letter. The shoeshine boys were around like a plague of insects. Every event breeds its own particular variety of con man, of hustler, and these urchins were what one had to put up with at Pamplona.

To keep them at bay, I appointed one to shine my boots, and continued to formulate sentences designed to make the recipient of the letter green with envy. I felt curious tugs at my foot, and looked down to see the little wretch trying to pry my heel off.

Ah, signor, the heel was worn. It is time to be replaced. I will do that now.

Like hell you will! I took the boot off and told him to put the heel back on. He hammered desultorily for a moment and handed the boot back. I put it on; at least no nails were sticking up to pierce my personal heel. He gave a final swish with the polish cloth and demanded an exorbitant sum. The boots looked only marginally better than when I had sat down. I gave him a couple of pesos and he began to wail loudly at the stinginess of the rich tourist. Nobody paid any attention, but he continued to caterwaul. I tossed another coin far over his head, forcing him to turn and scramble if a competitor weren't to grab it first.

He shook his fist at me, hurled what was obviously an insult, though I didn't catch it, and went off in search of more tolerant suckers.

Alan showed up with two other Americans who had just been assigned to the tent. He would show us the ropes: cheap places to eat, where to buy wine, and where to watch the running of the bulls from. In the cantina the wine was eight cents a liter — bring your own bottle. Basic rough red, it was guaranteed to provide a smashing hangover at no extra cost. This was when you could do Europe on $5 a day.

I don't quite remember getting back to my sleeping bag, but in the morning Alan and I traipsed down through town to hang on the railings and watch the running of the bulls. The bulls, having arrived by train the day before, were at the stockyards down by the railroad station, and the afternoon sport would require six of them, two for each of the three matadors.

The route from the stockyards to the bullring was maybe a half a mile long, right through the narrow city streets. All the side streets were barricaded with stout eight-foot tall constructions so the bulls could only go in the desired direction. Between the yards and the ring a simple pole was placed, blocking the way, and behind it milled the daring young men who wanted to run with the bulls. Women not allowed, though occasionally an androgynously dressed one would try.

Hanging on the barricade and looking down on the seething mass below me it seemed that more than half of the runners were Ivy League undergraduates. Button-down shirts and chinos definitely outnumbered the white pants and shirts and red scarves of the locals.

A distant cannon shot was heard, indicating the bulls had been released. The runners began to exhibit nervousness, but the policemen in charge of the pole refused to budge.

"It takes about two minutes for the bulls to get here," said Alan, "and those fellows definitely enjoy holding up the runners. Courage, or stupidity, is determined by how far back you start." Pushing and shoving was going on, the front line squeezed up against the pole. The police were smiling. The runners were not. It was now nervousness *in extremis*. Cries came from the rear to open the barrier. The cops continued to smile.

Finally they pulled the pole clear, and the front runners could barely keep their feet with the pressure from behind. The clutch of humanity, probably a hundred or more people, popped forward like the cork from a champagne bottle. And no sooner were the last ones past the barrier than a great voice made up of hundreds of small voices came up the street from the direction of the yards, "*Toro! Toro! Toro!*"

The heads of spectators leaning over the barricades began snapping back as the bulls came up the street, skimming their horns along the sides of the buildings, sweeping it clear. Looking the other direction I could see the last of the runners already losing heart and leaping up to be hoisted over the barricades by helpful hands, scrabbling to catch onto grated windows and second-floor balconies.

One dolt seemed petrified with fright, his back against a barricade, his eyes popping as the first bull bore down on him. He could not move. On-lookers from the top of the barricade reached down to pick him up, but he slipped from their grasp and fell to his knees as the bull thundered by, not touching him. That galvanized him, and he was up and over the fence in less than a second.

Damn, that looked like a good time!

The rest of the bulls tore by, big beasts, with big horns, and behind was a smaller mass of screaming humanity, people who had jumped over the barricades and were now chasing the bulls. It had become a big sandwich act, with the live beef in the middle.

Alan and I went over to the *plaza de toros* to watch the second phase of the morning show. When we got there the bulls were being ushered off-stage, their masculine rage mollified by the presence of a dozen cows with padded horns. Knots of daring young men stood around the arena.

The bulls secure, the cows were turned back into the ring for the pleasure of the masses. Homemade capes appeared, and the novices were acting as though there were a talent scout in the seats, whirling and twirling and often getting knocked down.

One group formed a large rugby-like scrum, about 20 people in a wedge, and faced off a cow which seemed quite perplexed as to just what was going on. The cow was foolish enough to approach the point of the wedge and lower her head, and as she did the lead man moved forward and gripped her around the horns. As this one man held onto the cow, she tried to dislodge him, but the scrum was holding fast. The cow backed up, moving her head as best she could, dragging the scrum along until people began to lose their footing and the unity unraveled.

"Looks like fun," I said to Alan.

"Doesn't look like fun to me," he replied, perfectly happy in his role as voyeur.

We retired to the square, breaking our fast with fresh bread and hot coffee. "Best to stay on your feet 'til noon," advised Alan, "then go back to sleep for a while and get up in time to see the fights." Sound advice.

The city of Pamplona, once the capitol of the Kingdom of Navarre, was an old place with narrow streets and traffic problems, not helped by the influx of thousands of visitors for the festival. At some point in the morning I saw a chain of revelers, mostly locals but with a goodly assortment of tourists intermingled, singing songs while dancing the jota and snaking through the streets. A Navarran let go of the waist of the girl in front and invited me to become a link. Fair enough.

Everyone had red scarves around the neck or waist, red berets on the head, a symbol of the festival. One tourist whispered to me that it was a not-too-secret indication of the city's political bent. I refrained from spoiling his theory by not saying that Navarre had been entirely pro-Franco at the time of the civil war, and was to this day. Red was merely a color, not a sign of leftist persuasion.

This was a bacchanalian revel, and botas, the leather wine-skins, were being passed up and down the line. At an intersection our conga-line came across a religious procession headed towards the cathedral. A short, heated discussion took place between the clerics and the hedonists as to who had the right of way, and the clerics won. We stood and watched as robed and hatted representatives of the church proceeded along in a stately fashion, carrying some religious reliquary. As soon as they had passed our musicians resumed the beat and off we went, gliding down the cobbled streets.

I was not much of an aficionado of bullfights, but the San Fermin fights were said to be very good. The best matadors came, not for the money, but for the glory. To show well at Pamplona was very much a feather in the hat and a move up in the ranks of the matadors, which meant more money somewhere else. And the bulls were good, too, the breeders wanting to show their best.

Despite the overlay of blood and death, the visual effect was one of an exuberant ballet. The bull had his role, the two horsemen had theirs, the three assistants had theirs, and the matador attempted to outdo himself and the competition. He would be rated on two major factors, his poise and his willingness to accept risk. Once the bull began the charge he stood erect, and if the crowd saw him as the epitome of tranquillity as he gracefully swept the cape around his thigh, the horn coming within inches of his suit of lights, then the applause was great.

And the thousands of spectators, of course, were part of the drama and highly critical of all the actions taken by the matador. The majority were locals, sitting on the cheaper, sunny side of the ring; with tourists and VIPs choosing the shade. Sitting in the shade that first afternoon I noted that the feckless visitors around me cheered at anything, whereas the sunny side was far more selective. Good work was greeted with great cheers, while poor performance was met with silence; nothing vulgar, like booing or hissing, was heard, just silence.

A highlight of the afternoon was the arrival of an interloper, or *espontaneo*. It has long been the practice for young men to try to attract the attention of a matador-patron by jumping into the ring and making a few passes before being hustled away. It is a dangerous way to catch the official eye, and police try to catch these young hopefuls before they get into the ring.

Not today. The bull had been piqued by the horseman, and the matador had come out to make a few passes before the banderillero was to place the festooned barbs in the bull's neck. The matador stepped back to receive his applause, his assistants watched the bull. Then a body toppled over the retaining wall, and a young man in ragged shirt and trousers got to his feet, a stick and a square of reddish cloth in his hand.

The bull saw him. The assistants saw him. The crowd saw him. The bullring was suddenly quiet. The lad advanced towards the bull, who pawed the ground and lowered his head. The *espontaneo* stopped and held out his homemade cape. The bull charged. A good pass. The crowd cheered. The matador held up his hand to stop his assistants from moving in and distracting the bull. The bull stopped, turned, the young fellow advanced, stopped, and completed another pass. He may have lacked the ballet-like grace of an experienced matador, but it was an impressive display of courage; more applause. A third pass. Then the capemen moved in to occupy the bull and lead the young fellow away, but gently, and the matador touched him on the shoulder as he passed.

The kid was definitely in. Maybe even got a job brushing the suit of lights.

After the fight it was another evening of roaming the streets, drinking, dining, dancing, until at some point after midnight I collapsed in the tent.

Alan woke me early. "Are you going to run?" Of course.

We went down to the barrier. Already the runners were getting in position. I climbed over the barricade and wormed up to the front of the pack. No fool, I.

The moment approached and the cannon went off in the distance. The police waited to lift the barrier. And waited. A sensation of panic emanated from the runners. Even the local champions at the back started to yell to let us go through. I was getting a prickly sensation and gauging my chances at a leap for the nearest barricade.

Finally we were let go, and I began an easy pace. It was like running down a miniature Broadway, the narrow street with tall houses on either side giving a canyon-like atmosphere. The heads above us were looking well behind us, trying to see the action. I let more frantic runners go by.

The houses give way to an open area that separated the city from the arena, bordered with a high, strong fence, the top lined with spectators. This led down to the tunnel that ran beneath the seats at the bull-ring. It was long and narrow and dark, maybe eight feet wide, seven feet tall, and over 100 feet long. No lights.

As I entered I could hear noise behind me indicating the bulls were getting close. I ran through and emerged into to the sunny ring, continuing on until I merged with a clutch of sweaty types catching their breath. Looking behind I saw other runners, and then a bull, two bulls emerged — thoroughly out of sorts.

As the bulls rampaged about most of us jumped over the five-foot wall that surrounded the actual ring, waiting until the cows appeared and the bulls lured away. Then it was back over the wall to play at being matador. The cows were certainly confused by having to cope with a hundred tormenters. Face one, and another grabs your tail. Knock one into the air or onto the ground and 20 others jump all over you. In time everybody was bored, and the authorities cleared us away.

I was back again that afternoon, now sitting on the sunny side of the ring. I cheered when my neighbors cheered, was silent when they were silent.

A new bull came out. The matador, one of the favorites, appeared in his suit of lights and made a several excellent passes. The crowd loved it. The matador stepped back to receive the applause, while his assistants kept the bull's attention.

The matador was facing the VIP box, lapping up the attention, his back to the action. As he bowed to the clapping crowd the bull turned his head away from the capemen and noted the shiny backside.

The bull began to turn, to paw the ground. The crowd could see what was happening and began to yell warnings. It all sounded like applause to the matador, who bowed lower. The bull began his charge. The crowd was going wild. The matador thought it was more hysterical adulation for his prowess.

It was a most astounding sight with thousands of people looking on one bull charging one man, and that one man completely oblivious to it all. The noise was absolutely deafening, and all the matador could think to do was to bow lower; the conceit of the fellow boggles the imagination.

Wham! Fortunately for the matador it was a square hit and the bull's horns went on either side of him, but the fellow was tossed a good 40 feet, right out of the ring.

I cheered. My neighbors didn't. Social error on my part. I thought they should send the bull off to stud as a reward, but instead another matador dispatched him. Bummer.

Next morning I was once again at the barricades, again with a monumental hangover. But this time I wasn't going to be one of those first-in-line wimps, this time I hung around at the back of the crowd. The cannon went off, the barrier was eventually lowered, and I was trotting up the street.

I could tell what was happening behind me by the sounds of the crowds hanging on the fences. The more noise, the closer a bull. I was still between the buildings when the first bull swept by me. Big boy! Then the second, more than half a ton of very angry meat on the hoof. I had two in front, and four behind. Let's leave it that way.

I was trying to stay up with the bulls in front when I broke into the open space, and I could tell from the sounds above me that I had a bull on my butt; "Toro! Toro! Toro!" I looked beside me and saw another tourist running for all he was worth. I had no idea how close the bull was, and did not dare to try to leap up on the fence. Instead I was headed for the dark tunnel — just the place to get gored and trampled.

My adrenalin was pumping like mad, but there was still a reserve to be called on. I had been a lousy track-man in high school, but coach would have been proud of me in that 100-foot dash. I was fast! And I could hear big noises behind me. The other runner and I were still side by side as we cleared the tunnel and immediately cut to each side — inches in front of the bull.

I'd had my fun, that was for sure.

That night at dinner I was celebrated and toasted by my temporary friends, as we sat at a long table in one of the cantinas. As I acknowledged my transient moment of glory one fellow passed out, face down in his lentil soup. To prevent his drowning his neighbor kindly turned his head sideways, but did not remove the bowl of soup.

Next morning I calculated the chances of my surviving two more days of this fun and frolic. Not good. If my head didn't split wide open from the daily hangover, something else, like a bull's horn, would get me. I hadn't even fired up the Bonneville since I had arrived. Time to leave, while the leaving is good. Alan was writing in his journal; he looked up and said, "You are one crazy man."

I loaded the motorcycle and headed towards Madrid. It was a beautiful day, and as I climbed up and over the Sierra de Cantabria I was feeling exuberant. I had run with the bulls! I was brave! I was reckless! I was a man! To prove that, I kept the throttle twisted hard, scraping pegs around the curves, charging up the road.

At the top of the pass a group of back-robed seminarians were having a stroll through the mountain meadow, and passing them at speed I gave a wave. Some waved back, others made the sign of the cross.

Hurtling down the hairpinned road on the south side, accelerating down the straights, braking heavily for the turns, I knew that the young priests-to-be were aware that I had had a little bit of divine intervention on my side. Which I needed, as those skinny little brakes soon got really hot and began to fade; I slowed down. No point in being too foolish.

Mastering the art of drinking from a bota bag was essential to enjoying life in Pamplona during the St. Fermin festival. No photos exist of that moment in time, but Clement was still using a bota bag 25 years later, here in Death Valley with partner in crime, Craig Stein.

Peru 1998

Our little group had been on the road for ten days and not a cloud had blemished the sky. Now we were climbing upwards, the dirt road snaking around the folds in the mountain range. Even while keeping a dust-free half-mile apart, I could see several riders ahead as they swing out around a curve and then ducked back in to hug the hillside. We were well above the tree-line, nothing but low shrubs and sparse grasses on the slopes. Way, way down in the valley far, far below were the green squares of small fields along the Paucartambo River.

We were ascending the last, the easternmost, ridge of the Andes Mountains, a low summit by local standards, only 11,500 feet. The narrow, two-rut road slipped around an outcrop, continued to ascend, and we found ourselves on a minor saddle, the road dipping briefly before ascending again.

Here Flavio, our indomitable multi-lingual leader, stopped and pointed in the distance, where a line of clouds lay on the horizon, and said, "Once we reach those clouds, that is the Acjanaco Pass; then it is 50 kilometers and three hours straight down on a bad, muddy road into the Amazon jungle."

Oh yeah! Give me more of this badness!

* * * *

Back to the beginning. A magazine had called up and asked if I would like to take a trip to Peru. Is the Pope a Catholic? Yes, of course. A Peruvian tour operation was looking to approach the American market, and wanted someone to write a story on a new route it had laid out, starting along the Pacific Coast and going over the Andes Mountains and finally dropping down into the Amazon Basin — where the road ended. Sounded like a very interesting trip, and fun to boot. The only drawback was a long day on airplanes. I could put up with that.

Flying into Lima, or anywhere, after midnight is never a pleasure, but it becomes acceptable when cheerful people greet your flight-ravaged body, take your bags, hustle you into a van, whisk you away from the airport. And right through the city.

Lima, home to about a third of the 30 million Peruvians, is a big, modern city, and like most big, modern cities, never sleeps. Even at one o'clock in the morning the streets were full of traffic and people, vendors still vending on the sidewalks. I stared out my window, but I hadn't come to Peru to see modernity, I had come for antiquity and adventure.

Finding our way into a seaside suburb we arrived at a quiet, small hotel, where I was tucked into bed and fell sound asleep within minutes.

Come morning, and the somewhat reasonable hour of seven o'clock, our small group met at the breakfast table. Introductions all around, with an English couple and a Dutchman being the other clients. Juice glasses and coffee cups were full, bacon and eggs to satisfy the stomach, and the first, of many, instructions to come from Flavio, head of Inca Moto Adventures: "Be ready to leave at nine o'clock."

Into the van, down the coast 150 miles. After three hours we pulled up in front of a discreetly elegant, if slightly aged, hotel on the coast. We were at the edge of the Paracas Natural Reserve, an 800,000-acre parcel of seaside real estate dedicated to preserving nature. Formal roads did not really exist in the reserve, which was all hard-packed coastal desert. The authorities allowed vehicles to roam as they wished, as long as they don't crush the plants (there weren't any except in little hideaways) or ran over the animals (never did see any mammals, only a few birds). The desert got virtually no rain, but tire tracks were always wiped clean by the nighttime winds.

Anybody got a compass? GPS? Satellite phone?

Lunch was provided at an outdoor table by the swimming pool, and afterwards we were introduced to our motorcycles, Honda XR600Rs, all prepped and polished by Oscar, the sweep-master. He drove a big Toyota pickup with our luggage and enough spare parts to build three new motorcycles, plus a large auxiliary gas tank. And a pile of Pink Floyd tapes that could keep a 1970s disco running for a week.

Our motorcycles were noted for their light weight and had only the rudimentary kick-starters, since an electric starter motor and bigger battery would add at least 30 pounds. Considering this trip would be more than 80 percent off the asphalt, the less weight we would have to deal with, the happier we would be.

This is why our leader, Flavio, told us to back off on the throttle before we come to the very top of a ridge. Surprise. No telling what might be on the other side.

A seaside lunch break in the Great Ica Desert has sweepmaster Oscar providing sandwiches and cold drinks on a bluff above the Pacific Ocean.

After learning the all-important starting drill we were going on our break-in ride, to see how we would fare in the rough — and the assembled foursome had dirty skills ranging from minimal to fairly good. Most of the Paracas lies on a large peninsula where tectonic plates had squeezed together some ten million years ago (so say the geologists), creating a crenellated wall of small hills at the edge of the sea, their windswept slopes now as smooth and hard as a good gravel road. Up and down we rode, up 40 degrees, down 50, up 50 degrees, down 60. Anybody (most of us) not familiar with the superlative torquey qualities of the motorcycles soon found how easy it was to run up a slope that would baffle and terrify the average street rider. Another skill learned.

After several hours we did not want to stop, until we all were parked on top of a small butte and Flavio pointed out that our headlights were minimal and the moon would not come up until late. Back to the hotel it was, with beer and wine and fish and much discussion about the future; we were pumped!

The next day was a southerly run along the coast; no roads, just keep the ocean to your right and you'll be okay. But stay away from the cliffs, or you won't be okay. We pranced and galloped, charging along like we knew what we were doing, but relying entirely on our leader to show us the way in this trackless, barren land — and Oscar to find us if we did get lost or broken down.

An old pisco distillery in the town of Ica provided lodging for the night, the owner's hacienda now turned into a hotel. Distillation still went on in the back the Bodega El Carmelo, which turned out quantities of delightful Peruvian alcohol. Pisco is a clear brandy made from muscat grapes, and mixed with a little lime juice this pleasantly sour concoction gave me dreams of grandeur, images of riding my motorcycle through an endless sequence of sand dunes, through the clearest sky on earth, through almost impenetrable jungle. We could thank the Spanish missionaries who had brought the vines to the new world in order to make sacramental wine.

Ica lies in the valley of the Ica River, close to the Andes, one of the few fertile zones in Peru. Agriculture is the city's main business, and most of the 50,000 inhabitants derived their income from the fields. Five hundred years ago it was the capital of the local Indian culture — until the Spaniards conquered the place in 1553. Little remains of the original residents, except in the museum.

The next day was back to the desert, which rolled on and on and on in a most beckoning manner, like a siren luring a sailor of yore to his doom. The throttle was to the stop as I headed towards a great hill somewhere in the distance. Two miles, ten miles, I could not tell how far it was.

Pre-Columbian Indian tribes lived along the rivers flowing through the Ica Desert, the air being so dry that, when buried, the skeletons and their clothes would be preserved for centuries.

This was, and is, the Great Ica Desert of southern Peru, about 50 miles wide and 500 miles long, separating the Andes Mountains from the Pacific Ocean. The desert is not flat, but has hills and valleys, the arid earth swept clean by millions of years of wind, and never a drop of rain. I could ride in any direction I wanted, at any speed I wanted, until I ran out of gas. Exhilarating is way too tame a word to describe this sensation — it was soul-stirring.

I headed full tilt upwards and arrived at the top of a bluff. Flavio had advised us always to back off just before reaching the top, or else we could be in for an unpleasant surprise. I followed instructions — and came to a stop at the edge of a sheer cliff which dropped straight down hundreds of feet to the narrow valley of the Big River, or Rio Grande. A dozen or more rivers do flow from the mountains to cross the desert, but rarely does green grow beyond the immediate riverbanks.

I looked behind me; plumes of dust rose out of the desert floor as the others rode towards me, headed for my vantage point. This was great "adventure" touring, truly great.

An hour later we were riding along the river's roadless valley and I saw what seemed to be bones, and skulls, on the ground. Stopping, I saw that dismembered skeletons lay all around. Flavio came up, looked, shook his head, and said, "Grave robbers." This prehistoric Indian cemetery had lain un-noticed and untouched for centuries, until found by modern-day thieves who dug up the graves to take what artifacts had been buried

Peru 1998

The old-fashioned suspension bridge serves to get people across a number of rushing rivers — motorcycles should go one at a time just in case there's a weight problem.

In the Andes this road is considered a first-class highway.

A bridge can be a pretty basic affair in the hinterlands of the Peruvian Andes — but definitely strong enough to hold a motorcycle.

with the dead, scattering the bones in their haste. Desecration, but collectors and museums would pay good money for these items. Contemporary inhabitants, poor and often unemployed, were more concerned with providing for their families than in preserving the past. Understandable.

Late that afternoon we arrived at the dunes of my dreams. Coming over a rise in the desert, there to our left was a wall of smooth, scalloped sand stretching as far as the sunglassed eye could see, any blemishes removed by the nightly wind. For ten miles or more we were careening along the dunes, picking up speed on the hard flats, charging up the soft slope, beginning to bog, arching downwards before the bike sank in (you hoped), and rushing back down to the flats to repeat the same process over and over and over. For a road rider like myself, this was better than any roller-coaster I knew of.

The next morning Flavio had reserved for culture, and he put us in light planes to fly over the famed Nazca lines, giant outlines of birds and beasts and geometric shapes formed into the Ica Desert by the Nazca Indians a thousand or more years ago. For purposes which remain unknown. UFOlogists claim these were guiding points for spacecraft flown by extra-terrestrials. Maybe. Maybe not.

After lunch we departed for the mountains, the Andes, stretching over 4000 miles along the western flank of the South American continent, with many Peruvian peaks reaching more than 22,000 feet. As the condor flies, the Andes are not a terribly wide, range 150 miles or so. But as the road goes, up and down, up and down, into a valley, over a pass, beside a river, scratching up a steep slope, it is a whole lot longer. From leaving the desert at Nazca to arriving in the jungle would be over 600 miles — which may not sound like much, but I promise, it was no simple journey.

Riding the Andean byways was a treat, with the road being paved in small part, but mostly rough dirt on which the motorcycles were in their element. On the second day in the mountains we attained our greatest altitude, a modest 14,411 feet at the Huachujasa Pass between the two towns of Puquio and

When the water
is not too deep
bridges are not
even necessary.

Our group was the
main event at any
Andean village we
stopped in.

Most markets
have vendors who
sell fresh-squeezed
fruit juices as well
as bags of coca
leaves which,
when masticated,
serve to reduce
any hunger pangs.
And the bag
costs five cents?
Cheaper than
eating.

Chalhuanca. This is the continental divide, with the Pacific a scant 150 miles to the west, the Amazon River meeting the Atlantic 3000 miles to the east; rather a poorly balanced continent, one could say.

The road spiraled down, spiraled up, crossed crashing rivers, sometimes splashing through a ford, or over a steel girder bridge, or even a narrow, swaying, pedestrian suspension bridge. On the road we ate at little cafes, where grilled steak and fries was always an option, the more daring trying treats like roast guinea pig. Very tasty.

The towns had an illusion of prosperity, the main road leading through the central square, often with a twin-towered church on one side, a colonnaded facade for the government building on the other. But away from the center narrow dirt streets led past hundreds of shabby little dwellings, with dark-skinned women carrying water jugs filled from the public pumps. Many of the Andes Indians were migrating from the countryside to the towns in hopes of finding a better life, and generally found misery instead.

One can't go into the Andes and not be aware of the existence of the coca bush, which stands six or so feet tall and grows on the east-facing slopes. There are several uses for the coca leaf. Locally, dried leaves are used as a herb to cure various maladies, or as a tasty tea, and, when chewed, as a mild stimulant, rather like the way we drink coffee or knock back a Red Bull.

If you stuff a wad of coca leaves in your mouth, and it has to be a big wad, two or three ounces, you don't really get high, just mildly anesthetized. And you lose your appetite; this effect is rather useful in a culture where food is sometimes hard to come by. And the by-product we call cocaine? The locals don't even know what it is.

Here is the legal product of a coca plant — a tea made from the leaves and quite soothing to drink, preferable to the chamomile we have in the U.S.

The Cathedral of Saint Dominic in Cuzco has been holding masses since its completion in 1654, and is the great backdrop of the Plaza de Armas, the city's main square.

Pre-historians and archeologists believe that Machu Picchu was built in the 15th century as a country estate for one of the Inca emperors, a fellow named Pachacuti. The three main structures are very much in the classic style of that era.

After several days in the mountains we arrived at the Navel of the Universe, the city called Cuzco founded by the Inca emperors in the 12th century, now the epicenter of the tourist trade in Peru. While Flavio and Oscar fiddled the bikes, which had endured considerable abuse at our hands, we spent a day in and around the city.

The center of this intriguingly historic place was lined with colonial-era buildings and souvenir shops. All standing on the stone structures built by the Incas before the Spaniards arrived in the 16th century. Empires come, empires go, but remnants of the past stay on.

A few miles outside of the city was the Inca fortress of Sacsayhuaman, a construction that would have done any European proud. It has always been a question as to how the Inca craftsmen, with no metal tools, could construct a 40-foot-high wall of massive stones so tightly fit a knife blade would not go between. That mystery has never been satisfactorily resolved.

Huayna Picchu is a peak that soars more than a thousand feet above the ruins at Machu Picchu, with a gnarly trail going to the top for the tourists who want an exceptionally fine view.

The next day a slow train (the only kind in that part of the world) took us to the ancient Inca religious center of Machu Picchu, the most famous ruins in South America. High on a mountain ridge dozens of buildings had been made of stone retrieved from the valley far below. This was the home of high priests and their attendants, and was never found by the Spaniards. Eventually this last remaining Inca outpost was abandoned, then stayed unmolested and hidden until an American archeologist refound it in

The train from Cuzco stops here in Agua Caliente, in the Urubamba River valley at the foot of the mountain on which sits Machu Picchu; a bus to the ruins takes 20 minutes, by foot it is two or more hours.

This aged Russian helicopter was sold off as Soviet army surplus, and would fly tourists from Machu Picchu in half an hour, about three hours less than the train ride and five times as expensive.

1912. Of course the local Indians all knew of the place, but they did not mention it as they preferred that the foreigners stay away.

We returned to Cuzco somewhat more quickly in an elderly Russian-made helicopter — quite exciting when I realized that in this steep terrain there was no margin for error. Or engine failure, as there would be no point to auto-rotating down to a 30-degree slope; the copter would then roll down the rest of the way to a rushing river.

It was time for our last foray, into the Amazon. We crossed the Acjanaco Pass and were thumping down a harshly angled road, into heavy fog, splashing through deep mudded ruts, beneath waterfalls plunging a hundred feet or more, with nothing but an adroit twist of the handlebars to keep us from sliding over the unguarded edge and tumbling down and down and down.

Another ridge, another valley, but eventually the road will go over the Acjanaco Pass and begin to drop down to the Amazon basin.

It was a great descent. From the treeless mountains we slowly wound down through layer after layer of vegetation, from the barren hills down into the lushest of tropical forests. We were now entering the Manu National Park, a modest five million acres in size, roughly the size of Kentucky and Tennessee combined. This huge park is supported by the United Nations and preserves both the forest and the Indian tribes which live therein, free of credit cards and television.

For the ladies in the remote Paucartambo Valley this is every-day dress.

Dropping down on the eastern-facing escarpment of the Andes Mountains the road goes past many streams, all of which end up in the Amazon River, the largest river in the world as determined by the flow of water.

On the edge of the park an extremely limited amount of tourist business were allowed, and we had accommodations at a remote lodge that had been completed just weeks before, the Manu Cloud Forest Lodge. To edify the reader, rain forest exists below the 3000-foot altitude, while cloud forest goes from 3000 to 6000 feet. This was our last stop — from here we would return to Cuzco and the inevitable airplane.

With special permission, and another day, we could have gone into the park to the very end of the road, where wheeled vehicles met boats on the tributaries of the Amazon River. No thru road indeed!

The lodge was a delight, designed with the intention of providing the guests with maximum access to the forest outside. The rooms overhung a frothing river, and the windows did not need screens, as no biting insects existed. A leisurely dinner, and then long talking into the night over many glasses of rum and fruit juice. We had just one more day of riding, and we wanted more than that. A good trip is when you don't want to go home — and we did not want to go home, did not want to return to our loved ones. At least at the moment. Maybe if we all sat there and talked about how wonderful life was, and what a fine adventure we were having, by some small miracle all our plane reservations would be moved back a week.

But home we had to go. Morning came, and with it a fine drizzle to accompany us all the way back up the mountain. After cresting the mountains at the Acjanaco we broke free of the clouds and rode back down into the Paucartambo valley, and from there it was more mountains and valleys, and views to absolutely die for, places where we could see 20 or 30 miles away, and nothing but the thin dirt road to show that man had been there.

And back to Cuzco, a farewell dinner, many pisco sours, goodbyes and regrets, and in the early hours of the morning Flavio hauled our drunken bodies down to the airport to begin the long trip home. It was over. Damn.

Clement's first visit to Peru was in 1969, with a pack on his back, and low-budget travelers were allowed to sleep in a building in the Inca ruins at Machu Picchu — very fine!

Queensland, Australia 1974

On my way to Queensland I stopped at Ayers Rock, or Uluru, which stands over a thousand feet above the desert floor, and is almost six miles around at the base.

Life was simple. Some might say idyllic. My tent was pitched under palm trees bordering a long expanse of pristine white beach, the warm waters of the Coral Sea lapping gently on the shore. Right behind the tent was my motorcycle, a BMW R75/5, which had just carried me from Perth, way in the west of Australia, across the Nullarbor Plain, up past Ayers Rock and through Alice Springs, and over to the Pacific Ocean. Two hundred yards away a small store with a fronded porch sold bread and meat pies and cold beer. Scattered up and down the beach at respectful intervals were other layabouts such as myself. Of an evening we'd gather around a fire, not for warmth in this tropical latitude, but for the communality that a small flame and glowing coals creates.

263

Queensland, Australia 1974

In 1974 visitors to Ayers Rock (now having reverted to its Aboriginal name of Uluru) could climb to the top of the huge sandstone monolith; the place has great religious significance to the local Aboriginal tribes and climbing is no longer allowed.

Clement may not have climbed Mt. Everest, but he did climb Ayers Rock in 1974.

We'd tell stories of traveling in strange and obscure parts of the world, hear about this good hotel in Bangkok, that great camping place in the Yukon, the best hiking trails on Mount Kenya, the excellent cheap food in Cuzco. When a valuable bit of information came forth, the pads and pens would appear and the particulars scribbled down. It was 1974, and the traveling was good.

It should be noted that Clement packed a small Olivetti 22 typewriter on his motorcycle, and carried it around for 3 years.

And so to bed. To rise with a yawn and a swim, maybe take a day-trip out to Green Island on the Great Barrier Reef, check at the post office in Cairns for mail. Even travelers need to take a vacation, and this stretch of northeast Australia was a fine place to do nothing for a while.

Riding past a hardware store in Cairns one afternoon I saw two BMWs and a Suzuki pulled up in front. BMW types being a fraternal lot, I stopped mine. Mitch and Greg were diligently mending Mitch's BMW sidecar rig with hose-clamps and baling wire, and tearing Suzuki-riding Rupert up one side and down the other for having been so stupid as to buy 20 pounds of muesli.

"We might need it," said Rupert plaintively, showing me a large

As I headed toward Queensland, the dirt road north through central Australia from Port Augusta to Alice Springs was very lightly traveled, maybe ten cars a day, and the rough camping was magnificent.

Northern Queensland was noted for its rustic bridges, put together by locals rather than the government department of transportation, but they seemed sturdy enough for the motorcycles.

bag full of nuts, raisins, dried fruits and rolled oats. Very healthy. "Try some," he said, proffering the bag. I took a handful and chewed; not bad.

"Stow it in the car," said Mitch, grumpily; "you can eat it all yourself."

They were camped north of town in a very little community called Port Douglas, and headed up to a place called Cape Tribulation for a week of hunting, fishing and trapping. It had to be a week, because the ferry across the Daintree River to the Cape only ran at high tide on Sunday. From there it was 40 miles to the end of the dirt road.

Come along, they said. It'll be grand.

We arranged to meet at the campground in Port Douglas the next evening, which was Saturday. We would take off from there bright and early Sunday morning.

Port Douglas was at that time a rather sleepy, quasi-dead-end town, catering to retired types with limited funds who had a hankering for tropical climes. The main street had half a dozen small commercial establishments, including a pub. Any serious business was transacted in Cairns.

We met at the campground as arranged, knocked back a few beers while cooking supper, then strolled up the pub along about dark, and sat there slowly drinking our lagers. Most of the customers were elderly, active grey- and white-haired types who loved a pint and a bit of a gossip. They had been accountants in Sydney, housewives in Melbourne, and found that life up here was good, property, cheap. We drank to that.

Did we know there was going to be some live music that evening? No, we did not. Well, Ralph and Edna were going to play the saxophone and piano, and we were in for a treat. A right good time. That called for another round.

Sure enough, about 9 o'clock Ralph and Edna appeared, both somewhat past retirement age but looking very fit. A great bustle began in the back room as they set up, and Mitch and I made sure we had front-row seats and fresh pints. Half of Port Douglas seemed to be arriving, chattering, moving chairs around.

The lights dimmed, the music began. I cannot remember the

names of the tunes, but they were reminiscent of an Australian Lawrence Welk. "Waltzing Matilda" popped up on occasion. In between numbers Ralph would tell slightly off-color jokes, much to the delight of the audience.

At some point my slightly sodden brain began turning over. This was a big night for Port Douglas, and all these oldies were having a fine time. It would be nice if I could do something that would make it pleasantly memorable. Had I been a whizz at the piano or sax, I would have volunteered to do a little jamming, but as it was my musical skills had peaked with the triangle in the third grade.

However, this was the year of streaking, that quaint pastime in which a person would shed all of his, or her, clothes and run swiftly past large groups of surprised people. Headlines around the world reported streakers in Times Square and Golden Gate Park, outside of Buckingham Palace and inside the Louvre. Obviously, while most everybody in Port Douglas might have heard of streaking, I doubted that anyone had ever seen a streaker. I myself had never seen nor been one.

But, the call was upon me. Give these good honest folk an evening to remember. I had a long shirt on, and the room was dark, with spotlights on the act. I discreetly slipped off my strides (Australian for pants) and passed them to Mitch, much to his surprise. I unbuttoned my shirt. Timing was everything. Just as Ralph and Edna finished a number I leaped up, dropping my last garment in Mitch's lap, did a two-second solo in front of the spotlit stage, and dashed out through the brightly lit bar onto the darkened street. Behind me was pandemonium.

I trotted naked down the darkened road, laughing maniacally, passing a young couple embracing. "Evening," I said, and jogged on. Two minutes later I was at my tent, digging out another pair of pants and putting them on. Half an hour later Mitch and the others showed up, fit to be tied, still hysterical with laughter.

My impromptu act had been an unqualified success, the hit of the night, with much applause after the initial shock had worn off. From in the back of the room they had heard voices asking, "What happened? What happened?" The lights came

on and explanations were given to those who had happened to be snoozing. One very little and very old lady had come up to Ralph and said, "I missed it. I missed it. Can't you ask him to come back?

I just hope Ralph and Edna didn't mind being upstaged for a moment.

* * * *

In the morning we awoke, broke camp, loaded the bikes, and headed north. We turned right on a little-used dirt road which led across flat land through tall grass and eucalyptus trees for several miles. The road ended at the Daintree River's edge.

A small hut had several cars parked outside, and a flat-bottomed boat pulled up to the landing could hold a car with ease, a large truck with difficulty. Our Charon was smoking a pipe and chatting with one of his fishermen friends.

"Sure, take you across. But it's right sticky the other side," he noted; "been raining a lot."

We four musketeers loaded the three solo bikes and the sidecar outfit on, and got handcranked across. Our boatman said there were a couple of cattle farms and a few vacation homes on the far

We're loading up the ferry which crosses the Daintree River and was, at the time, the only access to Cape Tribulation.

When we talk about sticky mud, we mean sticky mud — the kind that gets between the fender and the tire and stops any forward motion. Solution? Remove the offending fender.

side, and that was it. Plus 40 miles of bad road.

"Hope you make it," the boatman said, "but if you get into trouble you can always hike to a farm. They have radios and can always get in touch with us out here." Cheerful thoughts.

We immediately entered hilly country, and I understood what "right sticky" meant. The red earth on the road was that cloying stuff which just packs in wherever it sticks. Within a mile three of us had to remove our front fenders as the mud had jammed the wheels. We solo bikers were traveling feet down, like outriggers, while Mitch was having a hell of a time trying to keep his three-wheeler from sliding off into the trees.

After a few miles the road flattened out, the mud turned to gravel and sand, and we were running parallel to the sea. No sparkling white sand up here, just mudflats.

"Great for crabbing," said Mitch, as we found a grassy promontory sticking out into the sea. A stream had crossed the road a quarter-mile back, which would do for the water supply.

We set up tents, and then Mitch set about emptying his sidecar. Mitch was a swagman, an Australian hobo, a motorized knight of the road. He had given up on civilization and women some years back, and decided to see his country at his leisure. When he needed money he would go into the outback and get a job in a mining operation mending machinery.

He liked traveling by motorcycle, but in much of the continent there is no water, so he needed a way to carry a few gallons. Hence the sidecar.

Which was also useful for putting useful things in, and things he had. A large pot for communal cooking. A grill to put over a fire and set the pot on. Enough tools to strip his motorcycle down to the last nut and bolt. A kerosene lantern and kerosene. Three fishing rods. Two crabpots. A .22 rifle. As well as two cases of beer, a small sack of flour, a tin of oil, a can of coffee, several cans of condensed milk — and the bag of muesli.

"We'll eat fine out here," said Mitch, selecting a rod with which to prove the point. "Live off the land. The way a bloke was meant to live."

The other two were somewhat less frontier-like. Greg was a

carpenter, working around Brisbane, and he had come north for a look-see. On the way he had met Rupert. About the only thing they had in common were motorcycles, as Greg was a quick-witted, good-looking lad, while Rupert was a tall, gangly fellow, a bit slow on the uptake, but good-hearted and careful in his thinking. Riding together they had met Mitch, whose idea it was to come up to Cape Tribulation.

Desolate it was, and beautiful. The cape itself was an uninviting hump sticking out between Cooktown and Cairns, and passing sailors had given the place its name. A hundred years ago, if you wrecked on these shores you were in no real danger, but it was a long hike to get to anywhere. Still was.

We were a male-bonding version of "The Swiss Family Robinson."

Forty miles of beach run south of the infamous Cape Tribulation — which is now a World Heritage Site well-known for its eco-tourism; our beach-riding would be frowned upon today.

Mitch had no luck with the rod. We did not have grilled fish for dinner, but sardines from a can and the last of a loaf of bread. The next day Mitch set out his crab pots, then he and Rupert were surf-casting. While Greg went off in search of hallucinogenic mushrooms in the cow pastures.

For dinner we had sardines along with our home-made chapatis, a thin, unleavened bread made out of flour and water.

The third day Rupert kept fishing, the pots kept crabbing, and Mitch went off hunting. Mitch was in a foul mood as he ate the last of the sardines and some chapatis.

That is Mitch on his sidecar rig out on Cape Tribulation, fording a river, hoping he is not going to flood the carburetor intake.

The fourth evening Rupert mixed his muesli into the flour and made rather tasty chapatis.

Greg spent most of the day zonked on his mushrooms, Rupert was content to have had his muesli justified, and Mitch was determined to wring a meal from the land or the sea.

The fifth evening I broached the idea of finding a farm and asking if we could buy some food. And got a long lecture from Mitch on bludging; a bludge, according to his lore, was the lowest of the low, a person who lived off the efforts of another. If you were actually in danger of dying, it was fair to seek help, but until that moment you should never ask a favor. We were in no danger of dying, and in no way would he countenance any of us going to ask for provisions. He would be successful tomorrow. Until he began to understand his own tribulations.

Muesli chapatis again the next evening, flavored with Greg's mushrooms. Mitch inveighed against altered states of consciousness until his consciousness was altered and he fell asleep by the fire. I was counting hours until I could get my teeth into a good piece of dead cow.

Saturday morning we were visited by shipwrecked people. Two men and a woman appeared in camp as we were making coffee. They had been walking much of the night under the light of the moon, their sailboat having run aground the evening before. Since we were leaving the next day, could we take the woman into Cairns; the two men would go back to the boat.

Mitch spent the day fishing, crabbing, hunting, to no avail. It was muesli chapatis for dinner, the last of the beer, splitting four cans five ways, and two fingers of whiskey. Our guest was quite complimentary.

"Very good," she said. And since Rupert was the chapati chef, he beamed bright enough to light up the darkness. And Greg was being quite attentive as well.

"She's a bludge," said Mitch as the two of us wandered alone up the shore; "all good-looking women are bludges. And a lot of women who ain't good-looking." I asked him about his misogynism; all he said was that he had been married once, and that had been enough of women for him.

We packed up in the morning, eating the last of the muesli for breakfast chapatis. "You done good," said Mitch to Rupert, grudgingly. He packed his rifle and crab pots and fishing gear in the sidecar, saying he was going to head out to Mount Isa and get a mine job for a while, then take off for the northwest coast. Greg and Rupert were headed back to civilization and work.

We got back to the ferry without incident, the road having dried out considerably. The boatman looked at the passenger and asked, "How'd you get here? I never took you across."

We rode back together to Cairns. The ship-wrecked one was dropped at the bus stop, where she had to make phone calls to get the salvage operation in progress. Greg made sure he had an address. Then us men-folk went off to eat.

Over steak and fries and beer Mitch snorted on about women making trouble. Greg smiled, and said he did like them, on occasion. Rupert allowed as to how our ship-wrecked guest sure was pretty. Dissension was appearing in our ranks.

We said our goodbyes after supper.

The Nullarbor (No Tree) Plain separates east from west Australia, and the dirt road that traversed it was dead straight; as a local said, "When you get up in the morning you can see where you'll be that night."

Rajasthan, India 1997

I've been a lot of places, traveled to many countries, but if I had to give the nod to just one as being the single most fascinating, I would say India. It has dramatic geography, with mountains and deserts and jungles and sea-coast, and history that has been going on for more than 5000 years, with remnants of the far distant past scattered across the sub-continent. Ancient ruins are all over the landscape, an indication of cultures come and gone, which could be defined by the more than 200 languages and dialects that are spoken. Among the 1.2 billion Indians English is the most commonly used, and then Hindi, followed by 21 other official languages. India is about one-third the size of the United States, with four times the population, which means that much of the country is quite crowded, although much remains almost primeval.

This is one American's view of India. "The land of dreams and romance, of fabulous wealth and fabulous poverty, of splendor and rags, of palaces and hovels, of famine and pestilence, of genii and giants and Aladdin lamps, of tigers and elephants, the cobra and the jungle, the country of a hundred nations and a hundred tongues, of a thousand religions and two million gods, cradle of the human race, birthplace of human speech — the land that all men desire to see, and having once seen, by even a glimpse, would not give that glimpse for the shows of all the rest of the world combined." Which is how Mark Twain described the place in one breathless sentence a hundred years ago, and it still holds true today.

A dozen of us had flown from the U.S. to the airport outside of India's capitol, Delhi, where our guide met us, simplified the paperwork, and then hustled us onto a bus. Which took us away from the urban complications to a pleasant hotel spread out over several acres. Unfortunately for our celebratory instincts the hotel was just over the line into the state of Haryana, which happened to be dry, in the alcoholic sense; fortunately several colleagues had bought bottles of duty-free liquor on the plane, and the hotel restaurant had all the mixers we needed.

Come morning we were fed a western-style breakfast, and then trooped out to meet our mounts — identical Indian-made 500cc Enfield Bullets. The background of these India Enfields is unburdened by romance, merely politics. In the early fifties the Indian army was buying hundreds of British-built Royal Enfield Bullets, preparing to do battle with both Pakistan and China. In 1956, to absorb these large orders, the rather small English firm set up a subsidiary near Madras to build these utilitarian singles. The English company went bankrupt and closed up shop in 1971, while the Indian operation acquired a life of its own as The Enfield India, Ltd. In 1995, appreciating the value of history, it became Royal Enfield Motors.

We all proved vaguely competent in learning the starting drill, since the bikes lacked electric legs. Then we rode them around the grounds at the hotel to familiarize ourselves with right-side shifting, easily done when there is no one around, no emergencies to react to. However, an hour later we were in the midst of vehicular anarchy, trying to thread our way through urban traffic, with grossly overloaded Tata trucks and impossibly crowded buses bearing down from every direction, dodging plodding camel-carts and buffalo-carts and pony-carts carrying everything from hay to sacks of cement to rusty iron bits, with rickshaws and motorized three-wheelers sneaking into the odd nook and cranny, available slivers of space filled by the ubiquitous bicycles, cud-chewing cows lying in the middle of intersections, comfortably confident in their sacredness, chugging tractors pulling trailers filled with whatever, pedestrians stepping out into this maelstrom without looking left or right, dogs and pigs dashing out to seek their next incarnation beneath some unguided wheel, horns blowing, brakes screeching, exhausts bellowing huge clouds of black diesel fumes, policemen whistling into the noise-filled void . . .

And then we found ourselves puttering through a magical valley, hillsides and flat land dotted with temples, a small lake, egrets and cranes, and when we stopped our engines there was not a sound to be heard, the quiet of absolute peace. Such is life in India.

This was to be a 1500-mile journey taking place mainly in the Great Indian Desert, which covers most of the state of Rajasthan, India's answer to the American Southwest. Beginning in Delhi we rode southwest to Jodhpur, down to Mt. Abu and Udaipur, back to Agra (of Taj Mahal fame) and Delhi. This course was chosen to keep us mostly on scenic back roads and to see some of the remarkable sights we would pass by, from magnificent temples to abandoned palaces, from luxurious hotels to gypsy encampments, from walled cities to desert camel markets, from liveried servants to snake charmers.

Before the start, our guide was explaining the do's and don't's of the trip and said that it was essential that we keep each other in sight. When someone asked if it wouldn't be possible just to get a route sheet and go off on one's own, he allowed as to how the roads were not always marked, that the occasional directional sign would probably be in Hindi, and a wrong turn could put

This is an atypical street scene, as usually our little band of Bullets would be struggling to get through traffic in any urban environment. But the occasional lull was welcomed by all and always short-lived.

This was the average road that our guide led us along in the Great Indian Desert, entirely fine until a large truck would come our way and — might making right — force us off the asphalt.

you out somewhere west of nowhere. And in case of a flat tire wouldn't it be nice to know that help was coming up behind?

Behind the Bullets was a 20-passenger bus carrying a secondary guide, a driver and an assistant driver, two mechanics and their two assistant mechanics, with trunks full of spare parts, and our baggage. Down-sizing is not a concern in India; why have one person do the job when you can have two or three for almost the same wage. Every evening the wrenches (metric, British Fine, and Whitworth) came out and the bikes were re-tuned, and every morning they would be started up and warmed while we consumed a leisurely breakfast. Bags would be collected from our rooms, and we would appear about nine o'clock to commence the riding day.

The most important device on the motorcycle was not the brakes, not the throttle, but the horn. India lives and dies by the horn. Anytime you do anything in a vehicle, any movement at all, you sound the horn. Every truck has a reminder writ large on the tailgate: HORN PLEASE. Our very low-decibel units were not terribly authoritative, but could occasionally attract the  attention of a pedestrian carrying a sheep over his shoulders who was about to step in front of the motorcycle; I would suggest that future travelers pack a pair of 120-decibel FIAMM hooters.

Indian drivers ostensibly adhere to the left side of the road, although a more realistic definition is that they stay on the best side of the road. Many of the secondary roads are just one lane of deteriorating asphalt, about eight feet wide, and should two trucks meet the drivers are both supposed to put the left wheels on the wide shoulders. Sometimes they forget. Or, appreciating that motorcycles would barely dent their iron cow-catchers, would not bother to move over for our column.

As our leader pointed out, trraveling alone would be problematic, as most road signs, while having Arabic numerals, used Hindi script.

One of our group tries out a donkey for size; he allowed as to how the Enfield Bullet was considerably more comfortable.

This mode of irrigation was probably developed a thousand or more years ago, and is still useful today; feeding a bovine costs far less than buying a pump and gasoline.

Most of our journeying was on these small roads, as we traveled the byways of Rajasthan, appreciating the subtle differences between our 20th century machines and the farming techology that dated back 2000 years and more. The fact that the average Indian earns less than $2 a day, and that it is cheaper to make babies than to buy gasoline, might have something to do with all this quaint antiquity.

At the other end of the transportation infrastructure are the few miles of divided four-lane highway that exist in the country. Many Indian drivers treat this oddity as two parallel two-lane roads, so you are never quite sure as to the wisdom of riding in the fast lane. The carnage on such roads can be quite impressive, perhaps seen by the government as a bloody attempt to slow the growth of the burgeoning population. I believe that these multi-lane roads should be dedicated to Shiva the Destroyer.

Much of the Indian attitudes towards life and death might be attributable to the Hindu religion. To grossly oversimplify a very complicated and very ancient theology, a Hindu believes in a Supreme Being, which manifests Itself in thousands of different gods, including Shiva, and the goal is to avoid the potentially endless cycle of reincarnation and go directly to Nirvana. The gents who set up this theo-corporate structure some 5000 years ago were no dummies, wanting to keep the power in their own Brahmin hands for the foreseeable future. They carefully arranged matters so that even the most miserable human on the face of the earth would accept his lot in hopes that the next time around would be better.

Our accommodations were generally rather spectacular. Battle your way across the windswept desert, golden sunlight filtered through the late afternoon dust storm, a great fort looming on the horizon; slip inside Khimsar's gates, and cold beer would be served on the battlements. Or an elderly palace in the Sariska forest, home to many tigers, built by some maharajah when times were flush, four dozen spacious rooms, peacocks mewling on the lawns, gin and tonics on the verandah, a pickup game of cricket. Or a Moghul garden at Samod, acres and acres of carefully planted flower beds and ornamental hedges, exotic

Building a temple is a good way to curry favor with the Hindu gods, and a hundred years ago some rich fellow created this small lake with an island and ornate structure near Pushkar. He's no doubt enjoying many rewards.

We were not allowed to take the motorcycles into the Sariska Wildlife Sanctuary, but hoped to quietly sneak up on a tiger or two with our pedicabs; no such luck.

Cannons on the wall of the Jodphur fortress, built on a hill 400 feet above the city, have not been used much since the British took control in 1818, and then gave it back to India in 1949.

tents all around the edge; not just any tents, but sumptuous living spaces that would put most California condominiums to shame, with carpets and soft beds, and fully equipped bathrooms.

Running water and flush toilets were often a bit on the gambling side. After all, these palaces and forts were built long before indoor plumbing became the standard, and sometimes the showers and other devices Americans are accustomed to were not quite as efficient as at a Motel 6. And electricity might be in short supply.

Food was abundant, usually prepared as a buffet with a dozen silver salvers offering curries, rice, lentils, lots of nourishment appealing the vegetarian crowd, as well as a chicken and a mutton curry, with little boney bits of the animals giving excellent flavor. This nourishment, as it was on the tourist route, was not overly spiced, a sensible precaution considering the often delicate Western stomach. Eating down at the Jodphur equivalent of Denny's would put hair on any Westerner's chest and fire in the belly.

Our plucky little bunch of travelers coped with India quite well; we didn't necessarily merge with the culture, but dodged around it as we did the trucks. Anyone taking a trip such as this should pass no judgement on societal shortcomings such as poverty, lack of sanitation, seeming disregard for the future, but only observe the beauty all around and survive the traffic. To do otherwise is pointless.

Late one afternoon I was riding alone on a long, straight road, knowing that our 16th century fortress hotel was just ten miles ahead, and with visions of a cold Tusker beer in my head I was pushing the Enfield a bit hard. Only to feel the over-heated engine seize; I immediately pulled in the clutch and coasted to a stop. We had just come through a small town with a very crowded main street where I had stopped to take pictures, and I knew that everybody but the bus was ahead of me, and that bus might not show up for an hour. I felt no danger, and I had a bottle of water with me but dammit I wanted a beer!

I put the Enfield on the centerstand and for a few minutes admired the setting sun, fast becoming a bright red orb over the

285

distant horizon. Sunsets are beautiful, but only good for so long, and after a few more minutes I gave the kickstarter a prod. The piston cycled around. I turned on the ignition, went through the starting drill, engine fired and I was on my way to a cold one — with a very light hand on the throttle.

That evening I told the mechanics what had happened, fully expecting them to rip the engine apart and put in new rings. Come morning the bike ran perfectly. I asked what had been done. They had pulled the spark plug, poured a teaspoon of oil in the cylinder and kicked it over a few times. Not to worry. Indian ingenuity.

As the old India hand Rudy Kipling put it, "The end of the fight is a tombstone white with the name of the late deceased, and the epitaph drear, 'A fool lies here who tried to hustle the East'"

That is the Taj Majal, India's primary tourist attraction. Built in the 17th century, this was a tomb that a Mogul emperor created to honor his beloved deceased wife. All widowers should be so affluent.

Sahara 1965

Photo by Arnie Friedman

The rising sun was still low in the east, the golden disc barely above the dead-straight horizon. In front of me were 2000 square miles of the flattest land on earth. Better than a billiard table; if I had had a very tall step-ladder I might have seen the curvature of the earth, but my eyes were less than six feet above the surface. I was idly considering riding my motorcycle across this flatness to a place called El Tozeur, which should be about 75 miles east-southeast. This being in 1984, the days before Global Positioning Satellites, I was planning on doing all this with a hand-held compass that my father had used in World War II.

"You're nuts," said Arnie. "Hold on; I want to get a picture of this. This might be the last picture of you ever. Here, look at me." I turned around. About a mile behind Arnie I could see the low-slung town of Nefta and the green of the date palms where we had spent the previous night. We were on the northern edge of the

287

Chott el Jerid, said to be the largest dry lake in the world. What if I got lost, missed El Tozeur, and ended up heading straight into the heart of the Sahara Desert — which is really big, over three million square miles? Or if the crust of salt broke and the motorcycle got stuck? Or the engine quit?

"Let's go back to the hotel," I said, throwing a leg over my BMW R80G/S. "They should be serving breakfast about now."

"First smart thing you've said this morning," replied Arnie.

This was in Tunisia, and I was traveling with a small guided motorcycle tour. I was back in Tunisia in 1991, on my own, on an R100GS, and then eight years later in Morocco on another GS. All three times I hovered along the northern fringe of the desert, having great fun racing along the hard-pack surface, other times frolicking on the edge on the mighty sand dunes.

However, my most memorable time in the Sahara was in 1965 when I left my motorcycle at home in Massachusetts and joined my sister on a trip in an aged VW bus from Algeria right across the desert to Nigeria.

It's a tough trip, no matter what you're in or on. It's been done on motorcycles, but it sure was a lot easier on four wheels.

* * * *

College and military service being done by the summer of 1965, I had rewarded myself by riding my motorcycle from the Atlantic to the Pacific, returning to Massachusetts relatively broke, with the idea of buying a new suit and getting a job on Madison Avenue. Until my sister called from Italy with a better offer: she and a friend were planning on driving a VW bus back to Kenya, crossing the Sahara Desert from Algeria to Nigeria. Would I care to come along?

That first night in the Sahara back in 1965 wasn't quite the romantic scene an armchair traveler would like to expect. No oasis, no date palms shading a small pond, no blue-cloaked Tuaregs and dromedaries, not even a sand dune in sight. But it did have a great view of the great void we were about to enter.

That day we had descended from the Atlas Mountains to a ridge just above the desert city of Laghouat, looking for an uninhabited place to park the van and spend the night. It was a well-camped site we were on, lots of people having been here before us. with fire-blackened rocks in a circle, bits of trash scattered about, and the stony desert stretching off to the south well beyond where the eye could see. On this rainless spot hundreds of vehicles had left their tire prints, oil had been changed, cans discarded. Anything burnable had been burnt, including old tires. Not a pretty sight on this wintery late afternoon.

We began preparing supper on the northern edge of the greatest desert in the world, and as darkness arrived our perceptions changed. The dim lights of the distant city did not intrude as the black curtain rolled back on probably the most magnificent sight of the heavens above that I had ever seen, a million trillion stars coming into view. I did not bother to ponder the origin of my universe, only laid back to admire it.

We rolled into Laghouat in the morning, the old town all painted white, with building-block houses, minareted mosques, and jelaba-robed men and veiled women cruising the streets. This place offered the last bank and last real garage for the next 1500 miles. Joni sat at a cafe sketching while Cynthia and I went off to find what we thought we might need for the trip. Our preparations consisted of two spare tires, three large plastic water containers, and a 20-liter jerrycan for extra gas. No Land Rover, Rolex-watch, Abercrombie & Fitch sort of adventuring for us, this was the minimalist approach to Saharan traveling.

We met a German whose VW van had collapsed 800 miles south. He had had to load the van on an empty truck and then ride in his van on the back of the truck for four miserable days. Much to the delight, he said, of the Arab truck drivers. He was rather soured on the desert. He did give us his big 50-liter drum for spare fuel, since he would not need it now, or ever again. He had had it with traveling in remote places.

Our next stop was Ghardaia, 150 miles away, and the road was said to be more or less paved that far, so the trip would not be arduous. We hustled along at a goodly clip, reasonably sure of our destination due to the latest Michelin maps of the Algerian and Niger Sahara. These were quite good, right down to pointing out waterholes.

Much of the Sahara is covered with hardpan, called **reg**, which is where the roads are; the soft sand is called **erg**, which moves with the wind and obliterates everything in its path.

We are leaving the southern edge of the Atlas Mountains and arriving at our first town in the Sahara proper, Lagouat; from here on travel can get iffy.

Small oases sometimes could not make the economic grade and would be abandoned, the residents moving to a larger community.

The Sahara Desert is divided between erg and reg, the erg being the shifting sand seas of romance, the reg being the rocky hardpan of reality. There are no roads in the erg, as any attempt to make a permanent passage would be futile, covered up in the first sand-storm. Fat-tired vehicles with compasses (then) or GPS units (now) do traverse the sand-seas, but the drivers had damn sure better know what they are doing.

Our road was considerably more mundane, a thin layer of pot-holed macadam running across the reg, skirting the ergs, sometimes covered in thin sand. Occasionally a nearby sand-dune would have shifted and covered the right of way; the road would be absolutely straight, and a 10, 20, 40-foot-high dune would block passage. No problem, the trucks would merely make a path around on the reg, semi-permanently altering the line of communication.

We only hurtled moderately, as the van was a '59 model with over 100,000 kilometers on the odometer. The tool kit consisted of a lug wrench, a plug wrench, a bicycle wrench that would fit eight different-sized bolts, a pair of pliers, and my Swiss Army knife. The sole concession to the trip was the extra-large air-cleaner, which filtered everything through an oil bath.

I was appointed Head Mechanic. I professed total ignorance about the workings of such a vehicle, but Cynthia rationalized that since all three of us were equally ignorant, I might as well be the one to suffer dirty fingernails. Anyway, it was her trip, she was in charge, and I better do what she said; mutiny would be dealt with harshly. I changed the oil in the air-cleaner every day — a filthy job.

For a European, going to North Africa is the equivalent of an American's going to the deserts in the southwestern U.S. Get on a ferry in Marseilles, France, or Genoa, Italy, and next morning you wake up in Algiers or Tunis. In the winter months a hundred or more motorcycles and four-wheel-drives will storm down the ramp and dash south, looking for adventure. They'll dash around for a week or a month, then head back to catch the boat home. It is desert touring akin to a trip to the Loire Valley or the Great Smoky Mountains National Park.

In order to defeat the sun, much of the warren-like construction of desert towns, like here in Ghardaia, involves covered markets interspersed with occasional open areas.

Where Americans are accustomed to the omnipresent used-car lot, the Sahara is full of used-camel lots.

Kids are kids all over the world, and these children are curious as to what these camera-weilding people are all about.

For proper desert traveling you have to disappear into the wasteland with no return ticket. Cynthia had told some friends in Nigeria that we might be there for Xmas, and that was all the planning we had.

Our next stop was El Golea, via an unpaved road that was reasonably well-traveled, and we passed a vehicle every hour or so. Most were heavy trucks coming back from the deep south, not overly laden. A lot of goods went into the desert, very little came out. The 175 miles was steady, if uninspired, going. The town of El Golea, built around an oasis, was now suffering the indignities of the automotive age, with a gas station and trucks parked wherever they pleased.

The next stretch to In Salah was over 300 miles, and friendly folk in El Golea said that *le piste* (the track — we were leaving the world of roads behind) was *pas bon* (not good). They were quite right. We bought a couple of loaves of bread and some tins of sardines; sardines are a staple of the desert, along with sweetened condensed milk, although it is best not to eat them together. Rather coarse Algerian red wine was an alternative to water.

We went to the Prefecture, local government headquarters, and asked the police if we should do anything special — like tell them we were headed south. Going south is not a good idea, we were told, the track is very rough. We appreciated the advice, but

Stuck! Rule #1 in the Sahara desert: Do not drive at night, because the difference between a hard surface and a soft one is difficult to discern.

This is the valley where the VW was skimming along on top of the smooth, windswept crust of sand — until we got to the end of the valley and it all roughed up.

In Guezzam is a small Algerian army post and waterhole on the border with Niger, and caravans form up here to trade in salt and other commodities.

told the spit and polished fellow we were going anyway.

"Fine," he said, "I will radio to In Salah and tell them to expect you. How many days do you think it will take?"

Three, we thought, and the gendarme asked us to please make sure we checked in at the Prefecture at In Salah when we arrived. We filled up with gas and water, and headed off into the arid wasteland, et cetera; no pavement, just tracks. The trip took on a slightly more serious note, and we paid a good deal of attention to not getting stuck. The wintery days were short, and we always set up camp before it got dark.

Camp was simple. Cynthia and Joni slept in the van, while I had one of the first "pop-up" tents on the market, a Thermos. A "pop-up" did not need any stakes or ropes, just two long fiberglass poles, each one made of five sections, that fit inside and expanded the tent to its proper dimensions as seen on many tents today. This was very useful — until a wind came up and I would have to go into the tent to prevent its being blown away. We had a one-burner stove that ran off gasoline, and a stew or thick soup would be the evening's fare. Only occasionally would we find any sort of wood, so a cheerful campfire was a rarity.

That next morning I began to feel remarkably seedy, having succumbed to some minor malady. I was achy and nauseous and bad-tempered, and the car was acting up. I reset the points, and the problem went away. My sister thought the best cure for my bad attitude would be a cold beer. She determined to push on to In Salah. However, nightfall came about 40 miles short of our goal.

A basic rule in the desert, we had been told, was not to drive at night. It was hard enough determining the quality of the sand ahead in the daytime, impossible in the beam of a headlight. We were in an area of thin sand, with dozens of tracks running side by side; we chose a wrong one and got good and stuck.

Where we spent the night.

In the morning I groused into my coffee that we were surely going to die out here. We did not have our get-out-of-the-sand techniques well honed, and while we struggled to free the van a truck came along, heading north; it stopped beside us, a hundred

The market place at In Salah is where the desert inhabitants come to meet and chat, since they may only get to town once or twice a year.

No point trying to gussy up a desert house with paint, but mud walls can easily be decorated.

A sack of flour, a little water, and a few twigs of wood are all that is needed to bake the unleavened bread that the Tuaregs enjoy.

yards away. The driver, co-driver and mechanic cheerfully pushed the VW to sounder sand. We were on our way again.

In Salah was a traditional desert community, where any sort of arability was much too valuable to be built on. The oasis proper served as a garden for date palms and a few other fruits and veggies, while the mud-brick town was on the north side. Desert towns closed themselves off to the outside world; no great boulevards entered, no welcoming arch to pass under, just blank walls of the backs of the most recently built houses. Sometimes it was hard to find one's way into a town.

To add to the image of desert hostility, a large fort sat half a mile out in the desert, a French tri-color flying from the ramparts. Algeria had only been a sovereign nation since 1962, and part of the deal with France, the ex-colonial masters, was that de Gaulle and his *force de frappe* could continue experimenting with atomic bombs at the test site a hundred miles further south.

We were cantering along across the desert towards the town, looking for a way in, and I aimed for a narrow cut between two walls. Too late we realized that the approach was half blocked by drifted sand, and our progress down the alley grew slower and slower until we sank to a halt. Right beside a squad of Algerian soldiers who were taking a break from the Sisyphean task of shoveling sand. They demonstrated no great interest in helping us, but after a chat with the NCO in charge, and the exchange of a couple of packs of cigarettes, we were pushed clear.

The town was of reasonable size, with a small square, a hotel, numerous shops, and requisite Prefecture. Yes, they had received the cable from El Golea. When would we leave for the next town, Tamanrasset? This afternoon. How long did we expect to be on the road to Tamanrasset? Three days.

It was nice to know that the police had actually sent the cable, but we had no idea what the search and rescue procedures were. If any. Would there be an all-out effort to find stranded travelers, notification of the embassy and all that, or would the cable merely be filed or discarded, the presumption being that the travelers had merely failed to notify the authorities? We never did find out. Probably just as well.

We loaded up with bread and sardines and cigarettes, the last being an excellent bargaining chip. Then topped off the gas, filled the water, and looked for sand mats. Sand mats are strips of perforated steel planking that can be carried along and, when necessary, laid on soft sand and driven over. Slow going, but better than being stuck. Ideally we should have had eight, but all we could find were two. Better than nothing. By late afternoon we were off, leaving town through an eastern approach which was not sanded in. Now the adventure was really beginning!

A couple of hours out the engine made a funny noise. Then another. We stopped. I opened the engine compartment and looked, which was about all I could do. I was hoping that a loose wire will be self-evident, and I could put it back in place and be hailed as a mechanical genius. It was not to be this time. Then I closed it, started the motor, and we continued on. And the engine made another funny noise.

Funny noises are seldom fun, especially with many miles of bad piste ahead. Go on? Or back to In Salah? Discretion won out, and we would head back. But it was late, and having learned our lesson about driving at night, we camped.

Late morning found ourselves rolling between the fort and In Salah, and a French soldier in fatigues was striding along. We stopped to enquire if he knew of a garage. Why? he asked. I described the problem. *"Zut, alors! C'est mon metier* (That's my profession)!" He was the head wrench at the fort, and said to bring the VW by next morning.

We checked into the hotel, more for the joys of a shower than anything else. A Dutch couple was there who had given up on the desert when the wife fell seriously ill. They were waiting for the weekly plane to fly her out, as the doctor thought that three days of beating across the desert would not do her any good. The doctor was probably right. They were even unhappier than the German fellow in Laghouat.

In the meantime several French officers had started chatting up the ladies, inviting us over to the mess for a drink that night. An honor. We informed the police of our changes in schedule (they were quite understanding), and gussied ourselves up as much as possible for the evening's happy hour.

Under dusky skies we drove to the fort. It was a large establishment, right out of Beau Geste, with 30-foot crenelated walls and huge gates opening into a giant courtyard. Security was non- existent, no one challenging us as we drove in and parked with some other civilian vehicles. The mess was ecumenical, a high-ceilinged room for all ranks, quite boisterous and loud, and many bottles of Algerian wine and French Ricard doing the rounds.

Ricard is a traditional drink of the Foreign Legion, a clear, sweetish, liquorice-tasting, highly alcoholic liquid, a distant cousin of absinthe. Its most interesting attribute, other than getting you drunk quickly, is that when mixed with water, it turns milky and white. I rather like it. My sister didn't, but she did not want to hurt the hosts' feelings. Throughout the evening she would take my empty glass and pass me her full one, which I would drink, and then both glasses would be refilled.

By the time we came to leave, I was schnockered. But I must have been holding my liquor well as I ended up in the driver's seat. Fortunately there weren't many highway patrolmen out there, nor other cars. Unfortunately, the portals of the fort opened out towards the desert.

We drove out, and looked for the lights of the town. We couldn't see any. All the celestial constellations any star-gazer could wish for, but no beckoning electric light. Desert towns running on generators do not waste electricity. I kept on driving. Then I got the brilliant idea that if I drove in a big circle, I would eventually come across the town. And bigger circles. Eventually even the fort disappeared. There was I, driving around the desert with not the slightest idea where I was or where I was going, and I had a paid-up hotel room that I wanted to go to.

At some point headlights came towards us. I stopped, and the headlights pulled alongside. It was a French civilian who had just come from the fort, he had seen our headlights careening around the desert, and out of curiosity had come to see why they were going round and round. He led us back to town.

I had a vicious hangover the next morning. So did Joni.

My sister thought it all quite funny. At the appointed hour we delivered the van to the mechanic. The job took only minutes. Apparently there was something built into the distributor that was designed to eliminate ignition static in the car radio, which we didn't have, and these things could go bonkers in the dry Saharan air. Eliminate the eliminator, and we were fixed. Back on the piste to Tamanrasset.

We camped out the first night at a water hole a mile or so off the beaten track that the Dutch couple had told us about. It was the size of a swimming pool, deserted, with no trees around, and the Michelin map had described it thus: potable water, but with little green animals. The only vegetation was from desert melons, which looked luscious but were so bitter that nothing could eat them. Plant life had learned survival techniques, which was as much to foil the animal predators as the heat.

On a huge broad stretch of wind-swept reg we learned why travelers had gone to the effort of building little rock cairns every mile or so. The blowing sand had obliterated any signs of the track, except for these small piles of rocks. In our three-person van the driver would drive, trying to avoid the soft places, the shot-gun passenger would keep an eye peeled for the next cairn, and the back-seat passenger would look out the rear window keeping track of the last cairn, so we always had a reference point.

Through all this the scenery was magnificent, very varied and very large, with steep escarpments and deep canyons, rolling dunes and table-flat hardpan. It was the hot and dry equivalent of the cold and icy polar zones.

Tamanrasset had its own particular charm. Adventurous tourists would fly in, take a day trip into the Hoggar Mountains, and return home to thrill the neighbors with tales of derring-do. A much smaller number would drive down in a fully equipped Land Rover or the like, and use that as the turn-around point. Occasionally motorized over-landers, like us, kept on going to Niger.

We were told by the authorities that the Niger side of the border had been closed the week before, and no vehicles were going through. We went looking for information. Apparently the closure of the frontier was due either to a Niger national holiday or to an army maneuver, nobody quite knew which. No trucks were headed that way, and we wanted one for company. The track was in rough enough shape that we had been advised not to go it alone, to follow a vehicle that knew the way.

It was quite possible to die out there if you screwed up and got lost. It had happened to lots of idiots and wise men as well.

Early morning we woke up cold; even a desert in tropical latitudes can get chilly in winter. Going to the Prefecture to check on the situation, we found an army truck loading up. Headed for the border! The lieutenant in charge took a fancy to the ladies and said he was leaving at nine o'clock, but it would not be politic for us to be seen accompanying him. He would wait for us 50 kilometers south of town.

Sahara 1965

Some people and animals are born to life in the Sahara desert, like these two Tuareg boys and their young camels; they know how to survive.

Lt. Mohammed of the Algerian army is chatting with some Tuaregs who are setting up a camel caravan; the truck is rapidly putting the camel out of business.

Clement has never met a camel he liked; here he is in southern Algeria with army Lt. Mohammed riding pillion.

We went tearing around trying to get things done, like buying provisions and gas, including the 50-liter drum. The food supply was limited, with nothing but sardines available. Bummer; I was looking forward to tinned beef. Although we were well over 200 miles from the border, this was where we needed to check out of Algeria with the immigration and customs people. Stamping our passports, they told us, "*Bon chance.*" Good luck.

Those first 50 km. had been recently graded and there was no possibility of getting lost. However, Saharan grading consists mostly of pushing soft sand into the ruts so you could not see where the ruts were. It made for interesting driving.

We found the truck, stacked high with supplies for the border post, with three Tuaregs riding on top of the stack. In the cab were Lieutenant Mohammed and the driver. We took off. The truck maintained decent headway, but not the van. It got stuck, unstuck, stuck again, unstuck again, and stuck some more. We had to lighten the load, so we moved the 50-liters of fuel to the truck.

It was supposed to be a one-day run for the truck, and evening found both the truck and the van stuck at about the two-thirds mark. We made camp. Lt. Mohammed allowed as to how the track was in worse shape than he had ever seen before. That was bound to restore our confidence.

In the morning Lt. Mohammed was not happy; he was far behind schedule. The driver of the diesel-powered truck had an interesting starting system in these cold climes; he wrapped a fuel- soaked cloth around the carburetor and set it on fire to warm the diesel and the venturis. He got the truck unstuck, and then everybody pitched in to unstick the VW. Mohammed ordered the truck to go straight to the border post. He, and his briefcase and his submachine gun rode with Cynthia and me, while Joni moved to the truck, which disappeared into the glittering dawn.

We were making okay progress, and then came into a valley about three miles wide, where we bumped and bashed along fairly well over the hardpan until we came to the edge of a thin sand surface which stretched as far as we could see. We stopped on the stones and sampled the sand with our feet, rather like

In northern Niger salt is made by evaporation from the same water that the inhabitants of the town drink — a bit too salty to be refreshing.

These are the cakes of salt that are still used to preserve meat and other food in the desert, as has been done for thousands of years.

testing ice on a pond for thickness. That little bit where sand and stone met was soft, but just beyond it had developed enough of a crusty surface that it seemed it could support the narrow VW tires — as long as speed was maintained.

We got a strong running start, accelerating on the gravel, shooting over the soft sand and onto the slightly harder variety; I could feel the sand trying to drag the van down, but as long as I kept it in third, we were moving at a good clip.

I got the VW into fourth, and soon we were cruising at 50 mph on this highway of sand that was several miles wide and many miles long. If all Saharan travel were like that you could take a Cadillac across. Especially if you ran ten psi in the tires. The wind-scored scenery was spectacular and gorgeous and bleak, but we stopped for nothing, fearful that we wouldn't get going again.

It is a truism that many of the best sights that a traveler sees are passed without stopping.

After half an hour the walls of the valley began to close in, and Lt. Mohammed was looking nervous. As the valley funneled down to about 100 yards across the sand was getting softer and more rumpled, chewed up by the wind and the few vehicles that came through. I had the van floored, but stuck we got. Get out, jack up the van, put our two sand mats under the rear wheels, drive forward, get stuck again — things got rather boring.

The bad section was only a quarter mile or so, but it took us three hours to get through. Finally we reached hard ground again. Then saw the army truck returning with a dozen soldiers waving rifles from the back. The truck stopped and the raffish crew jumped to the ground, looking peeved. We stopped, the lieutenant got out and walked over to the soldiers, leaving the gun behind, but taking the brief case. A couple of minutes later they all whooped and clambered back on the truck.

The rest of the ride to In Guezzam was easy, but I asked Mohammed what the peevishness had been about. Well, he admitted, he was the payroll officer, the money was in his briefcase, and the soldiers had thought he had absconded.

We were allowed into Niger, and had more adventures as we

continued on to Agades and Zinder. At one point we ran out of gas, and as we came to a stop I, the pessimist, cried, "We're going to die out here!" My sister, the optimist, got out of the van with cameras in hand, heading for a Tuareg family she had seen camped a half mile back up the road, and said, "No we're not; help will come." Which it did.

Of all the trips I have taken in my life this one, despite being without a motorcycle, was the most exciting.

After crossing the Sahara, Clement decided that he could use a slightly damper climate, and headed up the Congo River on a barge — and began his checkered literary career.

In 1991 Clement returned to Tunisia, here at the Roman ruins at Dougga, and again decided not to attempt crossing the Sahara. Wise fellow.

Scandinavia 1984

Postcard of a 24-hour time-exposure of the midnight sun, except in reality it is like a triangle, with the sun scraping along the ocean at night to get back to where it will rise in the morning.

I had long heard about "the midnight sun", but I did not really understand what it was. Yeah, you see the sun all night; so what? Until that June night near Hammerfest, Norway, when I was lying in my tent on a small hill, looking north over the Arctic Ocean. Night? That was rather a misnomer, as at that latitude, 300 miles north of the Arctic Circle, and at that time of year, the summer solstice, there was no night.

I watched the sun drop slowly to the northwest, until it disappeared behind an island some miles off-shore. I fell asleep, only to wake an hour or so later to witness a most astounding sight. The sun had reappeared, heading east — east!? — just above the surface of the ocean. Actually it was on the far side of the North Pole, where west was east. I was entranced as that golden orb, its brilliance substantially muted by a considerable portion of the earth's atmosphere, but making it richer and oranger, like being seen through a great polarizing filter, kept moving along the horizon until it appeared to stop, and then began moving upwards and westerly. Like a great triangle with slightly curved lines. I fell asleep again.

How does one end up camping out 300 miles north of the Arctic Circle? If the travel gene is in one's DNA, as it definitely is in mine, one doesn't need much of an excuse to take a trip — preferably to a place one has never been before, along roads never traveled. Like a trip to The Land of the Midnight Sun, as northern Scandinavia is often referred to. And here was an opportunity, as I had been sent to Europe to test a new motorcycle and I could go wherever I wanted. The magazine was willing to pay for a week on the road, but I added another three weeks of my own time and money.

Not being a very accomplished photographer, Clement pushed the button about 3 a.m. to get this picture.

This trip had begun two weeks before in West Germany, where the folks at BMW had been kind enough to loan me their latest luxury touring motorcycle, a K100RT. From Munich north to where the paved road ends at the edge of the Arctic Ocean was about 2000 miles, I would do a gentle loop up and down, 28 days, 4000 or so miles, piece of cake.

Even time for a little sidetrip through East Germany to Berlin to have a look at The Wall, and ride through Checkpoint Charlie. I expected a few East Berliners to be attracted to this flash motorcycle, but obviously nobody wanted to be seen talking to an obvious Westerner, and I was totally ignored. I got a few furtive looks when I parked beside an outdoor cafe, on the Lindenstrasse, sat down at a table, and ordered a coffee; nobody pulled up a chair to talk about that motorcycle.

West Berlin was pleasantly raucous, but I wanted to head toward the midnight sun, my destination being Nordkapp, Norway. Or North Cape in English, the northernmost point on the map accessible by paved road. I had been in Fairbanks, Alaska, a few years before, but the Dalton Highway, the dirt road to Prudhoe Bay, at 70 degrees, 20 minutes North, was not open to public traffic — until 1981. Nordkapp was even further north, at 71.11 with paved roads approaching from both sides. That way I could do a loop rather than any lengthy repetition.

Leaving West Germany I was on Denmark's Jutland peninsula, which is a continuation of the great northern European plain, stretching north from the Alps to the Baltic Sea.. Turning east I crossed the bridge to the island of Fyn, where Hans Christian Anderson brought his tales to print. Denmark is comprised of Jutland and about 500 islands, the two biggest being Fyn and Sjelland, where the capital, Copenhagen, translated as "Merchants' Harbor", is located. Great city, that one; being very flat, transportation is mostly by bicycle, with extensive pedestrian zones. A delightful amusement park, the Tivoli Gardens, provides fun for children and adults alike.

I also took a trip to nearby Roskilde, where the Viking Ship Museum reminds one of an always changing world. A thousand years ago the Viking warriors and merchants did pretty much as the pleased in northern Europe, their reputation spreading from the British Isles to the Volga River in Russia. All due to their development of the longships, seaworthy vessels that could take on an ocean or a river. Like me, the Vikings always sought new places, wherever their waterborne craft would take them, while I was content with my motorcycle.

The harbors in Copenhagen, Denmark, were home to many wonderful old ships, the kind of vessels that bring the sea stories of Joseph Conrad to mind.

In Oslo, Norway, is a museum dedicated to the Viking explorers, with examples of the boats that carried them all the way to North America long before Chris Columbus arrived.

Part of the traveling experience is the attention that should be paid to local fare, like the traditional Danish smorgasbord. The term is abused by Americans as "all you can eat", generally meaning heaping your plate indiscriminately with mounds of fried chicken and potato salad, but the real smorgasbord is a much more complicated concept, requiring a certain amount of coaching in order to be done right. Fortunately I was staying with a friend in the city, and he took me to what was rated as the best smorgasbord in town — at the railway station. Some ten different courses were laid out on long tables, with multiple choices in each course, and I was discreetly informed as to the arcane etiquette. First we admired the plenitude, from the silver tureens holding soups to platters of cold meats, and a stunning array of desserts. No rush, as all the food would be available through-out the evening.

After sampling several soups I moved on to the herring course. Scandinavians love these little fish, and they are done up in half a dozen delicious ways, pickled, marinated, baked, et cetera. Next was a course of other kinds of fish, and then cold meats, then hot meats, veggies, salads, desserts, winding up with fruit and cheese. I did pretty well. And the bill was a modest $8.

Departing Copenhagen I rolled northwards to Helsingor, site of the Kronenberg Castle, putative home of the fictitious Hamlet, of Shakespearean fame. And less than three miles from Helsingor was Helsingborg, Sweden, separated by the Oresund Straits; a 20-minute ferryboat ride took care of that.

Sweden is large, the biggest country in Europe, covering over 170,000 square miles — of which 90 percent are covered with lakes and mountains and trees. The major city is the capital, Stockholm, cheerfully called the Venice of the North, but it has no gondolas, and increasingly congested streets and bridges that connect the many islands. The city was expanding as the great majority of the nine million Swedes live in the southern quarter of the country. Which meant the northern regions would not be suffering a glut of humanity. All the better by me.

I did go and see a new museum housing the *Wasa*, a great battleship that had slipped down the ways in 1628 into the Baltic

Photo reproduced courtesy of Road Rider magazine, 1984..

Clement was traveling alone, but any time he saw motorcyclists along the way, he was invited to join them.

Photo reproduced courtesy of Road Rider magazine, 1984..

Just as getting to Alaska is a goal for many American motorcyclists, riding up to northern Norway and the Arctic Ocean provides the same impetus for Europeans.

Sea — and immediately turned turtle and sunk. Apparently not a good design? It lay entombed and forgotten in the cold mud until rediscovered in the early 1960s, unentombed and brought to shore. An impressive sight. And a reminder that the Vikings of a thousand years before understood the basis of sea-going craft much better than these later Renaissance naval architects.

Time to head towards the Arctic. Traveling north reminded me of being in an Ingmar Bergman film, with few people and much time for contemplation. But instead of contemplating Bergman's favorite subjects, mortality and loneliness, I was luxuriating in the vastness of northern Sweden, hundreds of miles of two-lane road through thick forests, the mixture of civilization and wilderness. With the wilderness patiently waiting for us mere mortals to make a mistake, so it can reclaim what the mankind has covered in concrete and asphalt.

The best way to approach the sparsely inhabited north was by camping. The hotels were few, expensive, and patronized by salesmen and businessmen. Campgrounds were everywhere, and I could either pitch my tent or rent a little hutte for less than $10, using my own sleeping bag and the communal bathrooms. Camping was a much better way to meet people, as camping types are quite gregarious. Most campgrounds were by a lake or river, and there would be a sauna on site — after which I was expected to jump into the very cold water. It takes a peculiarly Scandinavian genetic makeup to appreciate that kind of suffering, and I must admit that I lack that in my own DNA.

Angling over towards Finland, skirting the top of the Gulf of Bothnia, the northern tip of the Baltic Sea, I was cheerfully waved through the border. Even in those pre-European Union days such crossings were pretty much non-events. I aimed the BMW at Roveniemi, a small city right on the Arctic Circle — 66 degrees, 17 minutes north of the Equator — with a large sign saying that on the south side was the Temperate Zone, on the north side, the Arctic Zone. And true to form a busload of Finnish tourists was swarming the place, clicking away, offering photographic proof that they indeed had journeyed to the Arctic. One of the drivers came over to look at the BMW and told me that this was the

A short ferry-ride takes the tourists over to the island where Nordkapp is located.

turn-around point of their trip, and in half an hour they would all be headed back to Helsinki, ready to tell their friends they had been to the Arctic.

But I was going north as far as the road would take me. Rolling through the forested landscape I stopped at a lonely little store to buy something for supper. The shop was run by two talkative elderly ladies who spoke not a word of English; between themselves they were probably chatting in Sami, the language of the Laplanders. Since the cans did not necessarily have pictures of their contents on the labels, we had a cheerful exchange of mis-information. An hour later I followed a dirt road a little way into the trees and did some free-camping. And heated up whatever was in the can; fish, if I remember correctly.

Next morning I exited Finland by taking a dirt road over the top of Lake Inari and into the northeasternmost corner of Norway, less than 25 miles from the Russian border. I did not see a single Finnish border guard, and only one Norwegian policeman who did not even have me stop. Scandinavian compatibility. I spent my first Norwegian night at a campground in Kirkenes, where the town was having its annual rockfest, hosted by a band that had come the 1800 miles from Oslo to entertain the youth. Riding over to the Russian border, where a small Norwegian military

presence was to be found, I thought idly about seeing if I could get into Russia. Discretion, fortunately, took hold.

The night in Kirkenes was noisy, crowded with young people who had come from miles around.

And with a never-ending mid-summer's night, the music went on until 3 a.m., more noted for its volume than its quality. A traveler should also be attuned to local music, but I'll take an accomplished flamenco guitarist over amplified and badly played rock.

Next day the road took me west, over several low mountain ranges, and my first glimpse of the Arctic Ocean, towards Nordkapp, which is actually on an island; The ferry for the short trip was full of tourist vehicles, from motorhomes to motorcycles, all headed for the same destination. A dozen bikes rolled off the boat for the 30-minute ride to the cape. Unfortunately the place was fogged in, which made for really bad photography. Tourists were spending a good deal of time in the Nordkapp gift shop, sending postcards to friends to prove they had been there. Setting up my tent in a campground I hoped the weather would clear — but no luck. Dang! But it was a good evening, with a trio of Swedish bikers who were on the road for exactly the same reason I was, to see a place they had never seen before.

A common sight: cows grazing along the hillsides of one of the many small fishing villages that can be found on the northwestern coast of Norway.

Northern Scandinavia is mostly forest and water, as the above scene in Finland shows.

It was a brisk summer day in fjord country when this shot was taken; the triangular rig is where fish are dried for the winter.

If one wanders off the main roads one can find all manner of lovely things, like this rustic, but reliable, stone slab bridge.

Photos reproduced courtesy of
Road Rider magazine, 1984..

I arrived in Hammerfest the next evening, with a clear blue sky, watching the triangular passage of the sun. Very much worth the trip. Those who have seen a fiery meteor flash across the night sky have a great memory. Those who have witnessed the brilliant curtains of the northern lights, the aurora borealis, have a memory. Those who have seen the midnight sun move through the sky, they also have a memory. Words do not do the event justice; it must be seen.

After Hammerfest I began a long run down the Norwegian coast on Highway 6, one of the most entertaining motorcycle roads in Europe, never straight for very long, and with ever-changing views. The road was well-maintained, too, as it is kept open all winter; Norwegian engineers have learned that a good base is essential to asphalt's surviving hard winters, preventing the frost heaves that plagued New England roads I grew up with.

From Hammerfest down to Trondheim was a thousand miles of twisted bliss, with a hundred side-roads going off to the islands on my right, or the mountains on my left. I had expected forests, as I had seen in Sweden, but instead in these northern latitudes found openness, with low hills, dark ocean water, the rocky islands lying just off-shore. I sat on a deserted stone beach, quite content with my solitude, feeling a little like Bergman's knight who plays chess with Death on a similar beach.

In a sheltered cove I might find a fishing village, boats moored along the main street, cow grazing on the summer grass. Boughten meals were rather hit and miss. The bigger towns had tableclothed restaurants which charged lots of money, but the average down-home eatery offered pretty dull fare. Cafeteria style was the norm, which was convenient since that meant I did not have to cope with a menu in a strange language, but the offerings were tediously bland, mostly boiled veg and maybe a boring chop. I expected fish and chips shops in all the little seaside towns, but they did not seem to exist. Reindeer burgers were quite tasty, but the only consistent food was the polzer, a sausage that was much too much like an American hot dog to really appeal to me. However, the scenic pleasures more than made up for any gastronomical failings.

This was Clement's campsite in Hammerfest, where he really got to appreciate the midnight sun.

Nordkapp is quite a tourist destination, so souvenir shops do a great business whenever the whole coast is clouded in. There is even a Nordkapp Motorcycle Club — though nobody was at the clubhouse when Clement stopped by.

Photos reproduced courtesy of Road Rider magazine, 1984

Below Trondheim the character of the coast changed radically, from low hills to steep mountains, becoming that famous fjord country of song and travel brochure. My reason for this trip was being rewarded richly, as I had never fully imagined what this part of the world could be like. It was beyond my expectations, both in the pleasure of riding and the pleasure of seeing.

At every fjord-crossing was the ultra-efficient ferry service, many of them having a small lounge with the inevitable polzer available. The beauty of these narrow fjords is that the mountain slopes descending to the water are often near vertical, created by glacial forces of millenia past, and the road hairpins down, down to the ferry and then up, up. While waiting at Balestrand on the Sognefjord the harbormaster told me that the water in the fjord was several thousand feet deep right off the ramp. A car had rolled in a few years before, and while the occupants were saved, nobody even thought to try to retrieve the vehicle.

In between the fjords the road would run over the saddle in the granite mountains, the sea unseen in the distance. In this part of Norway there were many tunnels, built because it was often easier to go through a mountain than over or around. These usually had no lighting, and it paid to pay attention as one approached a tunnel, with a sign indicating whether it would be 100 or 2000 meters long. Yes, stop and take the sunglasses off. The roads were great sport, the scenery lovely, but by the time I got to Bergen three weeks of traveling had gone by, and I was supposed to catch a plane in Munich before long.

This meant that rather than ride the southernmost part of Norway, reputed to be the most beautiful part, I turned inland and crossed over the rather barren mountains of Hardanger Vidda, where the wind and the weather make vegetation hide behind the rocks. At a small cafe on the top of the plateau a local motorcyclist said this was a favorite destination for the city riders from Oslo, the capital. Down to Oslo, where I had a quick look-see at the Kon Tiki and Viking longship museums — rather different craft perhaps used at roughly the same time. Then it was south to Sweden, a ferry from Goteberg back to Jutland, and a long run back to Munich.

I would love to go back, to do that loop around the base of Norway, go back to Nordkapp and watch the midnight sun again — so many places to ride, so much to see, so little time.

∿∿∿∿

This signpost in Narvik, Norway, says that we have come 672 kilometers down from Nordkapp — and that Paris is still 3257 km. to the south.

South Africa 2006

Official emblem of the Valley of Baboons, or Baviaanskloof Wilderness Area.

"Okay," said our leader, "tomorrow is going to be tougher than today was. If anybody wants to go back the way we just came, there will be no shame in that. We should all know what our capabilities are, and if you were stretched thin today, tomorrow will be worse. We will have a helicopter with a doctor on board overhead, just in case." Or words to that effect.

Heck and tarnation! When I was offered an all-expenses paid tour of the Baviaanskloof Wilderness Area, I hadn't expected this. But, as my civics teacher in high school liked to say, in for a dime, in for a dollar. Back then I could actually buy things with a dime, like two single- scoop ice cream cones or a Captain Marvel funny book. I'll stick it out.

* * * *

Our little group of 15 riders was down in the southern part of South Africa, Cape Province. I had skirted the Baviaanskloof some 30 years before without even knowing it was there. I still have a map from that trip, dated 1972, and while it shows the Baviaans Mountains, it would be another 25 years before the area was considered a national asset, and a prime tourist destination. The Wilderness now covers about a million acres, with two-thirds being publicly owned, the rest, private, the owners amenable to the Wilderness restrictions. If you can make more money milking tourists than cows, why not?

That first trip of mine was done under the auspices of apartheid, that benighted era when whites ruled the country and every other color was relegated to second- or third-class citizenry. I had planned on spending several months in South Africa, but after one week I realized that I could not abide the segregation. I was on my BMW R75/5 hustling along the coast road, called the Garden Route, from Durban to Cape Town to catch the next ship going to Australia. Back then some shipping lines ran passenger ships like buses, but instead of waiting a half-hour for the next one, it could be a month. But sea travel was inexpensive, and I could take the bike along as cargo.

I had been given the name of a third-generation English couple who lived in the seaside town of Knysna, and very hospitable they were. And willing to talk about the future. Their son was working in Cape Town, 300 miles to the west, but their daughter was going to university in England, and they were worried she might not return. Themselves, they could not see leaving, as they had never known anything other than this part of the world, but they also knew that it was just a matter of time before the Boer (Dutch-descended whites) controlled government would have to change its racist ways. And they just hoped that the transition would not be too violent. That did come about in the early 1990s, and while the road to integration has been rocky, it has generally been peaceable.

The next morning I bade my hosts good fortune and rode on to Cape Town and found that a Chandris ocean-liner would be arriving in three days, and I would be on my way to Australia. The fellow filling out my paperwork asked me how much my motorcycle weighed. "Four hundred pounds," I said. "Ah, how convenient," he said; "400 pounds is your baggage allowance, so we will take it as your baggage. No extra charge." Ships may be slow, but they are a lot more pleasant than flying and you can take a lot more luggage.

Since the end of apartheid I had been back to South Africa twice, and each time the place looked happier and healthier.

The purpose of the whole trip was for BMW to show these American moto-journalists just how good its two-wheeled SUVs were on the back roads.

Now I was on my fourth trip there, this time compliments of BMW motorcycles, which was introducing two new models, the sport-touring K1300GT, and the latest version of its two-wheeled SUV, the R1200GS.

Our little group of 15 consisted of eight moto-journalists and seven people from BMW, including the head of BMW's motorcycle division. After spending several days hurtling along well-paved roads on the GT models, we found ourselves one evening at an elegant resort on the coast with wonderful views over a manicured golf course and on to the Indian Ocean. The

Mandatory stop at the Cape of Good Hope with photo ops so we could boast that we had been there.

At one restaurant stop the owner appeared with a boa constrictor and asked if any of us would like to try it on for size; Clement volunteered.

This two-tracked road is in the middle of the Lelievlei Nature Reserve, where we stopped to look at spectacular views of the ocean to the south, the mountains to the north.

Knysna tourist board has grown fond of calling its little piece of paradise "The Garden of Eden" — though there is not an apple tree to be found. I had long ago forgotten the name of my host couple of some many years ago, so I could not see if they were still there.

At dinner we were told that we would getting on the GS models in the morning, heading for some rougher roads, and since the company had overspent its budget, we would be camping that night, but they would provide sleeping bags and MREs "Meals Ready to Eat" in military parlance. Which meant that all I had to do was to put my toothbrush in my pocket.

After breakfast we went outside into the beautiful dawn, and there, instead of our sleek road-going missiles, sat a long row of ultra-functional machines, with knobby tires to cope with the dirt roads, big gas tanks that could carry us 300 miles, and panniers to hold the clothes we would shed as the day got warmer. Bottles of water were handed out and stowed.

It was a truly gorgeous morning as we headed out of town, beginning with a few miles of pavement then turning inland onto a dirt road going uphill to the Lelievlei Nature Reserve. South Africans have realized that what they have long taken for granted, which is the natural bounty all around, is highly saleable to the eco-tourists. And eco-motorcyclists. At the top of the hill one of our guides was standing in the middle of the one-lane road directing us left onto a very narrow, very steep track. It was a tough go, maneuvering these 500-pound bikes up the gnarly path, but we all made it to a small grassy area at the top where we collapsed in relief and took out our bottles of water. And admired the splendid 360-degree view, with the ocean to the south, mountains to the north.

"This little excursion was a secret test," said our leader, "to see how you would cope with the rest of the trip. You all passed." Oh, good, I thought, I barely made it up here, and now they are promising more of the same.

We went back down to the road, another exercise in gnarliness. Then it was over Prince Alfred's Pass (named for a son of Queen Victoria who visited South Africa in 1867) and back to blessed pavement. Briefly. We stopped for lunch and then turned off the asphalt and headed into the Valley of the Baboons — a translation of Baviaanskloof. We had been told that the valley, between the Baviaans and Kouga mountains, was home not only to baboons, but also Cape buffalo, zebra, and leopards. As well as the African black-footed cat, a five-pound version of the big wild felines. However, I imagine that these sharp-eared creatures, hearing the exhaust note, albeit well-muffled, of 15 motorcycles, decided not to stick around, and the only critturs I saw were the occasional domesticated ones.

The dirt road was quite reasonable, although the occasional sandy spots caused a couple of riders to spill. We cheerfully

The Baviaanskloof was mostly dry, but when two rivers came together it was wet for long stretches, with no telling what was under the front wheel.

went about 50 miles, passing just a couple of farms which now seemed to function mainly as tourist havens. The road we were on had actually been built in the 1880s to allow farmers to get their produce to market over in Port Elizabeth, and from what I could tell, little maintenance had been done since.

Finally we came upon one of our guides parked beside the road, who pointed the way up a little track to the right — and some of the softest sand we had seen. After struggling through the sand we arrived at our campsite   but it was more like a Cecil B. DeMille epic than any campground I had ever seen. A dozen large tents were set up in a semi-circle in a big two-acre field, with hot showers and toilets off to the side. None of this cot business, but comfy beds in each tent — one tent for each of us overly pampered journalists.

Drinks were provided, including some very worthwhile local red wine, and then at the appropriate hour we trooped off to the farm headquarters, a half mile away. A sumptuous table had been set up under a huge rock overhang, decorated with aboriginal drawings of a thousand or more years ago. The best china, the best flatware, and four glasses at each setting for water and wine. We were introduced to our hosts, as well as to the pilot and doctor from the helicopter, which was parked in another field. Then we proceeded to do justice to some six courses, all brilliantly prepared.

This is what the BMW company considers roughing it, with Clement having a tent with a very comfy bed all to himself and hot showers just a hundred feet away.

After being surfeited we were advised about the toughness of the next day, and told to wait until morning to decide. Then it was back to the "campsite" to sit in comfy chairs around a huge bonfire, drinking snifters of good South African brandy, telling jokes and lies. And then to bed. Although one person about three tents away chose to snore loudly.

Morning, and four-wheel drive vehicles ferried us up to a hilltop chalet where we breakfasted while gazing out over the valley, as well as east towards a rather ominous-looking mountain. Two of our indomitable group chose to return the way we had come. No shame in that — bloody wusses. We did feel that the helicopter was more for the benefit of the BMW vice-president who was riding with us than for any of us lowly scribes who could be replaced in an instant.

The rest of us suited up and headed east. Where the Baviaanskloof and Kouga rivers combined, the greenery got very lush, and we had more water-crossings then dry road. Sometimes we would go for a hundred yards in foot-deep water, never quite sure what was beneath our wheels, kept in the right direction only by the thick vegetation of each side. We stopped for mid-morning refreshments in what was almost a semi-tropical forest, and congratulated each other on having made it through the water traps. Only to find what was worse ahead — a steady climb up the face of a mountain over broken rock, any notable vegetation rapidly disappearing. All the dirt had long ago been washed away by the seasonal rains, and all that remained was rock, sometimes solid and slippery, more often deceptively small pieces that slithered beneath our wheels. A little too much throttle, the rear tire spins, spits out a few stones, the bike slips sideways, and the rider (me) is looking down a very steep slope. The higher we went, the steeper the slope, the longer the fall. Not for the faint of heart. And I was certainly glad to have done training at an enduro school on one of these bikes the previous year. Up and up we went, and then came to a beautifully desolate plateau, the Bergplaas, covered with boulders and shrubs and what seemed to be stunted palm trees, with million-dollar views in every direction. I could imagine some wealthy South African trying to convince the local authorities to allow him to build a house up here — with its own helicopter pad.

On the far side of the Bergplaas we crossed over the 3770-foot Combrinck's Pass, the literal high point for our trip. But what goes up must come down, at least according to Isaac Newton, and we began our long, necessarily slow, descent to the Gamtoos River. Fortunately, this road was in far better condition that what we had just come up. Finally, to the bottom and blessed pavement once again. Our leader used his satellite phone to communicate with the helicopter and tell them that we were all safe and sound, and they could go home now.

It really was a stunning ride, and showed not only the aptitude of the motorcycles we would have to write about, but also one of the many hidden beauties of South Africa. I wonder what the trip would have been like on my street-going BMW back in 1974.

A happy rider is a rested rider, and Clement is undoubtedly both happy and rested — as anyone who has ever traveled with him knows. There are hundreds of photos from various parts of the world showing Clement napping along the way.

Soviet Union 1988

Flat, wet and dull was my opinion of the Ukraine after the first day on the road — and muddy. No wonder Napoleon's artillery and Hitler's tanks bogged down. The featureless land went on to the horizon, sodden and puddled, vast fields broken by occasional patches of woods and shabby villages, the sky grey and drizzly.

I needed a bathroom, or, better put, I needed to answer the call of nature. Public and most other conveniences were in short supply in the Ukraine. A muddy track went off from the pavement, between woods and field. I pulled off, parked the bike and retired to the privacy of the trees.

When I re-emerged, a motorcycle and sidecar were coming down the road and swerved onto my track, the rider's ancient greatcoat flapping in the wind, the plastic shell of a helmet (Soviet law required all motorcyclists to wear a helmet, but no standards for such a safety feature had ever been set) practically covering his eyes, and no gloves. It was a miserably cold, drizzly day, and he had to have some tough fingers. He saw my bike, and then me, and slammed on a brake, the three-wheeler slewing to a stop in a shower of mud. There was a definite advantage to the stability of a third wheel in these slippery conditions.

He stared at me, rough Slavic features giving no hint of interest, friendship, enmity — nothing.

I tried some friendly-sounding English words, like "Hi, how are you" and walked over, my boots squelching in the mud. "America," I said, tapping myself on the chest. That did not seem to get through. "A-mer-i-ca," I tried again, articulating the syllables. He looked at me through lowering eyes, pointed at me, and said, "America?"

Hey, we were getting along! This was 1988, the third year of glasnost (openness) and perestroika (restructuring), which concepts had yet to penetrate the hinterlands of the Ukraine, one of the 15 so-called republics that made up the Union of Soviet Socialist Republics. The then-head of the Soviet Union, Mikhail Gorbachev, thought that a little fresh blood within the Communist political framework would be good, hence his modest appeal for a bit of openness and restructuring amongst the government bureaucracies. His ideas would also allow for American motorcyclists to ride around and see for themselves what a great union this really was. Fortunately for the world, the appeal of this openness notion got away from Gorbachev a year later and his union collapsed.

On this wet day in the rural provinces a foreigner was still someone to be wary of, and democratic ideals were a long way off in the future. However, curiosity had obviously gotten the better of this Ukrainian chap, and he pointed at the motorcycle, a BMW K75. "America?" he asked.

I shook my head. "Deutscher," I said, and beckoned him to follow me. I showed him the license plate and the big D sticker on the fender that denoted to the constabulary of all European countries that the motorcycle was indeed registered in Deutschland.

He looked a bit perplexed, and pointed a finger at me, saying, "America," then at my bike, "Deutscher." Granted, his pronunciation wasn't too precise, but I got the drift. By now I was expecting to be invited home to meet the wife and kids and have a bowl of goulash, or at least for a trip to the local speakeasy for a shot of whatever and an introduction to his buddies.

I effected to admire his machine, which was a tawdry imitation of a German flat twin, circa World War II, very much like the Ural motorcycles now sold in the U.S. Except this would have come from the factory in the Ukraine along the Dnieper River, not the factory in Russia's Ural Mountains. In good Soviet industrial thinking, two factories producing precisely the same motorcycle were better than one factory, let alone two factories producing two different machines. The matter of choice did not figure large in the Soviet economic equation.

He obviously was not into mechanics, as he professed no interest in my liquid-cooled, fuel-injected, mono-shocked marvel of technology. I wanted to take a photo of him on his machine, and unleashed my camera with that intent. However, when I indicated that I wished him in the picture, too, he waggled his finger negatively in front of his face. I had to settle for taking a photo of his motorcycle alone.

Conversation was waning. He solved the problem by mounting his machine, kicking it into life, and taking off into the distance without so much as a wave, slipping and sliding the whole way. He disappeared from view. So much for meeting the family.

One thing I was fast coming to appreciate, after 70 years of Big Brother old ways died hard out in the Soviet boondocks. It just wasn't done to show interest in anything that didn't concern you.

I met up with my group in Lutsk late that afternoon. At the Intourist hotel, of course. We were a tour group of three dozen North Americans, with 24 motorcycles, a Mercedes sedan driven by Mike the tour director, and a VW van with most of our baggage inside. We had begun in West Germany (as it was then known), gone through Czechoslovakia and Poland, entered the Soviet Union at Brest, in Byelorussia (now Belarus), and were now heading for Kiev.

The Intourist guide, Helen of Kiev (center), instructing our group on preferred Soviet riding rules and regulations. In the background: As *pertroika* was loosening the economic restriction of the Eastern Bloc, an enterprising Polish capitalist bought a worn-out airplane and turned it into a popular restaurant.

The tour riders more or less gather in front of a bland Soviet tourist hotel in preparation for a leisurely departure in small groups — the lack of American's discipline made our guide very unhappy.

In Brest we had been joined by our mandatory Intourist guide, Helen of Kiev, a squarely built woman who obviously was accustomed to being obeyed. She had a sidekick, Andrei, whose main job was to rush off each morning before breakfast in his tin-can Soviet-made car and warn the police in the various towns along the route that a horde of motorcycles were coming through. Helen, a sensible woman, chose to ride in the comfortable Mercedes.

During dinner in Brest Helen instructed us that we should all leave in a group, stay in a group, and arrive at the next hotel in the group. The next morning the two dozen motorcycles left in one and twos and threes over a period of two hours; Mike allowed later that Helen was not pleased.

We had a raucous evening in Lutsk after the usual abysmal hotel meal. The kitchen staff obviously did not appreciate having to do the extra work that our group required, and did as little as possible other than ensuring that the meat and vegetables that eventually appeared were over-cooked. There was no joy in commercial Ukrainian cuisine. The town offered no entertainment, the hotel offered no bar, the rooms offered no television.

We took matters into our own hands; some entrepreneurial type on the staff sold us a very large jug of tomato juice, which was mixed with several bottles of vodka we had acquired at the border. Since the only chairs were on the landing where our floor warden had her desk, we congregated there and passed a fun-filled evening. We tried to interest the warden in a glass of cheer, but she gave us her most professional sour look and declined. After an hour of our jollity she gave up and stalked off. Probably to find and have arrested the poor person who had provided the tomato juice.

Breakfast was uninspired stale bread with even less inspired cheese, and after that was all eaten, a single cup of lukewarm ersatz coffee. It seemed to be a matter of principle for the surly staff to refuse to provide what we wanted when we wanted. The concept of good service, as has been noted time and again, was sadly lacking in an economy where the servant, public or private, had no incentive to do his job well.

Little villages we passed seemed to have escaped the worst of the Soviet authoritarianism, the places probably being too small to rile the authorities.

Again, Helen ordered us to leave en masse; again, we trickled out over a space of two hours. The hotel had packed us box lunches, and about noon a number of us were on the road that circled around a place on the map named Zhitomir. The town itself was, by Soviet standards, of military importance, and foreigners were not allowed inside without special permission. Which we did not have. The main road headed straight into town, and the bypass angled off at a road-block manned by many soldiers. Obviously Andrei had done his job well, as a military policeman stood out in front exercising his best "Turn Here" motions when my motorcycle approached.

The byway went through an unpopulated area, with heavy woods and fields, and then past a large retired gravel pit, which was now a series of small ponds surrounded by grass. It was noonish and sunny, and half a dozen of us stopped and investigated the contents of the box lunches. Boring bread, gristly sausage, processed cheese, and an orange were our fare. No champagne and caviar for us today.

A weak sun was trying to warm the place, and we were

cheerfully discussing the particular gastronomical pleasures of this trip, when four local motorcycles appeared, Soviet-made two-stroke tiddlers, each one with two young men on board. Nothing bashful about these fellows.

Obviously the word was out that a group of foreigners were having a snack on the outskirts of town, and they had come to see what profit could be made from such an occasion.

They weren't trying to intimidate at all, but this road was one of the few Intourist-approved tourist roads in the Soviet Union, so obviously they had had some contact with foreigners before. Several spoke a very few basic words of German. Our motorcycles, slick new German and Japanese models, did not interest them. Our clothes did. These fellows had a lot of rubles in their pockets, which they continued to show us, and they were willing to spend it for the clothes on our backs. And cameras and gloves and things like that.

There were two hitches to this. First, we needed everything we had. We all had one riding jacket, and if anyone sold it he would get cold in a hurry. Second, we couldn't use the damned rubles; there wasn't anything to spend them on, which was precisely why the boys were trying to buy our gear. We had to use hard-currency coupons to buy gas, and any hotel bar or souvenir shop would also require "real" money. There were few places to spend dollars, and no places to spend rubles: no nice cafes to order up some eggs and bacon, no liquor stores to buy some Stolichnaya, no shops with interesting things for sale.

In this alingual communication, the kids were persistent. But all they got out of their efforts were some pins and patches that some of the group had brought along to give away. Unabashedly capitalist were these boys, and having obviously had success before were a mite peeved at their failure with us. As we saddled up to leave there were no friendly waves of goodby, just sour looks of frustration.

In Kiev we were sequestered in a downtown Intourist hotel. Helen, who had chosen me as her confidant, was practically in tears as out motley crew dribbled in over a space of a couple of hours.

The Spasskaya Tower is the most visible part of the Kremlin in Moscow's Red Square — and the clock showed the official time in all of the Soviet Union, which covered nine time zones. Doubt that worked well.

The continued existence of St. Basil's Russian Orthodox cathedral in Moscow's Red Square is proof that Stalin was wise enough not to outlaw religion totally.

"Why cannot you be more like other people?" she asked. "Andrei was with another motorcycle tour this summer, and every morning they would leave together, and then in the evening they would arrive together. Why cannot you be more like that?"

"And what nationality were these other motorcyclists?" I queried.

"They were German."

"Helen, now you understand the basic difference between Germans and Americans. The Germans are regimented, the Americans are free."

"Some regimentation is necessary," she blustered, "for a society or for a tour group to operate. You are too unregimented. You must learn to do what I, the tour leader, say."

"No, no. The American way is that we pay you, and then you do as we wish."

The discussion could have gone on a long, long time.

Helen was obviously a Party member in good standing, with a good job. She enjoyed the perks that Intourist types had, and got to go on vacation to islands in the Indian Ocean every winter. She saw nothing, or would admit to nothing, seriously wrong with the way the Party ran things. Minor improvements could of course be made, but the basic system was all right.

The plan was to spend a night in Kiev, fly to Moscow for two nights, where we would see a few sights, admire some Czarist treasures in the Kremlin, take in the ballet, and fly back to Kiev to get our motorcycles. Which we did.

In Moscow when I complained, through sign language, to the floor warden at our flea-bag Hotel Belgrade that my one thin blanket would not be enough to keep me warm, she pointed to her cleaning-lady companion, who would have done any football team proud as a fullback, and signed that she would be happy to keep me warm. Raucous laughter. The Russians do have a sense of humor, though perhaps not particularly refined.

After an evening out soaking up culture, I did find two extra blankets on my bed.

At the airport next day I witnessed what I think of as the essential socialist-capitalist confrontation. Our little band of

339

Westerners had money to spend and there was a hard-currency gift shop on the concours. It was a small, glass-walled room, vastly over-staffed and under-merchandised. We went in and promptly cleaned the place out.

Then, because our plane was late (of course), we were led off to eat an inedible lunch. When we returned we found the four shop-girls restocking the shelves with all sorts of new tourist trash. Little wooden dolls that fit one inside the other; clumsily made little boxes with traditional paintings on the lid; pins and scarves and T-shirts with hammer and sickle emblems. Just the kind of junk one wants to take back to Aunt Agatha and Cousin Jimmy.

The materialist lust of many of our group had not been satisfied, but the door of the shop was locked. Inside we could see the staff leisurely unpacking box after box of souvenirs, just what these American men and women wanted. For half an hour our group was patient. Then they began to demonstrate to those inside that they really wanted to spend a lot of dollars and help resolve the USSR's foreign exchange problem, going up to the glass door and indicating on their watches that time was passing, and the plane might come.

The staff was not interested in the plight of these sordid capitalists. They knew that if they opened the door, the shelves would be swept clean, and they would just have to go back through the labor of restocking them. A bulging cash register would not make one iota of difference to their salaries.

After an hour our side was losing patience, and several people had their faces squished up against the glass, fistfuls of dollars at the ready. The staff activity demonstrably slowed, as if to prove that the Soviet system was superior to the American. I had visions of these irate consumers picking up a bench and smashing their way inside.

Fortunately, or unfortunately, the plane was called and we left. The collapse of the Communist State several years later came as no surprise to our group; they were just mystified that it had lasted as long as it did.

Back in Kiev, the group disposition was not improving. We seemed to be thwarted at every turn when it came to spending money: no souvenirs, no decent food, not even any local beer or spirits. When we went into the hard-currency hotel bar all they had was Heineken beer and Johnny Walker Red whiskey. We never did see a bottle of Johnny Walker Black, and political implications were drawn.

But the trip had peaked, and we were soon on our way West. Our next stop was at Rovno, where our VW van chose to expire with a broken engine. No problem, said the optimistic Mike, any mechanic anywhere in the world can fix a VW, using tin cans and baling wire if the necessary parts were not available. Except in Rovno. Not a mechanic in the city was willing to tackle the job. To the credit of Ukrainian talents, I was reasonably sure that the inability to fix the VW was a put-up job. If some local mechanic managed to repair it, the van would disappear back into Western Europe. If nothing were done, it would stay in Rovno, and eventually, after some bureaucratic machinations, reappear on the city streets patched up with bits of tin cans and suitable wire. Another tribute to the success of Communism over Capitalism. Mike did have to abandon the VW, squeezing the luggage into the Mercedes.

In the hinterlands of the Ukraine we could still find examples of the old wooden architectural style.

In Rovno we finally solved the local beer problem. Within an hour of arrival we had drained the last imported beer on hand, and the hotel send out for some local brew. A bit yeasty, but quite potable. And we still paid in dollars.

The next day, our last in the Soviet Union, was the best we'd had since entering the Evil Empire. It was bright and sunny, with beautiful panoramas and attractive old-fashioned wooden houses as we crossed the Carpathian Mountains. It was a small time-warp within the modern-day Ukraine, and a lovely one at that.

We rode down to the valley of the Uz River and the border town of Ushgorod. Nothing charming about that place. It had obviously been flattened in the last great war and completely rebuilt in socialist-modern architectural style. We put up at the inevitable Intourist hotel, and Helen laid on a great banquet for us, from caviar to chicken Kiev.

It was by far the most pleasurable meal we had had, and even the waiters, if not quite friendly, did not actively throw the dishes down in front of us. Wine and champagne appeared, toasts were done in vodka, and there were even dancing girls.

The Soviet society had proved to be prudish to a fault. Nothing even remotely resembling a naked woman could be found on a newsstand, though perhaps in back alleys seedy men offered filthy postcards. One exception was notable; if a statue were more than twice life-sized, bared breasts were acceptable, and heroic figures of noble women, standing 15 or 20 feet high, storming the barricades were to be seen in any city, stripped to the waist, wielding machine guns and bazookas. Though not nearly as comely as France's La Liberte.

At the hotel we were not about to be titillated to that degree, but the lights lowered and several harem-clad local ladies came forth. Breasts and buttocks were firmly defended by some sort of apparently bullet-proof material, but large expanses of large thighs were quite noticeable as they undulated about the floor. I muttered to the fellow sitting next to me, a proper Bostonian, that this show was quite risque by local standards. He harrumphed, "What do you expect from a sleazy border town."

The next day we prepared for the final run to the Hungarian border. Helen came up and asked if she could ride with me. We kitted her out with jacket and helmet and showed her how to climb up on the saddle.

Helen of Kiev kitted up and ready to ride pillion on Clement's motorcycle.

True to American form, many of our motorcyclists left when they wished, ignoring Helen's orders to travel in a group. The majority of bikes did go off with us, if only to see Helen on the pillion. Her short arms could barely meet around my waist, her wide bottom sitting like a duffel at the back of the saddle.

She seemed to love it, and when we all had to wait at a railroad crossing, while the rest of us stretched, she sat on the bike and held court. We were coming to like her, and she, us.

At the border we gathered en masse and the Soviet side did its usual bureaucratic, petty machinations until Helen collared the boss and must have read him the local equivalent of a riot act. Perfunctory stamping of passports then took place and we all made our farewells to our guide.

She told us, and I think with genuine feeling, that she hoped we would all come back, that she had found us very interesting. If a little bit fractious. Discipline was important, she concluded, and that is what America lacked. Other than that, we were a delight to be with.

Last seen, she and Andrei were standing side by side, waving at us as we moved off to the West.

Postscript: *In 1992 I received a letter from Helen, in which she inveighed mightily against the changes that were going on in what had been the Soviet Union. "No good will come of this," she wrote.*

Tanzania 1974

When traveling by myself, the question I was most often asked was: "Aren't you lonely?" In Asia and Africa family and friends generally take on more importance than they do in Europe and North America, where children are apt to leave the parental abode as soon as they can afford their own car. Or motorcycle. And I was certainly a prime example of this willingness to leave the known behind and face the unknown.

For me to arrive by myself, on a motorcycle, in some remote village was often the event of the day — or the week. If I had a companion, locals would be less likely to intrude; and if I had a VW bus, who knows what mischief I might have hidden under the back seat. Being alone, and on a bike with all my possessions easily viewable, was very non-threatening, and inviting conversation with the curious. When asked that question, I would respond: "Lonely? No. Look, I am talking with you."

Of course, there were sometime offers of companionship, be it a boy volunteering to be my unpaid servant, or a woman asking if I might like a temporary wife. Ah, yes, the distaff factor.

As is common with many of the spear side — the opposite to distaff — I enjoyed a number of transient and semi-transient "relationships" in my pre-marital years. The intelligent ladies who enjoyed my company would realize that I was not yet a "settling down" person, and when the time was appropriate, would kiss me a fond goodbye. Several times a less perceptive woman would tell me I had to make the choice — her or the motorcycle. She always lost. It wasn't my fault, but it seemed harder to find a good motorcycle than a good woman — that is a joke, by the way.

In a Tanzanian village I was offered a straight-across swap, a fetching young creature in exchange for my motorcycle. Barter is a perfectly acceptable way of doing business, to my way of thinking, and my BMW R75/5 was a handsome machine.

I pulled into a thatch-and-wattle community of a few hundred souls, looking for gas. Or petrol, as they called it. The local petrol station consisted of a 55-gallon drum in the back room of the only store. The shopkeeper's assistant cranked a handle, filled up a five-liter can, carried it to the bike, poured it through a funnel into the gas tank, and repeated the whole thing again.

The process attracted a crowd, which was only to be expected, as television had yet to come to blight the lives of these free-thinking folk. A prosperous-looking plump fellow, prosperous to the extent that his white shirt was intact, if not very clean, elbowed his way through the spectators, and announced that I should come to his house for a bit of refreshment after having replenished my fuel reservoir.

A good traveler always takes advantage of such impromptu invitations. There is no guarantee that a pleasant time will be had by all, and the social occasion can turn out to be excruciatingly dull, or embarrassing, or even dangerous. Or it could be an excellent adventure. As my semi-fictitious Aunt Agatha was wont to say about her gambling habit, "If you don't play, you can't hope to win."

By local standards, admittedly not very high, my host's establishment was proof of a successful life, with mud walls surrounding a little courtyard and a small house. An exhausted, crumpled wheel-less Land Rover sat on blocks in one corner of the courtyard, and beside it a very tired-looking Honda 90 leaned against the wall, so beaten and bashed and trashed that it looked more like a relic of World War I than a reasonably new motorcycle — it was probably less than five years old.

Dark faces peered from the windows. My host yelled something and two homemade chairs and a table were brought out. Me, I like an Adirondack chair, but such amenities were not to be found here at roughly latitude 6 South, longitude 33 East. The host excused himself, to come back in a few minutes with a slightly pleased smile gracing his round face.

We chatted idly about politics and religion, avoiding the stickier issues of Tanzania's economic decline at the moment. The man told me how much he admired my motorcycle, and what a beautiful machine it was, and he had a motorcycle, too, pointing to the dilapidated Honda, and was thinking of getting a newer, a bigger, a better motorcycle.

The social pleasantries included a benign interrogation. Where was I going? Why was I going there? How could I afford such a trip? And, cunningly, wasn't I lonely traveling alone?

An extremely fetching young lady appeared, trim, slim, and clothed in the omnipresent East African kanga wrapped around her hips, and a pleasingly sheer blouse. Bringing us tea and little meat-filled pastries, she positively radiated youthful good health and happiness; she adamantly refused to meet my gaze. A pubescent 14, I judged.

My host took note of all this in a sideways fashion. Very nice girl, no? he asked. Had I been in a larger town, I would have presumed that I had wandered into the local bordello, and that wares were being offered. This village was too small to support such an enterprise. But honesty being a good policy, I allowed as to how she was an attractive person, a credit to her community and upbringing.

Did I like her? Now the questions were taking on a distinctly personal tinge. I looked at him; he smirked. It is difficult to define or describe a smirk, rather like pornography, but when it happens, you know it. Something was up.

Why? I asked, preferring to front the problem. Directness was not exactly a local trait of renown, and my host was startled. But rallied quickly, as a good businessman should, and said that he would be willing to trade me the girl and his motorcycle for my motorcycle.

As a slave, I demanded to know, deciding that the mildly hostile approach was being called for.

No, no, he protested, as a servant, or perhaps a wife; I don't think he saw much difference between the two. Then I would have somebody to travel with me, to wash my clothes, to cook

Tanzania has some 20 national parks and conservation areas, of which Serengeti is the most famous. The authorities are acutely aware that to have visitors eaten by wild animals would not be beneficial to the tourist industry, so I had to see Serengeti with friends in a VW van.

On the other hand, the main road between Dar Es Salaam and neighboring Zambia went right through the Mikumi National Park, and no one minded what I rode or where I slept. I camped under a tree which was a noted lion haunt, but did not see a single one of the kitties.

my meals, to keep me company. He smirked again.

It brought a new angle to the age-old skill of horse-trading, except I did not need a new horse. I told him I had important business in the next country and that I had to get there quickly, which meant I could not be without a reliable motorcycle. He had the transportation theme figured out, swearing that the Honda had never failed him, and was more than adequate to carry two people plus baggage.

I didn't see any necessity of trying to force my Western values onto this gentleman, so I took refuge in the last resort of thieves and scoundrels — the bureaucracy. The lady obviously had no suitable documents for crossing international borders. I showed him my passport, and said it would take six months for my intended to get one. The problem of paperwork did have him bamboozled. I assured him, however, that were I ever this way again, I would surely stop by, and maybe reconsider the match-making offer.

Thanking the man for his hospitality, I rose to leave. He opened the gate to his courtyard so that the crowd outside could see him shaking my hand many times, saying loudly that we would see each other again. Over his shoulder I glanced at my unrequited love, who was looking quite beguiling. Straddling the bike I started the engine and went down the dusty street of a village I never knew the name of, riding off into the afternoon sun, a hundred children hooting and shrieking behind me.

I wonder what the US consular officer in Dar Es Salaam would have done had I showed up and asked for a passport for my new wife?

Many years later I did get married, and my bride brought along her own motorcycle as part of her trousseau. I still have the same bride, though her motorcycle has been upgraded a number of times.

Illustration by Gary M. Brown

Postcards sent by Clement often remained a mystery and undecipherable until he came for a visit — sometimes many years later.
And even then he couldn't always read his own writing.

Texas 1966

In the early fall of 1966 I bought a new Triumph TR6R, intending on riding down to Mexico. From Massachusetts an easy two-lane ride took me along to the Lone Star State. I woke up in a no-name motel somewhere in East Texas on a lovely Sunday morning; I had greenbacks in the wallet and not a care in the world. The engine of the Triumph was broken in and running well, the road was clear, and in a couple of hundred miles I would be at the Mexican border. Roast *cabrito* (young goat) and Dos Equis beer for supper. Little attention needed to be paid to the flat, straight road, and my thoughts wandered through various Texas-type subjects, like the size of the King Ranch, the size of the presidental ego (LBJ at the time), the size of our impending disaster in Vietnam.

Motorcycle thinking is different from car thinking. On a bike one has to remain alert, and the mind is always sharper, the thinking more constructive as a result; inside a car one becomes lulled into a false sense of security, reminiscent of that "Route 66" television series. Bang! An explosion! My thoughts were shattered. I was not crashing. I was not shot. The motorcycle was slowing. The throttle was not responding. I headed to the side of the two-lane road. We were stopping.

Putting the side-stand down, I lifted my right leg over the duffel bag bungied behind me and got off. I wondered as to whether or not I could define the problem. Coming from a family which considered a wheelbarrow to be sophisticated equipment, I was not a very technical person — but at least I had to make the effort. I knelt beside the engine and much to my surprise I could deduce the situation. A large hole was quite apparent in the front of the left crankcase. On closer inspection I could see the broken end of a connecting rod hanging down. A busted con rod poking through an engine case does make a hell of a noise. Whatever, it was clear I wasn't going any further that day.

US 59 stretched north and south of me as far as I could see, barbed wire and rangeland to both sides. Not a payphone to be seen, let alone a habitation. It could be a long day. Several cars and pickups rushed past, ignoring my angled thumb, heads turning to catch a passing close-up of this stranded motorcyclist. "Hey, Maude, guess what I saw today out on 59 . . ."

After an hour a two-door sedan, filled to the brim with a family, stopped. A fellow with a red neck got out, enquiring amiably as to my problem. I showed him.

"Victoria's only 15 miles down the road," he said; "there's a motosickle dealer there. I got some rope in the trunk. Think we kin tow ya?"

It sounded a lot better than waiting for a good Samaritan in an empty pickup. We stashed my gear in his trunk, then tied one end of the rope to his bumper, I held onto the other end after giving it a hitch around the handlebar, and off we went. With four kids leaning on the back seat, staring out the window. For a while they were slack-jawed, stunned at what their father had on the line. After a bit they began to make faces; I responded, though handicapped by my need to keep one hand on the handlebar, the other grasping the rope.

My savior took me right to the dealer, which was closed of course, being the Lord's day. The schedule in the window said the place was open Mondays. "Leave the bike here," he said, "it'll be safe. We got an honest town. Anyway, who'd want it now." He didn't have to chuckle, but he did. I couldn't blame him. Every man is proud of his own jokes.

The man regretted that he had only a small house, but he could offer me the sofa. Thanks much, but an inexpensive motel would do. I crammed in with the four giggling kids and got dropped off in front of an old-fashioned red-clapboard motel, twelve rooms all in a row. The sign advertised daily, weekly, and monthly rates; it was a cheap place, just what I was looking for.

The news the next day was good, and bad. By lunch the engine had been taken out and stripped. The problem originated with a defective connecting rod. The good news was that the shop would do the work under warranty. The bad news was that it didn't have any engine cases, nor, a phone call told us, did the Triumph importer in New Jersey; the cases would have to be ordered from England and air-freighted in. It would take at least a week. Maybe more.

Victoria was a nice town, but not really the sort of place I wanted to idle around for a week or more, eating up precious resources. I went down to a bar, or club as local drinking establishments were euphemistically called, and proceeded to honor that time-long tradition of drowning my sorrows.

After a while I was on a first-name acquaintance with the barmaid and I asked her if I she knew of any jobs. She was a pleasantly brassy peroxide blonde, who had seen 39 a few years back, with a cardboard brassiere poking at the pockets of her white cowboy shirt. Very Texas.

"You care what you do?" she asked.

"Nope. Anything."

A few minutes later a cut-off sort of fellow hiked on to the next stool. He may have been short, but his shoulders were real big.

"You looking for work?"

"Yup."

"Ever worked the oil fields?"

"Nope."

"Think you can learn?"

"Yup."

I had already learned that a third of Texans spoke non-stop, two-thirds used words parsimoniously. Handicapped by my strong Massachusetts accent, I decided that the laconic approach would be most suitable for me.

The deal was done. Sledge said he would pick me up at my motel at 4 a.m., and we'd head off to Beaumont, about 300 miles to the northeast. I left my motorcycle gear in care of the motel proprietor and at the prescribed hour I was ready. The horn tooted. I was off on a new adventure, never having imagined I would ever be working on an oil rig.

Sledge was driving his ten-year-old Buick; I put my duffel in the trunk and got in the back seat. Next to me was Art; next to Sledge was Red. When I shook Red's hand, it felt like all the bones were in the wrong places. They were.

We four made up a drilling team for one of the derricks of the Big Six Oil Company. The company sounded impressive, as anything with oil in its name sounded impressive, but Sledge said that it only had three old derricks. They were setting up one of the rigs in the Big Thicket north of Beaumont to tap into some natural gas. They knew the stuff was there after trying for oil in that place a few years back, but it wasn't until now that a pipeline had been built so the gas could be gotten out.

I dozed most of the way up, but Sledge occasionally gave a little bit of information as to what we were passing. "Bunch of bo'hunks live over there," he said at one point, jerking his thumb towards the west.

"Bo'hunks," I asked, "what are bo'hunks?"

"You know, Bohemians."

For a moment I had an image of a colony of artists out on the south Texas plains, but before embarrassing myself I realized he was referring to some Central Europeans who had probably immigrated a hundred years before, but still held on to their old names.

True Texans aren't much on sissified names, preferring Smith and Jones and Jack and Billy. They all agreed that they'd lose face having a Clement on their crew, and Clem was too damn hayseed, so they decided to call me Slim.

We checked into a low-bucks motel on the outskirts of Beaumont, two to a room, then went up to see the rig. We drove north for half an hour, the paved road running through thick brush. The asphalt was dotted with two-dimensional armadillos.

"Armadillos are born dead in the middle of the road," chortled Art, with a limited repertoire of bad jokes. Bad jokes are very much a Texas trait.

Sledge turned onto a sandy track, and the low-slung car pounded along, the sump and transmission smoothing the hump in the middle. After a mile we came into a clearing where half a dozen big trucks and a dozen men were finishing bolting the derrick into place, stacking up piles of drilling rod, making sure the motor was set. Off to one side stood a house-trailer; the drill boss came out.

I was going to learn fast. Once up, the rig would run around the clock, with three crews; it was the only way to make all this expensive hardware pay. The drill boss was always on site, and had responsibility for everything.

Sledge took me up on the platform and showed me the hole in the center of the rig. "This is where you work, Slim, with Art. You guys are the mudders, the holemen. Since you're cherry, you're the boll weevil; that's low man on this totem pole. I run the motor, Red's in the tower with the chain. We got the graveyard; we start at midnight.

"One thing to remember. This can be a dangerous place. We

got a saying, Let the iron fall. If something goes wrong, don't try to stop it happening, just get the hell out of the way."

Back at the motel I took a nap, dozing until Art woke me up. The four of us went across the road to a diner, where my three buddies were well-known. As they were in the bar next door. I was learning, but my Massachusetts accent kept the ladies at a distance.

At 11 o'clock Sledge said, "Let's go." We changed out of our clean jeans into the worst we had, piled in the car, and were off. Along the road, smack in the very middle of nowhere, we passed a roadside stand, fully lit, with a dungareed fellow sitting under the lights, contentedly chewing.

"Two bucks," said Red, and we each gave him two bucks. He came back out with bread, hotdogs, cupcakes and two quarts of milk.

I wasn't quite used to 24-hour drive-in grocery stores far removed from any sign of civilization, but that was the way of things in East Texas. The food was for our break.

On the sandy bit the headlights picked up a peccary, moving fast on its dainty hooves. Lots of animals out here, I was told, including snakes. Rattlesnakes.

The rig was lit up with big spotlights, but shadows were everywhere. We piled out of the car, put on heavy work gloves, and the previous crew took off. Crews were very independent. Each crew had different hangouts, stayed in a different motel. You knew your crew, and the boss man, but nobody else. Sledge would exchange a few words about problems with the previous crew honcho, and the same with the one that followed us, but that was it.

We were using 30-foot sections of drilling pipe, with a few dozen sections stacked upright by the derrick. Red, high up in the tower, would lasso a standing piece of pipe with a chain, Sledge would pick it up and move it over with the motor, Art and I would line it up with the previous section, Sledge would tighten things up, then start drilling. The motorman needed a deft touch with the clutch and throttle, and the tower man needed to be adept with the chain. Red, I was told, had once gotten his hand between the chain and the pipe, breaking just about every bone in it. This was a trait common to most tower workers; hazards of the trade, the oilfield equivalent of a Heidelberg dueling scar.

The drilling itself was a yawn. Sledge would set the throttle and the pipe would go round and round, with the drill bit eating away at the earth. It could take half an hour, an hour to use up a 30-foot section. In the meantime Art and I were stacking more pipe, making ourselves useful.

The fun came in the turn-around. That was when the drill bit got dull and needed to be replaced. If you were 300 feet down, that was ten sections of pipe which needed to be brought up, section by section, disconnected, stacked, and on and on. Three thousand feet, 100 sections. The drilling was easy, the turn-around was tough, and each crew prided itself on doing a quicker turn-around.

The first night was uneventful. About three o'clock we stopped for a 20-minute break to eat our food, putting mayonnaise on white bread and folding it over a cold hot dog; it tasted good. At eight o'clock the second crew came on and we were back in Beaumont by nine. Breakfast, to bed, get up in the evening, dinner at the diner, and then live it up a little, with no more than a couple of beers at the bar. It was pure common sense that nobody would go out drunk to work on the rig.

Nights two and three passed, and I began to fall into the routine — but the adventurous aspects of the job were wearing thin. I was glad knowing that I would not have to make a career out of this job.

On the fourth night we pulled all the pipe out, put a new bit in place, and I went to move a short, heavy-weighted section back over the bit. The trick was to shuffle the weight along the metal deck until it was in place, and Art would help me screw it on. Except it began to tip. Since it was just a short thing, about three feet tall, I made a move to stop it falling. Left-handed, stopping 100 falling pounds. Not a good idea, I thought, a bit belatedly as the sheer mass began pushing my hand down. I pulled my glove away, and by the time it hit the steel deck I was all clear except the tip of my little finger.

Crunch! I immediately righted the piece, brought it into position, and Art and I screwed it on. Then I took off my glove. The very tip of my finger, just half of the last joint, was about as thick as my driver's license. As thick as my fingernail, actually. Properly flat. Flatter than any of those armadillos.

I stuck my hand behind my back, not wanting to look at the mischief. Sledge came over for a look, blasphemed mildly, then trotted off the platform to rouse the boss man. Boss man came out with a clean towel, wrapped my hand, we got in his pickup and were gone.

Conversation to town was limited. He took me to the emergency room, gave the details to the nurse, and said he'd come by tomorrow. I was taken away, put on a gurney, given a dose of local anesthetic to numb my arm and dull my senses, and waited.

I was rolled around, moved onto an operating table, a sheet pulled up in front of my face, and, semi-comatose, listened to the quiet, competent voices of doctor and nurses. After a while I heard a nurse say, "We're about done, doctor; shall I write up the operation?"

"Sure."

A brief pause as, I imagined, she collected pen and paper, and the nurse asked, "What should I call it?"

"Amputation."

Jesus Christ to Glory! My left arm and chest had been secured with straps, but I rose up as best I could to rip away the sheet in front of me, to reveal what these blood-crazed, butchering beasts had done to me!

The doctor, a plumpish man with thin blonde hair and watery blue eyes, looked at me in surprise. My hand was still there, four digits visible, the fifth swathed in white bandages.

"What have you done?!" I cried.

"Very little," he said in the nasal East Texas drawl; "we just had to take off the very end of your little finger. Look at it as an advantage; you won't have to trim the nail any more." Texas humor. He left, taking his rustic bedside manner with him.

I was angry. An amputation without even consulting me.

What the hell did these backwater jerks think they were getting away with!? I fumed. But as one of the nurses pointed out while mollifying me, and reminding me that it hadn't been a very large amputation, to the doctor I was just some oilfield roughneck who needed some damage repaired. Roughnecks were not high on the list of those who should receive preferential treatment.

It was probably my first real experience with being a second-class citizen. I didn't like it. I hoped the doctor's Cadillac ran out of gas on the way home.

They put me to bed in a ward, and I slept through until lunch. Another doctor came to look at my little finger, protected by a metal hoop and wrapped in the whitest of bandages, and said I would be out on the morrow.

That afternoon the boss man came by to see how I was doing, wanting to make sure I wasn't going to sue Big Six. Not a chance; that was my fault. He said that Texas had a compensation board for just such accidents, and all I had to do was file my claim. He was followed by my crew, who stood around the bed and told me how stupid I'd been. In a friendly manner, of course. Red showed me his mangled right hand.

"Now that's an accident," he said, "had me in the hospital for three weeks. If I'da had what you had, they'da given me a band-aid and told me to get back to work."

They wanted me to come back. "We'll give you all the easy jobs," said Sledge; "won't hurt your little pinkie none."

Laying there on white sheets, listening to them joke and jibe, I was tempted. It was good ol' boy company, with lousy pay and bad working conditions, but a nice feeling of fraternity.

"Maybe. I'll call Victoria tomorrow," I said, "see how the bike's doing."

They left. I slept, woke, called, and heard that the shop expected the new cases the next day, and after that the engine would be back together and in the frame in hours.

I checked out of the hospital and took a taxi back to the motel. Art was sleeping. A call to the bus station told me there was a bus in the morning to Houston, and connections to Victoria.

The four of us went to the diner and the bar that evening, as usual. But the atmosphere had changed perceptively. I was no longer on the team. I was just a stranger hanging out with three buddies.

Shortly after 11 they all shook my hand and left. "Take it easy, Slim." "Write if you get work." "Send us some good tequila."

I'd be gone before they got back.

I sat with a beer and my bandaged finger, and two of the girls came over and sat down with me. It was a slow night.

"We heard you got hurt and was leaving. Wha'cha going to do?" one asked.

"Go get my motorcycle and head on south to Mexico."

"Wow! Mexico! I'd like to do that. I went to New'awlins once, and that was the best trip I've ever taken. But Mexico . . . ? My old man would never go for that. Too far, and too many furriners."

At 7 a.m. I was on the Greyhound.

I did file a claim with the Texas compensation board and months later got a check for $55: $15 for the loss of one section of one finger, $20 a day for two days loss of work.

Clement had no camera along on his Texas trip, but the Triumph did eventually make it to the Pacific Ocean – almost a year later.

Tibet 1999

Illustration by Gary M. Brown

There are three reasons to go ride Tibet: one, because you've had a fascination with the place ever since you were a child and your father gave you books with pictures of such places (that's me); two, you want to one-up your riding buddies ("Haven't seen you around the last couple of weeks; where you been?"); three, you're a masochist. Or you could be a secret agent on recon.

I love to travel, and must admit that the myriad of "organized motorcycle tour" companies have served to make traveling to exotic places much easier. There is a definite pleasure in letting someone else do all the arrangements — such as coping with the inevitable bureaucrats trying hard to justify their existence, exacerbated by the gargantuan Chinese government. Riding evil roads and suffering catastrophic breakdowns is nothing compared to the stultifying effort involved in coping with socialist paperwork, and here all that had been taken care of by an outfit called Lotus Tours (R.I.P.).

In 1974 I had been in Nepal on my BMW R75/5, and gone to the Chinese consulate in Kathmandu to request a visa to visit the so-called Autonomous Republic of Tibet. The Chinese, understandably, seemed singularly uninterested in having a lone motorcyclist wander through their hinterlands, as I was peremptorily told that I would have to make my request through Beijing. But here was an opportunity, and all I needed was money. When I asked the bank for a short loan, the bespectacled woman across the desk commented that if I should disappear in Tibet, she might have a hard time collecting the money from my miserable estate; my wife, who thought I should do this Himalayan expedition without benefit of spouse, co-signed. I'm not sure if she upped my life insurance as well.

So this short travel story is about riding across the Tibetan plateau and over the Himalayan Mountains from Lhasa to Kathmandu on an Indian-built Enfield Bullet 500, a somewhat less-than-modern machine. And it was a great trip, as close to a true adventure as any of these motorcycle tours have ever dared come; after all, "Bring 'em back alive" is the operator's motto, as dead clients are bad advertising.

Our two-wheeled trek took us over the aptly named "Roof of the World", the plateau's height averaging more than 14,000 feet above sea level, the road crossing a number of high passes, the tallest being over 17,000 feet — a tad higher than the highest road in North America. We followed hundreds of miles of muddy mountain roads, with holes big enough to swallow a Cadillac without a trace. Some days in the clear skies we could see a hundred miles in any direction, other foggy days we concentrated on avoiding the chasm on the edge of which teetered the slippery excuse for a road. At the beginning and end we had fancy hotels with luxurious bathrooms, in the middle we were in dirt-floored guesthouses with no running water. It was fun; not easy, but fun. And memorable.

Nine of us flew into Lhasa's airport, Gongkar, which happens to be some 60 miles from that austere provincial capital of Chinese-controlled Tibet. Our group consisted of seven affluent, middle-aged businessmen from Michigan, a 30-something dot-commer from Manhattan, and yours truly. And we were going to ride those 600-plus miles from Lhasa to the capital of Himalayan hedonism, Kathmandu, along the Friendship Highway. The term highway turned out to be rather a misnomer, as it more closely approximated a long series of mudholes going over the mountains, with dusty valleys in between.

And, I might add, that would be the longest 600 miles I have had the pleasure of riding.

The Michigan Seven, having garages bulging with Harleys and Ducatis and other pavement-oriented machinery, had originally planned to go to the south of Spain for their annual motorcycle extravaganza, when at the last moment the fellow in charge of organization heard about this Tibet trip and changed all the tickets. He claimed to have notified the others, but there seems to have been some disagreement about that; one gent looked around him at the godforsakenly desolate Lhasa airport and said, "Where the hell are we? This doesn't look like Marbella." The dot-com dude thought that the trip would be a good boast, and his tooling around New York City potholes for ten years on a BMW obviously made him qualified.

We idled away a couple of days in 11,500-foot Lhasa getting adjusted to the altitude, as we would spend a week well above 12,000 feet. And learned the all-important drill involved in kick-starting our 500cc Bullets as well. These ultra-utilitarian overhead-valve singles have been around since 1948, and not much had changed in 50 years. Our machines came with four-speed gearboxes, a compression release, and a manual spark-retard on the handlebar. If done according to instruction, the engine usually fired on the second or third kick. If done wrong, and the carb flooded and the spark plug soaked, that could be a problem.

Lhasa was quite different from the illustrations of my bookish childhood. After marching into Tibet in 1951 the Chinese have tried hard to eradicate the Tibetan culture — as well as revamp the city. Where there was once a medieval collection of temples and monasteries and houses and markets, with little winding streets, everything overshadowed by the magnificent Potala

Our group posed for the obligatory photo in Lhasa with the Dalai Lama's old home, the Potola Palace, in the background.

In Lhasa the Chinese police were making full use of their sidecar rig, carrying four officers to a doughnut shop.

Palace, there were now broad socialist boulevards and shoebox-ugly low-rise buildings.

But the Potala is still a sight to behold, soaring hundreds of feet up the Red Hill, a thousand rooms hidden inside its towering walls. This is supposed to be the home of the Dalai Lama, the leading political/religious figure in Tibetan life, but since his abrupt departure in 1959, to avoid the Chinese, the place has become a rather bleak museum. For a better look at urban Tibet, a mile or so from the Potala is the Barkhor district, where what remains of the old way of life in Lhasa is to be seen. The centerpiece is the Jokhang temple, the holiest spot for Tibetan Buddhists, full of monks and worshippers, with the permeating smell of incense and yak butter candles.

I advise the visitor not to try to understand Tibetan Buddhism, unless he has a lot of time to put into the study; it is full of buddhas and bodhisattvas and a great many revered lamas and other historical figures. Imagine a Tibetan coming into the Vatican for a visit, and trying to make sense of all the pictures and statues of Jesus and archbishops and the myriad saints. Just enjoy the aesthetic, as these Tibetan temples and monastaries are superbly beautiful.

After two days we got the 6 a.m. wake-up call, departure at seven. The journey was beginning; our troupe was more reminiscent of a D-Day invasion than a motorcycle trip: running point was our American tour leader, then the nine "clients", with the sweep done by a second American on the 11th motorcycle. We were followed by a 4WD Land Cruiser with a driver and Tibetan guide #1, and a bus with driver, guide #2, three mechanics from India with trunks full of spares, and our baggage. At the rear was a truck carrying our supply of gas. In other words, we had 10 staff for our group of nine — the way things should be in the world of luxury. Or in this case, the lack of luxury.

Day 1 would be a long day, 160 miles over the Kamba (15,820) and Karo (16,648) passes. Not that our leader wanted to go that far, but there were simply no towns to stop in along the way. We thumped out of Lhasa on the pavement, crossed the Brahmaputra River, and soon the pavement ran out. We began our 600 miles

Tourism is everywhere; on the first mountain pass after leaving Lhasa, the Khamba, at a lowly 15,800 feet, an industrious woman had set up this photo-op. It worked well; even one of our jaded motorcyclists couldn't resist a souvenir saddle-up on her well-decked out yak.

If one chose to explore the countryside off the main "highway" one could find some rather basic bridges — albeit strongly built.

of dirt, dust, mud and slush with a 4000-foot climb up to our first pass. The way was rough, but well-defined, the biggest worry being the mudholes that the occasional trucks had gouged out. It was a damp day, and had rained the night before; Tibetan dirt makes world-class mud.

At the top of the Kamba Pass our dot.commer, looking a bit blanched, said it was a good thing we were all experienced motorcyclists. I never saw him again. I went off ahead to take photos, and told our leader I would stop and wait in 20 miles. Apparently the dot.commer was on a straight stretch of road beside a lake, dipped into a large mudhole, powered out, but mud was covering his faceshield. Right ahead of him was a narrow bridge, but being a few degrees off course he missed it entirely, plunged into a creek, and knocked himself senseless. Fortunately the crash was witnessed by a rider behind, otherwise he might have been down in the little ravine a long time. The Michiganer pulled him out, and he was ambulatory but pretty beat up. He chose to return to Lhasa in the Land Cruiser and fly home — where he was diagnosed with a broken vertebra. The bike continued in the bus..

We spent a night in Gyantse, which has a magnificent fort sitting high on an unassaultable hill. At least until a small British expeditionary force, armed with modern rifles, arrived back in 1904, routing the musket-equipped Tibetan army and eventually forcing the 12th Dalai Lama to open his country to western trade. Though in the end no merchants ever felt it was worth their while to haul their goods across those mountains. In 1906 China and Britain signed an agreement officially placing Tibet in the Chinese sphere of influence, which document Beijing capitalized on 45 years later.

We then motored on to Shigatse; it was a dry day, and dusty — dusty enough that when a truck passed in the opposite direction, I could not see and had to stop. I made a small request of Lord Buddha to provide an early-morning light shower to quell the dust. Which I was not soon to forget.

Shigatse is the second largest town in Tibet, but at 13,000 feet has no airport. It is also home to the Panchen Lama, the

Yaks are greatly valued for milk, meat, and work, so when they go out to the fields the owner proudly dresses them up.

second most powerful man in Tibet; the Chinese thought they had this dude all bought and paid for and in their political pocket, but when we passed through he had been showing a very disconcerting side (insofar as Beijing is concerned) by praising the Dalai Lama. He has got nice digs in Shigatse, the roofs of the monastary buildings being done in shiny gold(!?) leaf, visible from ten miles away.

Here is your precis of Tibetan history. About 1300 years ago Tibet was a monarchy, but the king got swept up into this new-fangled Buddhist religion and decided that holy men would be better leaders then the drinking, wenching, carousing royal family. Over the next 500 years Tibet slowly evolved into a theocratic state, and gently bumped along into the 20th century. Occasionally Mongols would invade from the northwest, or Han Chinese from the east, but these interlopers would eventually get cold, suffer from the altitude, and go home. In 1949 the Communists took over mainland China, and in 1951 occupied Tibet, using that 1906 treaty with the Brits as a pretext, and declared it an integral part of their country. The tiny Tibetan army did not stand a chance. Eight years later the 14th Dalai

Lama snuck out and set up a government-in-exile in the Indian Himalayas — one reason the relationship between China and India has always been a bit rough. Then Beijing sent a few hundred thousand Chinese "volunteers" to settle in Tibet, and has assiduously been trying to Sinify the country over the past several generations. And, to a great degree, succeeding.

The food has also been, to a great degree, Sinified. We were not going to starve to death on this trip, but the food had a sameness about it that would soon wear thin on the old palate. We would sit at round tables, with a large lazy Susan in the middle, on which would be half a dozen small savory dishes all cooked in gallons of sesame oil — yak meat and bean sprouts, tofu and greens, chicken and veg, scrambled eggs and tomatoes — and in the middle a big pot of rice, and a big pot of soup. Breakfast, lunch, and dinner.

Occasionally we ate Tibetan, but that was mainly doughy dumplings called mo-mo, or a barley-based gruel called tsampa, or industrial-strength chapati-like bread. This was not a gastronomically inclined adventure. We grew to love the occasional plastic bowl of instant noodles — just add hot water and wait three minutes.

Back on the road, we slogged our way wetly up to Tso Pass, at nearly 15,000 feet, the narrow road a slick carpet of slippery mud. Lord Buddha was taking my request for early morning showers a little too enthusiastically. Tricky going, especially when it came to overtaking some truck grunting along at 6 mph, and we would have to dash(!?) along the shoulder while praying that the tires not lose their tenuous grip. I was roundly chastised by my companions for having had the temerity to ask for a damp day, and told that if I could not rectify the situation myself, they might use me as a sacrifice to placate the weather gods; dust was preferable to disaster.

At Lhatse the road split, one branch going to western Tibet, the other southwest to Nepal. This small town consisted of two rows of low, neo-socialist buildings facing each other on the main street. The leading, non-AAA-approved guesthouse put us in rooms on the second floor, with a common toilet at the

When a Tibetan Buddhist is up at over 17,000 feet like at Gyatso Pass he tends to leave a prayer flag behind, just to help his descent; Clement is contemplating kick-starting his Bullet at that altitude.

A flat tire gets repaired by the Indian fix-it crew traveling in the bus behind us, and attracts a few Tibetan locals as well.

A few of the boys are stopped at the La Lung Pass, at a mere 16,800 feet, to take a breather in the rather thin air.

end of the long corridor, carpeted years ago in bilious green; no running water, and very weak electicity for 90 minutes after dusk. At the restaurant on the first floor all the locals came to stare at us through the windows; we were the month's major entertainment.

Out of Lhatse we began our climb to the Gyatso Pass, attaining our highest altitude at a commendable 17,213 feet. It was a dry day, but leftover rainwater filled many a large hole and had soaked the countryside. The Bullets were okay as long as one did not miss a shift at a crucial point, leaving the rider sitting in neutral in a foot or more of mud at the bottom of a crater. At the top was a light covering of snow and our view was reduced to several hundred yards due to fog, but ten thousand multi-colored prayer flags placed by thankful Tibetans fluttered from the cairns and poles. Then we had to kick-start the Bullets, no mean chore when our oxygen intake was about half that of normal.

One could think that at 17,000 feet we might have had a downhill jumpstart, but the road was deep in sticky mud.

And I soon found out why all the prayers. My *Lonely Planet* guide to Tibet told me that ten miles further on were "Terrible roads 5 km either way." How true, if somewhat understated. I began the descent, and after a few miles rounded a corner and there in the narrow valley some 30 trucks and buses were faced off, nose to nose, victims of a small broken bridge and a truck that had half slipped off the single-lane track and gotten itself stuck good and proper. It was a mess, and half a dozen 4WD vehicles had tried to bypass the situation and gotten themselves bogged down in seriously slippery mud. But the Michiganer in our lead took one good look at the situation and figured that since we were headed downhill, we stood a chance of getting through. He hurled his motorcycle into the muck, spinning and churning and howling and sliding, but all the time making forward progress as he circled around the bridge and at last reclaimed the road. And we all followed his good example. I have no idea how our bus and truck drivers made it through, but they did.

The road smoothed out as we headed into Tingri, a village on a broad plain lying 14,500 above sea level. And from here we could see the central Himalayan massif, with Chomolangma (a.k.a. Mt.

Some riders stopped on the Tingri Plateau to get a shot with Everest behind them; Everest is not the big mountain, but the clouded peak to the left, much further away.

We did not take the turn-off to the Chomolangma National Nature Preserve, which is on the Tibetan, or Chinese, side of Mount Everest.

Clement after a hard day on Tibet's Friendship Highway; one look at his legs is ample evidence of having been through a lot of slippery-as-snot mud. And his face seems to indicate he has had enough fun for the day.

Everest) visible some 60 miles to the south, nearly 15,000 higher than we were.

To set the nomenclature straight, George Everest (1790-1866) was head of Great Britain's Great Trigonometrical Survey back in the first half of the 19th century, as well as Surveyor General of India, and did do his best to map the Himalayas. In the 1860s his successor thought it would be nice to honor him by giving his name to the world's highest peak. Since nobody who lived near the Himalayas had the foggiest notion who this Everest guy was, most sensible people thought the indigenous name would continue to be far more appropriate; Chomolangma, transliterating pleasantly to "Goddess Mother of the Universe", is how the locals refer to the mountain.

We put up at Tingri's Ho Ha Guesthouse, a lovely rustic place with well-swept dirt floors and an open-air toilet on the roof; one did get a superb view of the not-so-distant Himalayan ridgeline while attending to one's eliminations. A stove in the dining room kept the water hot and the gamblers warm; there was little to do in that village other than admire the mountains or play dominoes for money.

Morning was suitably cool; although we were on roughly the same latitude as Daytona Beach, Florida, we were some three miles higher. We rode out of town, across the plain and up a long, gradual valley, with the road climbing and climbing and climbing to the top, the La Lung Pass at 16,809 feet. Followed by a dip and then another pass, the Tong, at 16,796 feet. From there a steepish, twisting descent alerted us to the possibility of rapid reincarnation if we were foolish enough to run off the minimalist road.

The valley broadened with villages, yaks ploughing and children herding flocks of sheep and goats. And then the valley narrowed, the road hugging the hillside while a river roared and tumbled not far below. Finally we rounded a sharp curve to see the skinny town of Nyalam (12,375 feet) stretched out on the far side of the river; when the Chinese want to build ugly, they can do a superb job, everything a dreary grey with nought but right angles and small windows.

On this trip, Clement wasn't the only one to take a quick snooze when given a chance. With the China-to-Nepal border crossing ahead it meant all tired travelers could take a brisk nap while the boss handled the paperwork.

The bridge over the Botakoshi River is the border between China's Autonomous Republic of Tibet and Nepal, and there is alway traffic and trade.

We stayed at the Snowland Hotel, a concrete block with a loud disco below and howling dogs all around all night. With dinner on the inevitable lazy Susan. This would be our last night in Tibet, and our leader allowed as to how tomorrow's descent from the plateau would be one humdinger of a ride.

Which it was. The Bhotakoshi River plunges off the plateau and the road does its damnedest to stay with it. The steep, twisting descent was fraught, just plain fraught, with lethal drops off the edge of the road, huge pools of mud, the occasional waterfall to ride under — all the stuff of a good James Bond movie.

Down and down we went finally winding into the border town of Zhangmu, where a hundred trucks were waiting to get through to Nepal. The town is built on a 30-degree slope and the narrow road somehow zig zags down through it, two-thirds taken up by an unbroken line of parked trucks. We passed a checkpoint, and descended a further five miles down to the bridge over the Bhotakoshi and the actual border. Since our baggage bus could not get through the congestion, another truck was organized to come up from the bridge, have the bags portered from bus to truck, truck returned to the bridge, and the bags were again transferred to a Nepali bus. Good thing for the bottom line that labor was cheap.

From the bridge we bumped along for 20 miles through Nepali mud, and then found pavement. Blessed pavement! And we roared up to the hill station of Dhulikal and a very well-appointed resort with hot showers and a Swiss chef. Say goodbye to that lazy Susan!

The final day on the road was a short, if complicated one, as the road led us out of the hills and into the traffic-jammed Kathmandu Valley. We were warned that if we lost sight of the person in front, we could be lost in the maze of roads for two days. But we all arrived at the Shangri-La Hotel.

The trip was over. This little journey was no bed of roses, no five-star extravaganza; this was an adventure. And a good one. And I, for one, am very glad to have seen a little of vanishing Tibet, rather than to have never seen the place at all.

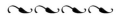

Tibet 1999

A trip to remember.

A prayer to return.

Viet Nam 1970-71

This photo of a pair of oxen pulling a cart, taken in the Highlands of Viet Nam, shows how traditional ways of life existed ... even with all the paraphrenalia of modern warfare just over the horizon.

Sunday, out for spin on my 150cc Vespa, Sally and I were heading back to Saigon at the end of a little day trip in the countryside, 30 miles at most, having had lunch with a friend who worked in a nearby town. We rolled along the much-abused two-lane asphalt through an ill-tended rubber plantation, then came into a small sleepy village. A few dozen houses were set back from the road about 30 feet, with all the shops closed on this day of rest. A cart pulled by a water buffalo was crossing the road. I slowed, shifted down, down again, came to a stop in neutral, the cart moved out of the way, I pulled in the clutch and something snapped. This was when the clutch and shifting mechanism were all on the left handgrip.

"What's wrong?" asked my passenger.

"Something broke."

So here we were, two round-eyes broke down in a village probably 15 miles outside of the city. With maybe two hours of daylight left. An elderly man who had been dozing on a rope bed got up and came over to introduce himself fortunately we both spoke French. "This is not a good place for you to be when night comes," he allowed.

Anybody who read the book or saw the movie *The Quiet American* can relate.

* * * *

Viet Nam was my generation's war, so I didn't want to miss it. Not that I had any notion that it was a good war, or even a sensible war, but I was very curious as to what this war was all about. The military aspects of Viet Nam had begun emerging in the American press while I was a freshman in college, had swollen discreetly under the Kennedy presidency, and had gotten blown out of all proportion to its importance by Johnson.

This book has stories about travel and motorized two-wheelers, and Viet Nam involved both, though sometimes the travel was compliments of the US Government, as was the Vespa motor scooter.

In truth I had long been interested in Viet Nam. When I was a wee sprat of a dozen years my father had worked for a year at NATO headquarters in Paris, and I had been banished to a boarding school in the French countryside. The most romantic figure in the place was an older Asian boy who had his own bodyguard; a son of Bao Dai, Emperor of Viet Nam, I was told.

I never talked with him, just remembered how dashing it was to have your own bodyguard. As Indochina became a divided Viet Nam, plus Laos and Cambodia, I imagined I had a personal interest, albeit somewhat distant, since I had gone to school with the son of the ex-emperor. The French bailed, the Americans came in. Eisenhower had underwritten the last years of the French presence and then supported the subsequent Diem regime, but quietly and discreetly. Kennedy was a different story; the Russian commies had smacked him a good one by building the Berlin Wall, and then the Cuban commies had hit him even harder with the Bay of Pigs fiasco. That's a lot of face to lose, as an Asian might view the situation. The Vietnamese commies weren't going to get away with anything, so he put in a lot of "advisors" to train the Diem troops in how to fight the commies. Late in 1963 Kennedy might have been deciding to disengage from Viet Nam, not wanting to get into a combat role, but history, as we know, took a different tack.

I decided to take a break from college and do my military service; this was in the early sixties, when JFK had just given his blessing to the Green Berets. Liking the look of the beret I volunteered, went through training, and was assigned to the 10th Special Forces in Germany. A lot of my colleagues had already served in ex-Indochina, with rare tales to tell.

I got discharged, finished college, and went traveling. In '66 I was in Nepal with a friend from army days who was working in a camp for Tibetan refugees. Originally our plan had been to go back to Europe from Kathmandu, but on the map we saw we were close to where the action was.

"Let's go see what all this noise is about," I suggested, and after a few minor adventures we found ourselves deplaning at the Saigon airport. This was the beginning of the Pentagon's effort to privatize warfare, and a quartet of American construction companies had bid themselves a billion-dollar job; however, they were hard put to find the warm bodies to fill the slots. We walked off the plane and into the arms of Raymond, Morrison-Knudsen, Brown-Root and JJ Jones, "biggest construction combine ever created." More popularly known as R-M-K, B-R-J, M-O-U-S-E.

My buddy and I had both been demolition specialists in the army, and he got sent off to honcho a gang of quarry blasters. I thought that was to be my line, too, but somebody saw "Harvard" on my application form and decided I would do better in the public-relations department, a decidedly curious concept in the midst of this war-torn, strife-ridden, guerrilla-infested society. PR is all smoke and no fire, and my job seemed to be to throw up smokescreens to conceal the incompetence of my employers. This was the year of the big US build-up, and everybody was in on the hustle. Privatizing war meant there was lots of money to be made, and to heck with the people getting killed.

Entire floating villages exist along the rivers of Viet Nam, with hundreds of families living in boats; sanitation was a trifle questionable.

This was net fishing in the Bay of Nha Trang, with a couple of dozen men rowing out to spread the net very, very early in the morning, then everybody working together to pull it in later.

I was getting paid extremely good money, tax-free, so I went to the Saigon office of an ex-GI who was in the business of selling cars. Any Spec/4 could order up a brand new Dodge hemi or big-engined Corvette and it would be waiting for him back home when, and if, he stepped off the plane. Boy oh boy, it was almost worth spending a year in the jungle. He also sold motorcycles, and I was interested in the new Honda 450. For delivery in Saigon. "Don't do it," he said. "You bring this bike in here, and for a week, a month, you'll be happy cruising Tu Do. But then will come the day you'll want to go a little further, and you'll go out in the country. And you'll do it again. And some day you'll get snatched. Pick it up at home. Don't use it here."

I took his advice and didn't buy the bike. I could walk to work and had a company car anytime I needed to go anywhere. Like to our infamous training site. RMK-BRJ had contracted to build a huge place where the locals — i.e. Vietnamese — could learn the subtleties of aerating concrete, grounding electrical transformers, and routing indoor plumbing. We were hiring lots of Koreans and Filipinos with these skills (learned from a long American presence in their countries), but the Vietnamese didn't know welding rod from re-bar. We were going to teach them.

A Navy officer from accounting came by my office one day and wanted to see how we were spending the Navy's money, specifically, how the construction on the training site was going. Everything RMK did was under Navy contracts, and his office made sure the Navy was getting what it paid for. Except they weren't. Entire convoys of RMK supplies would disappear, the contents of whole warehouses vanish from one inspection to the next.

On the outskirts of a steadily growing Saigon we found our training site — the skeleton of a building, with four floors of rough concrete and rusty ends of re-bar sticking out all over. The land it sat on was overgrown with weeds, the weeds surrounded by a barbed-wire-topped cyclone fence. Work had stopped months ago. Somebody hadn't been paid off, and the project had come to a halt. It was no longer a matter of finding the right recipient for the bribe, as the whole affair had become so confused that nobody seemed to know how to get the construction under way again.

The only happy person was the elderly Vietnamese watchman, who had built himself a comfortable hooch and was hoping this job would drag out for a long time. He locked himself and his dog inside and let the world outside go its own way.

We stared at this monument to incompetent bribery, and the Navy guy confided that this structure was barely noticeable in the figures. "We have over $80 million dollars in equipment unaccounted for," he said; "everything from boxes of blueprint paper to D-9 Caterpillars. This place is a disaster, and nobody cares."

It was a stupid war, stupidly conceived, stupidly fought. It was quite obvious to me, back then in 1966, that the Americans would eventually admit they could not win. It was just a matter

The US Government saw fit to issue Clement an International Harvester Scout for his transportation around Pleiku Province; in a pinch he found he could fit up to 12 people inside — and frequently had to do so.

Clement is trying to convince some Montagnard leaders that the Vietnamese government will provide food when their villages are relocated . . . or he will fill in the gap. The traditionally peaceful Montagnards, native to the mountains of Viet Nam , were there long before modern-day Vietnamese arrived from southern China and generally had a pacifist, merely self-defensive role during the war.

of time. It was a depressing thought; I quit the job and went back to the US with my ill-gotten gains and bought a new motorcycle.

To justify my existence I applied to graduate school to get a Master's degree in Southeast Asian studies, paid for by the GI Bill. Then I joined the US Department of State — and for my first assignment I was headed back to Viet Nam.

"Be happy to go," I said, "if you don't mind having someone who is acutely aware that we will eventually lose."

"Not at all," said the man in charge, "you might be just what we need." Nice words, but both he and I understood that reality and the White House were not on speaking terms.

Nixon did not want to take the rap for "losing Viet Nam", so the White House had developed a silly policy called Vietnamization: let the GSDs (gooks/slopes/dinks — as the locals were sometimes referred to by the irreverent American military) do it for themselves, while Americans advised them — just as Kennedy had done seven years before. Americans were very, very slow learners.

In mid-1970 I found myself beginning an 18-month tour in that rather pleasing country — if one could avoid the war. I would advise the Vietnamese civilian administration. First I did it on the district level, which was actually rather fun. Since I was reasonably competent in the French language, not Vietnamese, the powers saw fit to assign me to the Central Highlands, where a number of the native Montagnards spoke French. I was posted to Le Trung, the biggest district in Viet Nam, in Pleiku province; the country had 44 provinces, rather like American states, and these were subdivided into some 250 districts, like counties.

I lived in half a trailer in a mud fort with seven American soldiers and some 200 local troops. I would spend most of my days driving my institutional-green 4WD International Scout to friendly villages, enjoying a drink or three of rice wine, and talking about problems with the local chief. I had an interpreter along when at a loss for words. My arrivals were appreciated, as I always had something I had scrounged to give them, whether it was a sack of rice, a case of soda, or a box of bullets for their self-defense force.

Việt Nam 1971 - 1972

The overly-tall American civilian advisor became known as Ong Rau (Mr. Beard), which was a lot easier to say than Ong Salvadori.

The fellow in the short-sleeved blue shirt, Duc, was Clement's primary interpreter in Pleiku, speaking English, Vietnamese, and several Montagnard dialects.

Relocation time is never fun, as it means having to move an entire non-combatant hamlet so that the area could be a free-fire zone — which military types love.

After three months I moved up to the provincial level, where I soon became unpopular amongst the other Americans, civilian and military, for stating unfortunate truths. The White House wanted proof that Vietnamization was working, so every bit of information from the field was funneled through the embassy, which made sure only the positive aspects got sent across the Pacific Ocean. My provincial-level colleagues wanted only to do their tours of duty and get out of there, usually with a promotion if everything sounded good.

That was the great mistake of the war; probably every round-eye who worked in Viet Nam understood the truth, but nobody voiced it. Had the ranking military and civilians been told that they were there for "the duration," rather than a year or two, it would have been a very different war. We would either have never gotten involved in the first place, or have won it.

Thousands of mid-level American bureaucrats and military compromised their principles by serving in Viet Nam. They did not agree with the war, did not see any possibility of winning it, but if they were sent, they kept their mouths shut and justified it by saying, "This is what you have to do when you work for the government." They should all wake up in the middle of the night, every night, in a cold sweat. After another three months I found myself reassigned to Saigon. Big city. Big city problems — like too much traffic.

The bunch of round-eyes I worked with in Saigon was supposed to be advising the South Vietnamese Ministry of Land Reform on how to reform the land ownership system. The American thinking was that if every Vietnamese farmer got title to his own bit of land, he would love the government and hate the communists. The US embassy had been pushing this line of thought for years, and in a suitably oriental way, so as to neither hurt our feelings nor get land-ownership reformed, the Vietnamese had set up this ministry.

My job, if I chose to accept it — if not, I could catch the first flight home — was to serve as the American advisor to the Director of the Office of Public Information of the Ministry of Land Reform. Our ostensible job was to work out a plan by

When a
Montagnard
hamlet was
relocated just a
short distance, the
men would carry
the roofs of their
long houses to the
new site.

If you want rice
flour, you have to
make it yourself.
This hardwood
mortar and pestle
system was labor-
intensive but quite
effective.

Preparing a meal
in a Montagnard
relocation site was
generally a family
affair. Poor diets
resulted from the
constant upheaval,
as is apparent
by this little boy's
distended stomach.

which we could inform all the farmers that if they appeared at the right office on the right day, they would no longer be tenants of the land they tilled, but owners.

The American offices were in a high-rise, hermetically sealed, air-conditioned building that functioned only so long as the electricity did. When there was a power failure, we all went home; there were lots of power failures. I shared my spartan quarters with Mr. Duc, a sad-eyed older man who should have been a professor or a senator, but was making more money on the US payroll. The best and the brightest of the Vietnamese, like Mr. Duc, were caught up in the need to survive, and tried to stay out of the way of bullets and politics.

I would need a vehicle, of course. All my co-workers had Scouts or Ford Falcons, and I could have one too. But for what earthly reason? To drive to the beach at Vung Tao on a weekend? I was more interested in careening around the city, and four wheels were not the way to do it.

Down at the motor pool a self-important chief, local hire, explained what was available. This guy, dressed in black trousers and sparkling white shirt, with mandatory sunglasses even in the gloom of the garage, had a gravy job, and he knew it. Here he was in charge of several hundred vehicles, and as long as he kept superficially clean records, he was in Fat City. He undoubtedly rented out cars to his buddies, probably even sold one occasionally, covering his sins with a report that it was destroyed in an accident or stolen. The way the American civilians ran their multi-million dollar operations in 'Nam was a financial farce. The motor-pool chief was extolling the virtues of a Scout like the one I had had up in the Highlands. It made a good bush-basher, but a lousy town car.

Over in a corner I saw a dozen Vespa scooters. "I want one of those," I said.

The poor fellow was quite startled. "No, no," he said, "those are just for messengers."

"You can put me down as the official land reform advisory office messenger; I'm taking a scooter."

"But none of those are any good. They are all broken."

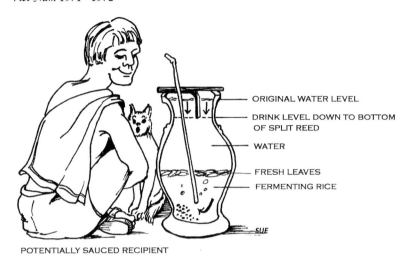

ORIGINAL WATER LEVEL

DRINK LEVEL DOWN TO BOTTOM OF SPLIT REED

WATER

FRESH LEAVES

FERMENTING RICE

SUE

POTENTIALLY SAUCED RECIPIENT

Montagnard rice-wine drinking etiquette

After a Montagnard dies, a schedule of gravesite events are held to commemorate the passage — all of which involve drinking copious quantities of rice wine. Not wanting to affront a local Montagnard chief in Pleiku, Clement was shown the proper drinking procedure and — reluctantly, of course — agreed to partake.

The Montagnard people were notably cheery, even in the face of adversity. Had war not descended upon them, they were content to lead a simple, rural life in the highlands away from modern strife and politics.

In the Vietnamese culture, death is merely a passage to another life and the deceased will still need money; to that end special funeral banknotes are buried with the body.

Good intentions gone wrong; the truck was trying to deliver supplies to a
Montagnard village, but obviously the bridge was not built with such a
vehicle in mind. More daylight, manpower and vehicles might be needed but
determination will win out. The supplies must get through.

This young man is being graduated as member of a village self-defense force
(some very young indeed), and is drinking a combination of rice wine and chicken
blood, with a bullet at the bottom of the bowl as part of the initiation. At the
end, the bullet is all that remains rattling around in the bowl.

What he said was true; they were not the pick of the litter. More like the cast-offs, and some had already been cannibalized. But sitting next to the chief's office was a shiny number.

"I'll take that one," I said.

"No, no, you cannot have that one."

"Why not?" I walked over, admired the polished paint and shiny chrome.

"No! You cannot have it!"

He was getting irate, not used to having his limited authority challenged. He was a foot shorter than I, with a mean look about him that I associated with the Saigon cowboys, young men who were out to fleece the GIs any way they could. And here was I, about to start arguing with some fellow who was supposed to be doing what I wanted him to do — like issue me with a vehicle.

"Give me a good reason why I can't have it. Who is it assigned to?"

That stopped him. He pulled himself up straight and said in an official tone, "It is my Vespa! You cannot have it!" He was truly distraught. Fortunately there was nobody else around, otherwise we would have gotten into one of those wretched face-saving struggles, which in the Far East often end in murder or suicide. Sometimes both.

"That's funny, I don't remember reading that the chief of the motor-pool was authorized to have a vehicle." Of course, I had never read anything about what the chief of the motor-pool was authorized, but that was beside the point. "Look," I said, "I'm going to take this scooter. You would be well advised to allow me to sign this vehicle out."

The poor motor-pool chief swallowed my hollow threat and it proceeded to expand in his gut. He was not one capable of oriental discreetness. His face contorted, his lips twisted, his eyes flared — and without a word he went into his office and pulled some forms from a drawer, along with carbon paper.

Ten minutes later I was happily scooting away.

It was an interesting year, working with the land reform program. It was too little, too late, and I never failed to remind visiting congressmen of that fact. I opened all the presentations with quotes from Lewis Carroll's Alice in Wonderland or Alice through the Looking Glass, and acquired the cachet of having an abrasive personality.

I got along famously with my counterpart at the ministry, a thirty-ish fellow named Hoa, who was polished, articulate, and whose only interest was furthering his own personal political ambitions. He wanted to be elected to the Senate from his home province, which was well up in the north of South Viet Nam, militarily unstable and low on the list of important places for his ministry to be concerned with. We could fly anywhere we wanted, but every third trip seemed to be to Quang Tri.

Sometimes of a Saigon evening he and I would get on my scooter and go down to the river to a cafe, have a couple of beers and discuss his career ambitions, and our differing views of contemporary reality.

"Hoa," I would say, "the Americans are going to leave, and because you are more interested in politicking in Quang Tri than getting the word about land reform out, you will lose the war." I must admit that I had a sneaking suspicion that if everything, including land reform and having a non-corrupt government, went according to the grand plan the communists might possibly lose. It was a silly thought, really, as American grand plans and South Vietnamese grand plans had absolutely nothing in common.

"The Americans will never leave," he would say. The not-so-subtle presumption was that we would lose too much face to ever leave. People like Hoa figured they had us where they wanted us.

"Yes, Hoa, we are leaving. Our troop strength is now down to 200,000 men, and in two more years the soldiers will be all gone. And then you will be overrun by the North Vietnamese, and any members of the government will probably be sent to prison, if not shot."

"You cannot leave," he would say, moving onto the philosophical plane, "it is you who are responsible for where we are today, and you now have a duty to protect Viet Nam." Good Buddhist thinking, but Americans are notorious for not adhering too closely to the ways of the Buddha.

"Hoa, I am leaving at the end of the year. And lots of Americans will leave before I do, and even more afterwards. Your government is near useless, your army has no desire to fight, and 90 percent of the population wants only for the war to stop, to hell with who wins or loses. You are doomed. And one of the reasons you are doomed is that you are not doing your job, because to give land to the landless might give the government enough popular support to fend off the communists." Pretty far-fetched thinking, but definitely part of the company line.

"You Americans," he said, "the only reason we have this land reform is to keep you happy. You think it will win the war; it will not. The only way to win this war is to have people like me in government, because I know how to keep the Americans happy so they will stay, and give us arms and money." Irrefutable logic.

I asked Mr. Duc how I could make Hoa understand what I was trying to tell him. "You cannot," said Mr. Duc. "You Americans have created Mr. Hoa; if you go away, he does not exist. He cannot imagine not existing. He cannot imagine your going away."

More irrefutable logic.

With airplane and car I saw the length of Viet Nam, the citadel at Hue, the Cao Dai temple in Tay Ninh, the nuoc mam (fish sauce) factories in Phan Thiet. I went from the swamps of the delta to the mountains of Ban Me Thuot to the beaches of Da Nang. I drank rice wine and ate dog-meat stew in the mountains, Algerian wine and lobsters on the beach in Nha Trang.

With my scooter, the girlfriend (she worked for an American newspaper) and I prowled the streets and alleys of Saigon and Cholon and Gia Dinh. Late at night we'd eat noodles off the street vendors' carts, where populist politicians like General Ky liked to appear. Then we'd rush home to beat the curfew.

Not that the curfew mattered much. The Saigon police, or White Mice as they were called due to their white uniforms, were not willing to risk their jobs by hassling round-eyes. However, if something did happen somewhere, and shots were fired in the night, the White Mice tended to be trigger-happy. And they might not see the whites of our rounded eyes before cutting loose. More than one night was spent on a friend's sofa.

* * * *

And how did we get out of our broken-cable problem? Our new friend said, "Come with me", and I pushed the Vespa along for a hundred or so feet to a house where remnants of bicycles and a rusty scooter frame were laying about. He roused the mechanic who brought out a few tools of his trade and fixed the problem. We were on our way in less than an hour. The mechanic accepted payment, our savior would not, but wished us good luck as we rode away.

My tour ended on the 31st of December, 1971. Nothing had been accomplished. I received a reasonable salary for my year and a half in-country, and left with no regrets. And not even a single Vietnamese that I could call a friend.

After Xmas I returned the Vespa to the motor-pool. The same chief was there. I had not seen him in a year, as maintenance had been done by a curbside scooter guru near my apartment.

But he did remember me. He was quite civil as I went in to his office to sign off on my temporary possession. "You go 'way from Viet Nam now?"

"Yes, I've been reassigned to Italy," I said.

"Vespa made in It'ly. You get scooter when you go It'ly?"

"No, but I will probably buy myself a motorcycle, a big motorcycle. There is no war in Italy, so I can go where I want."

"You are first 'Merican to get scooter from me," he noted. "I been here four years. No other 'Merican want scooter. Maybe you understand Viet Nam better because you have scooter."

He smiled. And outside his office I noted an even newer and shinier Vespa. Whatever happened, he was going to stay ahead of the game.

Zimbabwe 1974

In sun-drenched East Africa the wide-brimmed hat was quite useful, cooler than a beret, and was DOT-approved to 60 mph.

The beach and the warm waters of the Indian Ocean were off to my left, and the temptation to stay was great. But time was a'wasting and there was a world to be seen, so I clicked my Krauser panniers onto the BMW and began the process of strapping on the tent, air mattress, all the camping gear.

I had been staying at this very nice house by the sea, a little south of Mombasa, Kenya. The owner was an elderly Brit who had moved into his own guest house and rented the big place to travelers like myself. The Brit walked across what passed for a lawn and watched my packing. "So, you're off to Cape Town. That should be a good trip. The newspapers tell me you might have some interesting times at the borders."

That I would. Traveling through southern Africa in the 1970s was an exercise in broken-field running. In those years white governments were still trying to administer the essentially black countries of Rhodesia and Mozambique, as well as South Africa, and many border crossings were closed to overland travel as a result. But others were open.

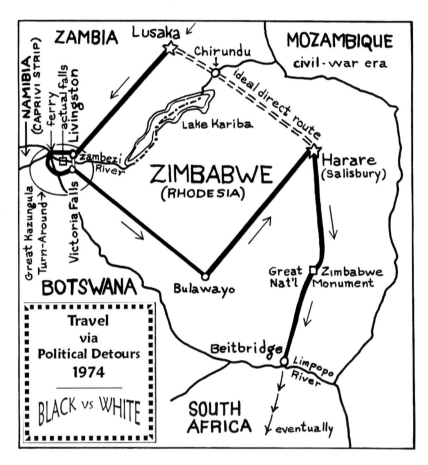

I bade my host goodbye, thumbed the starter on the motorcycle, and headed along the coast road. I had spent three months in Kenya, and was going to spend a leisurely month or two going south to the tip of the continent. The plan was to find a ship in Cape Town, South Africa, that would take me and the motorcycle to Australia. My route was going to have to go through Tanzania, Zambia (ex-Northern Rhodesia), detour into Botswana (ex-Bechuanaland), and then Southern Rhodesia (now Zimbabwe).

My route was as straightforward as possible in a geographical sense, although rather twisted by politics. The only serious sightseeing I had in mind was to have a gander at the ruins of Zimbabwe in Southern Rhodesia. I've always had a soft spot for large, aged constructions that have been overgrown by weed and bramble. I'd seen Angkor Wat, and Machu Picchu, and the Canyon de Chelly, and scores of European castles and fortresses and abbeys and churches that were succumbing to time and gravity. Any list would be incomplete without Zimbabwe.

The natural route on leaving Zambia's capital, Lusaka, would have been to go southeast to Chirundu, where I could cross the Zambezi River just downriver of the Kariba Dam, enter Southern Rhodesia and continue on to the capital, Salisbury (now Harare). An easy 300 miles. But life in this part of the globe has never been easy. Zambia and Rhodesia were not on speaking terms, let alone of a mind to allow traffic to pass back and forth. Also, Rhodesia was under international economic sanctions in an effort to make the white government give up power.

I was going to have to go down and do the well-known, at least among travelers in Africa, Kazungula turn-around. This meant riding southwest to Livingstone, then west to a point roughly in the middle of nowhere where a ferry would take me across the Zambezi — which is an 1800-mile long river — to Botswana, and then ride east into Rhodesia. Thanks to the muddled course of human events the distance from Lusaka to Salisbury had more than tripled.

Ah well, this would give me the opportunity to see Victoria Falls. Riding across the savannah heading towards the falls I was under a perfectly clear, blue African sky, the land flat and golden on each side of the narrow asphalt road, the boxer engine whirring comfortably along. About 60 miles out of Livingstone a small cloud appeared on the horizon, growing larger as I approached.

Long before Queen Victoria took the British throne the natives had called the falls Smoke That Thunders. I was seeing the smoke,

a cloud created by the moisture from the falling water, but it was not until I got a mile or so from the falls that I heard the thunder. The roar of a huge waterfall is a constant, and because it never varies it becomes quite tolerable. I pitched my tent as close to the falls as I could. At first the noise was overly intrusive, but once I became accustomed to the crashing of the water, the sound was wonderfully soothing.

The Smoke That Thunders are not tall falls, but wide ones, looking rather like Queen Victoria in her later years. A steel bridge ran from bank to bank just downriver from the falls, but hostile-looking men in uniform with guns glowered at each other from behind sandbags at each end. I was told foot traffic was occasionally allowed to cross, but never any vehicles. A large obstruction smack in the middle of the bridge made sure of that.

People at the campsite who had just come from the south told me about the Kazungula ferry's regular scheduled departures, at ten in the morning and four in the afternoon. Irregular crossings cost more. It took only minutes to get across. Botswanan customs and immigrations were perfunctory, and then less than an hour of bad dirt road would get me to Rhodesia.

I broke camp the next morning, rode west, found the ferry sitting precisely in the middle of nowhere, and paid a nominal fee for the privilege of circumventing white versus black rivalries. The ferry was merely a motor-driven barge which could accommodate several large trucks. One truck full of goods to sell in Rhodesia was heading south, as was a taxi crammed with people going to see relatives, and to sell whatever it was they carried in their bags.

We loaded, and as I stood at the front of the boat I could see a machine gun pointing at us from behind sandbags on the Caprivi Strip on the southwest side of the river, then a part of South Africa, now the easternmost tip of Namibia. There was probably one manned by Rhodesian troops to the southeast, but at least that was out of sight.. Not a friendly welcome.

The amount of river frontage that Botswana enjoyed was minimal, probably a quarter mile or so between South Africa and Rhodesia, just enough so it could serve as a back door from

A small herd of giraffe are wondering what this strange blue machine is doing invading their privacy out there on the African plains.

Clement shares a quiet campsite with a couple of domestic animals.

white to black Africa. All the proprieties could be observed, officials would not have to speak to each other, and borders would be closed, but essential traffic could flow through Kazungula. Convenient for merchants and travelers. The ferry was obviously making a killing, though I imagine the kickbacks were staggering.

Official Botswana stamping was done by cheerful bureaucrats in a small house set back from the river, and a modest exchange of money took place to secure proper passage. Outside was a sausage tree, a jacaranda of sorts that carries a sausage-like fruit which can weigh upwards of ten pounds. Local lore had it that David Livingstone the explorer had camped here, though I trust not under the tree, as those fruit could do one a mischief when falling.

The road east was a rudimentary affair, just a swipe with a bulldozer through the forest. After all, Botswana had no real need for this road, as hardly anybody lived up here. Its sole reason for existence was to benefit Zambia and Rhodesia. I soon came to a sandy intersection, where the little-traveled main road went

The Kazungula Road runs through lots of soft sand from Kazungula at the northern tip of Botswana east to the border with Zimbabwe — or Rhodesia, as the country was then known.

south towards Francistown, which would have had me staying in Botswana and avoiding Rhodesia altogether. The more-traveled and deeper-rutted off-shoot headed east to Rhodesia, and I wanted to see the ruins.

Down the sandy road a ways I came to the next border crossing and more cheerful functionaries stamped me out of Botswana. These fellows had a nice job, paid adequately, and their families lived in the little community that had developed.. No shopping mall, no movie theater, but their life was good. They lifted the simple barrier pole, and I was on my way, having spent less than two hours in that country.

Then I was in Rhodesia. The officials at the border, all white, were quite pleasant, quite glad to see me, and full of advice. Everybody understood what was going on, that this served as a quasi-legal circumvention of international law, and nobody gave a hoot. And they could commute from the relatively cosmopolitan town of Victoria Falls.

Along with my touristing activities, I also had the somewhat serious problem of a cracked battery, and I was looking to either get a new one or have something done about the cracked one. The folk at the border recommended my not stopping in Bulawayo, the next town of any size, as there were "too many thickheads." But Salisbury — now there was a proper town. Anything could and would happen in Salisbury. I could certainly get some help for my battery problem there.

I spent a night on the Rhodesian side of Smoke that Thunders, in the town named Victoria Falls. It had once been a minor tourist resort, but had fallen on hard times due to the politics of the era. The empty hotels and sour looks of the inhabitants backed that up. Livingstone had been much more cheerful, if equally empty. It seemed a white proprietor took it much harder than a black one if his hotel or restaurant wasn't full. The campground here was not nearly as pleasant as the one on the north side of the river, probably due to the surly type who took my money.

Next afternoon I was in Salisbury, enquiring as to places that knew about batteries. In a country under economic blockade one doesn't just rush up to your friendly BMW shop and buy whatever you need. One asks around, and was told that a new battery would be out of the question, but a couple of places did "battery repair". A new line of work. Close to closing time I pulled up in front of a shop that advertised boats. I explained my problem. Bring it by in the morning, I was told.

Walking about town that evening I noted there were white pubs and black pubs and at least two mixed pubs. Take your pick, but the segregated bars liked to remain segregated, and the integrated ones were in hotels, where people met to do business. I had expected a much more oppressive air, but it was nothing like that. At least on the surface that I saw. Obviously there was political and economic discrimination, but the city itself manifested a reasonably integrated look.

In the morning I went back to the boat shop. There was virtually nothing new to buy in Rhodesia, thanks to the sanctions, so they had a fix-it mentality. The shop made fibreglass boats, and as a side they did anything else that could be done with the material. I took the battery out of the bike and handed it over. Easy as drinking a pint, said the man. He would pour the acid into a container, clean the outside of the battery, mold a layer of fibreglass all around it, let it harden, put the acid back in — I could pick the bike up at five o'clock.

Which I did. And as I stood there admiring my travel-worn steed a stranger came alongside and said, "That your bike?"

I said it was, and he said it was the rattiest-looking motorcycle he had ever seen. I couldn't disagree. He introduced himself. Chris had a BMW as well, and invited me to come and stay with him at his house just outside of town, see how real Rhodesians lived.

It was a nice stay. We argued politically much of the time, which always adds spice to a visit. He claimed to have no personal animosity towards the blacks, only he had never met one that he wanted to see socially. It was standard colonial racism. Chris knew his days in Rhodesia were numbered, and he was already looking for a place in South Africa. He felt the white Afrikaaner was only a slight cut above the black, so he would go down to the Cape, where the English were in preponderance. And when

South Africa went down the tubes, as it inevitably must . . . maybe Australia.

He did not feel that he was being pessimistic, merely realistic.

I spent a couple of nights at Chris's farm, had a proper tour of the city, and several like-minded friends came over for dinner. We cheerfully agreed to disagree, and the evenings were really quite pleasant. A traveler has his or her own political views, and can voice them, but cannot expect to change the minds of everyone he meets.

After three days I thanked Chris for his hospitality and rode south to the ruins of Great Zimbabwe, which cover some 2000 acres. It was a well-tended site, as behooves a national monument, and there were little thatched chalets to be rented close to the ruins. Great.

Zimbabwe's centerpiece is the Great Enclosure, surrounded by 800 feet of wall standing up to 30 feet tall, with several buildings and conical towers inside — all built by local architectural experts placing rocks one on another. No mortar is involved, but

This picture is looking down at the Great Enclosure at the Great Zimbabwe National Park, which has 800 feet of wall surrounding it, much of it 30 feet tall.

Archeologists figure that the building of the stone structures at Great Zimbabwe
began roughly a 1000 years ago.

the place has been standing upwards of a thousand years, which
means it was not a bad construction technique. This enclosure
was presumed to be the king's residence, and highly defensible,
as behooves a king. On a nearby hill is another major structure,
called the temple, and all around the valley are the smaller houses.
Archeologists think that the place had some 25,000 inhabitants
in the 15th century.

Despite being 200 miles inland from the Indian Ocean, the
place was obviously a trading center, and artifacts of Arab, and
even Chinese, origin have been found. The authority of the
Bantu kings waned following the 1500s, and the first European
to talk about seeing such a place was a 16th century Portuguese
explorer, Gaspar Veloso. Over 200 building sites have been
found in this part of Africa, but Great Zimbabwe is the largest
and best preserved. After Veloso wrote about it in his journals,
Europeans did not refind the place until the 1850s. Some
Victorian historians decided it had to be the home of the Queen
of Sheba, preferring not to believe that it was a construction of
the indigenous Bantu.

I shared one of the tourist chalets with Alan, an English-born South African who had the blessings of a United Kingdom passport and was heading north for Cairo by thumb and bus, and then onto Britain. He was leaving the only country he had ever known, having migrated there when he was three, and did not know if he would ever be back.

We sat on chairs outside our hut and looked across the valley, drinking a bottle of Rhodesian-made red wine; a bit rough but not bad stuff. He saw no future in southern Africa because it have become impossible for black and whites to talk meaningfully between the races. The blacks had one agenda, the whites had another; the blacks knew they would win eventually, and the whites were determined to hold out as long as possible. Alan wanted to be a lawyer, but could not bear the thought of continuing to live, and working towards a law degree, in a society that contravened the very notion of justice under law. So it was off to a red-brick university in cold, wet England.

He said he might have stayed on in South Africa if he had been able to have any black friends. But everything was skewed, and he had not found that possible. Now he was soaking up a little African culture on his journey out.

It was a perfect full-moon night, and Alan and I decided to have a wander through the site. A local black youth offered to show us around, for a consideration, and we agreed on a price. Our guide, a mission-educated chap the same age as Alan, decided that the ruins needed some embellishment, and proceeded to expand on both their importance to the history of the area, and to the amount of treasure that had been found. I told him that was not what the guidebook I had purchased said, and he replied, "That book was written by a white man. This place is part of the black man's history, and only a black man can tell you the truth."

Perhaps he was right, but I do think he was falling prey to the same trap as some 19th century historians, slanting the truth to suit their own ends.

Alan and I wanted to talk about politics; our guide did not. As he put it, "There is trouble in politics." He wanted no trouble. The gap between black and white, even in the velvet darkness of the night, albeit moonlit, was too wide to bridge.

We wanted to know what our guide felt, how he saw the future, how he saw us. But to him we were at best transients, at worst provocateurs. It availed him nothing to speak frankly with us.

It was not a satisfying night, and I was discontented at the end of our stroll. I probably would have felt better if just Alan and I had walked around and discussed the injustices of the world and how to correct them, two white men giving the white man's solution to all problems. As it was, our guide interjected a rather heavy portion of reality.

"How am I going to earn a living?" ponders Clement. Got it! Write a story about going to visit the ruins of Great Zimbabwe on a motorcycle!"